Still on Call

WRITERS ON WRITING
Jay Parini, Series Editor

A good writer is first a good reader. Looking at craft from the inside, with an intimate knowledge of its range and possibilities, writers also make some of our most insightful critics. With this series we will bring together the work of some of our finest writers on the subject they know best, discussing their own work and that of others, as well as concentrating on craft and other aspects of the writer's world.

Poet, novelist, biographer, and critic, Jay Parini is the author of numerous books, including *The Apprentice Lover* and *One Matchless Time: A Life of William Faulkner*. Currently he is D. E. Axinn Professor of English & Creative Writing at Middlebury College.

TITLES IN THE SERIES

Michael Collier
Make Us Wave Back: Essays on Poetry and Influence

Nancy Willard
The Left-Handed Story: Writing and the Writer's Life

Christopher Benfey
American Audacity: Literary Essays North and South

Ilan Stavans
A Critic's Journey

Still on Call
Richard Stern

Still on Call

Richard Stern

The University of Michigan Press
Ann Arbor

Copyright © by the University of Michigan 2010
All rights reserved
Published in the United States of America by
The University of Michigan Press
Manufactured in the United States of America
♾ Printed on acid-free paper

2013 2012 2011 2010   4 3 2 1

A CIP catalog record for this book is available from the British Library.

Library of Congress Cataloging-in-Publication Data

Stern, Richard G., 1928–
    Still on call / Richard Stern.
        p.   cm. — (Writers on writing)
    ISBN 978-0-472-07090-9 (cloth : alk. paper) —
    ISBN 978-0-472-5090-1 (pbk. : alk. paper)
        1. Stern, Richard G., 1928–   2. Authorship.   I. Title.
PS3569.T39Z46   2010
818'.54—dc22   2009047782

This book is for my dear Nina (born 2005)
in hopes that one day, long after her grandfather is gone,
she will be able to find some of him in its pages.

Acknowledgments

Thanks are due the following publications in which sometimes quite different versions of the following pieces were originally printed: *Antioch Review:* "Reflections, Observations, Memories"; *Literary Imagination:* "Pages from a Journal: Afghanistan"; *Daedalus:* "On a Writer's Endgame" and "How the Stories Changed"; *University of Chicago Magazine:* "Becoming a Writer: The Forties" and "Then and Now: The Chicago Literary Scene"; *Sewanee Review:* "Glimpse, Encounter, Acquaintance, Friendship" and "On John Updike"; *The Republic of Letters:* "How I Got to Think the Way I Think" and "Individuality, Style and Other Forms of Identification" which was published first as an Adams Lecture by San Diego State University; *Seattle Review:* "Pages from a Journal: Rwanda"; *Tableau:* "Scattered Memories of the U. of Chicago English Department"; *The New Republic Blogs* Open University.

Contents

Preface

I'm TEMPTED TO SAY that this is an old man's book. The temptation is a geriatric self-inoculation, an excuse: "Please read this book in a charitable frame of mind because it's not as good as the books I wrote when young(er)."

This won't do. Why should the reader, who may have on his night table a dozen books, each one bought to enlighten, deepen and divert him from more vulgar, superficial diversions or from the tiring, perhaps deadening, routines of his life, choose to read a second-rate book, unless he's so devoted a fan of the author that the least effort of the now old brain somehow augments the special beauty, knowledge and feeling he's long enjoyed?

The book has been almost entirely written and assembled by a man in his late seventies. If that man, me, can be trusted to assess his powers, then he goes on record here saying, "In some ways, I'm a wiser, more knowledgeable and even abler writer than I was ten, twenty or fifty years ago. I believe that some of my opinions should be even more seriously considered, although in some cases, the weariness of age has stopped me from defining them as clearly or backing them up as carefully and fully as my younger self would have.

"As for some of the reflections, these have been marinating a long time and should thus be more flavorful than those written years and decades earlier."

This is the sixth book of the sort I call an "orderly miscellany," a book which includes different sorts of work, reportage, commentary, observations, poems (including translations), reviews, plays or playlets and fiction. Much of the writer's pleasure comes in its assemblage, the juxtaposition of pieces written on different occasions for different purposes now connecting to and playing off each other. Of course, all are connected to the author by whatever it is that constitutes his way of expressing whatever prompts him to write.

The hope is that the assemblage will reveal not repetition, a parade of old skills and tricks, but expansion and development. Yes, some may expose the deficiencies of old age. If such deficiencies as, say, senile garrulity diminish or extinguish a reader's interest, the writer has failed to do what he's tried to do, and that's to attain and stimulate a high level of mental energy. In short, this writer feels that he's still on call.

I

Coasting

MOST OF THE FOLLOWING PIECES are reflective, the longer ones more loosely held together than the essays in earlier miscellanies. The author is letting his sixty years of composition give him a visa to such liberty. I remember laying down strictures to a novelist friend of mine who, much younger than either he or I am now, was taking what I thought were shaky, if not improper narrative liberties. So, a character in his novel, dead in one scene, was alive in a scene which took place later. I'd missed my friend's point which was to emphasize the special authority of the narrative's author. Brecht had used such devices of "alienation" as having a set dressed in view of the audience, thus calling attention to theatrical artifice and contrasting it with the external actuality he wanted the audience to alter after it left the theater. The point of the greater freedom here is to call attention to the memory-heavy and nostalgic meandering of the older mind. For some, this will be a liability, for others, an enrichment.

Reflections, Observations, Memories

Familiar foolishness:

1. Do you promise to tell the truth, the whole truth and nothing but the truth? (Every court case, every witness, would go on forever.)
2. The TV anchor's "I'll see you again tomorrow night." He doesn't see us; we see him/her.
3. Love ya.
4. Have a good one.

That the carnage, savagery, starvation, ignominy, pain, fury, hatred and pity which rise from the news don't send us all to the loony bin speaks for the indifference developed by even the most sensitive and saintly of the world's privileged.

We write letters to the editor, send a check to a charity, moan to our lunch companions, or, like Proust's wonderful Mme. Verdurin reading about the loss of life on the *Lusitania* as she dips her croissant into her morning coffee, say "How awful," even as her lips curl with delight.

Now and then, we analyze and comment on this or that.

So I, on July 21, 2003, reading the caption on two wonderful photographs taken by Tyler Hicks of the *New York Times* the day before in the holy city of Najaf, decide that it does not represent what I see in them. The first photograph shows us the backs of seven U.S. marines in hard hats facing a crowd of mostly bearded and beturbaned men, some with arms raised in a salute of appreciation to something unseen by us off to the right; one man is raising a photograph of two white-bearded men. In the background, there is a group of mostly younger, beardless men, most of them seated on what seems to be a low wall. Six of these twenty or so men may be looking in the direction of the photographer or the marines. Two of them are raising their arms, one is standing with arms spread and seems to be shouting something in our direction. The second photograph is of eight men standing on a dais. Three of them wear turbans, one, the most prominent, is waving a sort of forked scimitar. One is taking video photographs of what is probably the crowd in the first photograph. The caption reads, "Iraqi protesters . . . pushed toward American marines yesterday in Najaf. The protest erupted after clergymen claimed that soldiers had tried to surround a prominent Shiite leader. Clerics, speaking to protesters from atop a mosque, below, demanded an end to the American occupation." The excellent article, by Neil MacFarquhar, spells out the complexities behind the photograph, the ignorance of the crowd that the marines and helicopters—which are not shown—had been called out as special protection for the visiting deputy secretary of defense, Paul Wolfowitz. It talks of the ambition of Moktada al-Sadr, "scion of a clan of beloved clerics," to assert himself by claiming that the Americans were bent on arresting him. "'Moktada Sadr and his supporters are trying to drag us into this kind of confrontation . . .' said a spokesman of the Supreme Council for the Islamic revolution in Iraq, the most established Shiite group . . ." It's clear that the crowd in front of the marines is not pressing against them. Only two or three men there are even facing them, and it is not clear what they are thinking. Some in the background fringe of younger men may be expressing indignation, but that is not clear. It does seem clear that three or four of the clerics are worked up and working up the crowd.

What is also clear is that there is much going on that brings people into the street and leads others to inflammatory oratory. It is all part of the complex events which led to the fall of Saddam Hussein and the attempts by many including, perhaps, Saddam, to vie for power in the post-war period.

I compare this to another photograph taken from the album of lovely Richard Rodgers songs to which I was listening while I read the paper. The photograph was taken at the final performance of the musical *South Pacific* in June 1951. It is the curtain call, and Mary Martin, the show's star, has her hands in front of her mouth and chin in what seems to be overwhelming surprise and pleasure as she sees what we do, the composer, Rodgers, in a sailor's jacket and round white hat, hands clasped in front of him, head bent, next to Oscar Hammerstein, the lyricist and writer, both presented by the play's director, Joshua Logan. Behind them, members of the cast are in various stages of jubilation and tearful nostalgia. One could look at this photograph for a long time, and find next to no space for misinterpretation, whereas in the first two photographs, there seems to be plenty of such space. The clarity comes from familiarity with Broadway traditions of celebration, farewell and public performance; the murk comes from ignorance of the political-social complexities of a very different culture.

3

I drove back from downtown Chicago along the Outer Drive immediately west of Lake Michigan on a mild, cloudy June day. I'd just bought cans of tennis balls at Sport Mart, where they can be bought cheaply. I pay with what's familiarly called plastic. Since I'm not using what I ignorantly regard as "actual money," the pleasure of getting a bargain is augmented by the self-pampering illusion that I'm not really paying. What occurred to me is that such postponement of payment, an example of artful separation from unpleasant actuality, is one of the fundamental components of human life. The pleasure comes from the illusion of escape, evasion, overcoming of a difficulty. What we call money, whether metallic or paper, is itself an instance of such separation. Instead of the exchange of commodities or services, instead of a brutal takeover by theft or conquest of what's desired, there is this almost weightless exchange which marks the way human beings have learned to live with each other.

Almost sixty years ago, I read in *God without Thunder,* a little-read book by the poet John Crowe Ransom, that the human separation from food, by cooking it, using utensils to cut and get it to our mouths, dividing the day into mealtimes, and finally the transfiguration of such times into occasions of conviviality, family intimacy, symposia and religious sacrament, is what differentiates people from animals. Ransom compared it to the democratic "separation of powers" which, although far less efficient than tyranny, elevates instead of degrades the citizen. (Isn't the function of religion itself the elevation of the weak and transient via at least the illusion of identification with more or less absolute power?)

Apropos "the elevation of the weak," I read in the *NY Times* (June 12, 2003) of "a Chicago man . . . Michael Garner, 39 [who] used an axe to break the arms or legs of a dozen people, then took them to the sites of pre-arranged car accidents. Mr. Garner made hundreds of thousands of dollars during the two years he led the scheme while the homeless victims made hundreds . . ."

Elsewhere the great newspaper reports on a Palestinian suicide bomber disguised as an Orthodox Jew who exploded a bus in central Jerusalem with bombs filled with nails and glass, so that not only were sixteen people killed but a hundred others were horribly wounded.

Then there is a picture of an Israeli soldier inspecting a long line of exhausted men and women waiting to go to work on the other side of a barbed wire boundary.

4

Every day, every newspaper reader and television watcher around the world is flooded with the injuries to the great social systems which constitute the orderliness of civic life. Most such readers and watchers have become addicted to these law-breakers. Not only do newspaper and television record them, but much of our literature, plays and films are built around them. Writers, dramatists and filmmakers understand the art of creating this derivative excitement which works on the emotions of audiences without damaging their flesh. I myself have spent much of my adult life either conjuring up such works or teaching students to understand and treasure them.

A year and a half ago, after fifty such years, I retired from teaching and, to a lesser degree, from writing them. I have entered another stage of life, the one often known now by a chess term which Samuel Beckett made the title of a play about it, *Fin de Partie* (some party!). *End Game.* It is this part of life which I want to talk about now.

Our memories are picture galleries in whose corridors a large number of images hang ready for re-inspection. There are also libraries of sounds, musical and non-musical, smells, tastes, movements and emotions. Another gallery is full of the slogans, mottos, poems, jokes and dialogue which constitute a too large portion of our active memory. There is finally a gallery of ever-deepening attachments to the past, not only to one's own past experience but to that of the often imaginary or dim remembrance of one's ancestry.

In Hungary for the first time in my life, it was almost a duty for me to think of my paternal grandfather, Adolf Stern, whom I remember vividly although he died sixty-five years ago. Grandpa was a Hungarian Jew, and those of my cousins who knew him better remember what they called his Hungarian temper and accent. My late cousin Ruth Worms Tishman remembered that he could not pronounce "th" and always called her—and my sister, another Ruth—"Russie." She also remembers that during the first three years of World War I, 1914–17, she and her sisters used to scratch out of the rotogravure section of the newspapers the faces of British soldiers. Grandpa was a partisan of Germany. When the United States entered the war in 1917, this changed, but she did not remember how or what Grandpa said to bring about the change.

I remember feeling happy when I saw Grandpa. He had white hair, parted in the middle, and a droopy white mustache. He dressed in stiff collar, cravat, gold tiepin, dark jacket, vest and pants. He was strong. When the laundress came upstairs with the wicker basket loaded with a week's wash, Grandpa hoisted it to show that he could. I sat on his knees, he gave me quarters. Only when I played checkers with him did I experience the man who could not bear to lose. When I crowned a king, he shouted, and once accused me, his beloved little grandson, of cheating him. I was bewildered; my parents calmed him, ended the game and later told me that I must never again play checkers with Grandpa. The last few years of his life, my father, my sister and I took him every winter to Grand Central Station and put him on the train for Palm Beach. The last time I saw him was beside the train in 1938. He died in Florida, a month before a ninetieth-birthday party, the invitations to which had been mailed out. I don't remember his death, only that one day my father, who almost never rebuked us, rebuked my sister and me for not condoling with him on Grandpa's death. I remember once again bewilderment. Who had said anything about his death to us?

What do I know of him beside what I have said? A handful of perhaps distorted stories: his being orphaned at seventeen; his being somehow enlisted by Count Esterhazy to work on a railroad; his working in a bar and there encountering a soldier who wished to recruit him for the Austro-Prussian War; young grandpa broke a beer bottle, threatened the man with its jagged edge, then fled, perhaps to Berlin where he met and married beautiful Rosa Wildman, the grandmother who died thirty years before my birth. In Berlin, she and Grandpa had the first two of their six children, then sailed for New York City where she bore the rest of them including my father; she died of puerperal fever after the last birth, that of my aunt Mildred. Grandpa, after peddling, cigar rolling and other jobs, became the businessman he was when I knew him, founder of Stern Merritt Inc., a firm that manufactured men's accessories including the red neckties he himself always wore, one of which he sent annually to his idol, Theodore Roosevelt, who once sent him a thank you letter, a treasure, which, like so much else, disappeared. In 1887, Grandpa named his last-born son, my father, Henry George, after the famous single taxer whose theories excited the likes of Leo Tolstoy. Grandpa's politics were not socialist or single tax; as far as I can guess, he named my father as he did because George was an idealist who ran, fruitlessly, for mayor of New York. Grandpa was a Republican who in 1912 became so furious at my father voting for Woodrow Wilson instead of the Republican Charles Evan Hughes that he kicked him out of the house. My father sneaked back in at midnight, let in by his loving stepmother, Leontine, probably on the instructions of Grandpa. Another of the extravagant grandfatherly gestures which memory has softened into cosy eccentricity.

What is the meaning of these scarcely documented anecdotes which stand along with a few sensuous memories as my grandfather? A grandfather myself, I wonder about my place in the heads of my grandchildren.

I already see my children turning me into a comic figure, one that releases some of the pressure I exerted on them at various times. Indeed, I already see that my oldest grandchild, a wonderful twenty-year-old girl, seems to regard me more realistically than her mother, my daughter, although the realism lies beneath a layer of affection, of love. Are there lessons here for historians, particularly for biographers?

5

One thing I can't remember is if in my first twenty or so thoughtful years I was ever overwhelmed by the sheer mass of event out of which thoughtful people try to make sense. Perhaps charitable oblivion erases this memory as it does many others. The algorithms which govern memory have been treated better by novelists than by psychologists, but I suspect that there's enough individuality in them to make it a serious occupation of the elderly. Why do we remember what we do? How much of what we remember applies to what we have to make sense of now?

What counts? What are the influences which lead to action or inaction?

What seems odd, strange, sometimes shockingly novel to an elderly American writer and professor may appear like matter-of-fact diversions and pleasantries to younger European, African, American and Asian intellectuals. ("The wildest dreams of Kew / Are the facts of Katmandu.") Let me try out a number of—let's call them—oddities which cropped up in the issue of the *New York Times* the day, April 29, 2003, I am writing this.

The art critic Michael Kimmelman reports from his recent trip to London. The headline reads "London Is Agog over Art, Especially Saatchi's." The article describes an exhibition of Titian paintings attracting "art besotted . . . mobs" to the basement of the National Gallery. Nothing shocking there, but when Kimmelman crossed the Thames to the Tate and other galleries and saw Ron Mueck's trompe l'oeil *Nude Man with Arms Folded Sitting in a Rowboat* and very small figures whose "forlorn and troubled expressions make them seem so vulnerable and childlike that they provoke the embarrassment of invading their privacy," something beside semi-mindless relaxation into an art critic's report occurred to me. Nothing exactly mind-blowing, but some of what Kimmelman called "the visual chestnuts" of Saatchi's old "Sensation" shows was agitating: *Marc Quinn's frozen cast of his own head in his own blood . . . Chris Ofili's*

9

glittery Madonna with elephant dung . . . Sarah Lucas's photograph of herself with cash stuffed between her legs or fried eggs on her breasts . . . Cornelia Parker's version of Rodin's Kiss *wrapped in marble strings . . . David Batchelor's tower of colored light boxes looming over Jim Lambie's eye-popping vinyl floor . . .* and the famous Damien Hirst's famous cow sliced up into parts exhibited in a row of glassy telephone booths aligned as in old-fashioned train stations. These roused me, but perhaps not entirely as the artists intended I should be roused from the spectator's complacent torpor.

The lust for novelty once satisfied by fantasies and myths, by sphinxes, dragons, griffins, plumed serpents and other fanciful creatures or, more physically, by exotic, difficult and dangerous voyages on earth and, more recently, in space has now overflowed the boundaries and proprieties of art, sex, family and crime. Almost every age offers similar violations often inflicted by the bored, the cruel, the idle rich and powerful. The violations occur when other powers are tightening the bonds of middle- and lower-class behavior. So out of the April 29 *Times* comes a list of strictures on schoolbooks inspected by Professor Diane Ravitch in her book *The Language Police: How Pressure Groups Restrict What Students Learn.* Here are things students are not supposed to find in their schoolbooks: Mickey Mouse, because mice and rats might upset small children; a mother cooking dinner, because it enforces a gender stereotype; stories set in jungles because they suggest "regional bias"; angry, loud, quarreling people, because they are not "uplifting"; birthdays, because some poor children can't afford to celebrate theirs; mention of cakes or cookies instead of healthy foods like yogurt and bran; words like "swarthy," "senile," "crazy" and "heroine" which could trouble the swarthy, the senile, the crazy and those driven mad by gender inequality. Old people must be described doing something active, not as weak or dependent; men must be considered nurturers, not, say, doctors, lawyers or plumbers. "Founding Father" is objectionable. I suppose Washington, Adams and Madison should be depicted along with their estimable spouses, Martha, Abigail and Dolley, as state-nurturers. Finally, children should not be shown as disobedient.

And we—rightly—complain of those Saudi schoolbooks which teach the inadequacies, if not sinful criminality of unbelievers, Westerners, Americans and Jews.

How much of this touches my own life in a way which would alter my decisions? Very little, if any. I may be amused, annoyed, disgusted, perhaps angry, but my day is not seriously altered by any of this. What is Hecuba to me?

I have offered two lists of oddities. Here is a third, which doesn't seem odd to me because it is part of the university life which for almost half a century has been mine. It is comprised of a few of the lectures offered this past week at my university. Any university member, indeed, anyone at all, can attend these lectures without paying a fee. Indeed, after many of the lectures, there are receptions with wine, cheese, fruit and vegetables, so that if one attended a number of them, one's weekly food bill could be substantially reduced. Our focus, though, is on intellectual diet. So: "Nero's Cultural Politics"; "Sexual Politics and the Enlightenment; Women Writers Who Read Rousseau"; a discussion with Vikram Chandra, author of *Red Earth* and *Love and Longing in Bombay;* a reading of his poems by (my former student) Campbell McGrath; a showing of Max Ophuls' *The Earrings of Mme. de* followed by a discussion and reception; establishing a Quarto text of *King Lear;* "Pheramones, Social Odors and the Unconscious"; "Religious Symbolism in the Fatimid-Tayyibi Tradition of Classical Arabic Poetry"; "The Dative Absolute in the *Kievan Chronicle.*" I attended the last four, because they are part of my weekly routine which includes a—once again free—luncheon seminar of the Humanities Division. A good lunch is served, and then there is a talk by one of my former colleagues, followed by a discussion. The luncheons occur during three of the four annual terms, and there are about eight lecture-lunches a quarter. I have learned a great many odd things in these hours. I could also attend other university lectures. Indeed, within walking distance, I could hear three or four authors of new books speaking at bookstores which offer their work for sale and signature. If I were bold enough to walk fifteen minutes in another direction, I could take the Number 6 CTA bus, the Jeffrey Express, downtown, stop at the Art Institute of Chicago, then cross the street to Orchestra Hall and listen to one of the world's greatest orchestras. I have not mentioned university and neighborhood concerts, many of them free, plays in local and downtown theaters and the movies showing all over the city. I have not mentioned the offerings on cable television. What I'm talking about here is the cornucopia of high culture offered in many centers of contemporary Western civilization.

What does this mean for a person like me?

I earned a living for over half a century as a college teacher and now live off a reasonably comfortable pension in a small comfortable house with a wife who has been my closest friend for decades. I have many friends in Chicago, around America, and indeed the world. My health is fairly good, I enjoy food, books, a little activity, some television programs and movies. In short, I have enjoyed the luxe provided by the inventions, industry, political freedom and stability of my wealthy country, where, I know, there are millions of men, women and children who go to bed hungry, have no regular place to sleep, no work, none of the comforts which are almost like second skin to me. Some are ill, some have been mutilated in family, national or tribal struggles. I sympathize with many of these, particularly if a skilled reporter has described them, or if I see them on the street.

6

My professional life has been spent thinking about, writing and teaching literature, the words, phrases, sentences, paragraphs, expositions, arguments, scenes, forms and situations which compose it. Almost all of us are language experts and sensitive to its variations and abuses. Those of us who do this professionally claim that we understand much about character from such usage. Let me illustrate what I mean by quoting a few words of the American general who devised and executed the war plan in the Gulf War, General Tommy Franks. I want to move from a look at his remarks to my speculations about the political situation of which he is a part. First, though, a contrasting quotation from one of the great generals of our bloody Civil War of 1861–66.

> Some men may think that modern armies may be so regulated that a general can sit in an office and can play on his several columns as on the keys of a piano; this is a fearful mistake. The directing mind must be at the very head of the army—must be seen there, and the effect of his mind and personal energy must be felt by every officer and man present with it, to secure the best results. Every attempt to make war easy and safe will result in humiliation and disaster.

Here are General Franks' remarks:

The threat creates its own battle space. That is epiphanous. This guy [Saddam Hussein], because of fear brought about by isolation from the regime or whatever, likes to aggregate. That's a powerful piece of information for which the regime will suffer greatly.

The first quotation is from the memoirs of William T. Sherman published in 1875, the second is recorded in a news story in the *New York Times* on April 13, 2003. General Franks' remarks were made not from the battlefield in Iraq but from U.S. Army headquarters in Doha, Qatar. He was not to set foot in Iraq for days and then only in a secure area, heavily protected by guards. General Sherman, like his greatly admired chief, General Ulysses S. Grant, was frequently shot at by enemy soldiers, and if he didn't exhibit Grant's almost superhuman indifference to bullets, he was more often than not with his soldiers in the midst of battle.

Of course weaponry of the American Civil War was not as deadly as it was in the Gulf War, and communication with lesser commands was of an entirely different order. General Franks had not only a view of one part of one battle but many views of many battles, and he had them in what is now called "real time," that is, as they were occurring. Moreover, the war General Franks observed and commanded was not a war of almost-equals—though the armament and manpower of the North greatly exceeded that of the South—but what is called in today's nomenclature an "asymmetric war," a David and Goliath war, except that David is not only much smaller and weaker than Goliath but unable to find any stones to throw at him.[1] More, after a very short time, David's brain was not communicating with his arm.

My interest here is not in the war itself. Despite the vast changes in armament, transport, logistics and medical care, parents, children, siblings and spouses on both sides experienced the same fears and mourned the same way they did in Homer's time. Here, though, I want to call attention to the linguistic gulf between the two American generals, though not emphasizing the fact that General Franks is speaking "off the cuff" and that General Sherman was writing his memoirs in comparative tranquility years after the war.

To find a contemporary equivalent of the language of General

---

1. 2006. This was written well before the so-called insurgents had turned the war tide.

Sherman, one can go to almost any reasonably well-written book. An easy place to find its equivalent might be the sports pages of today's newspapers. Indeed, in the same issue of the *New York Times* from which I've taken General Franks' remarks, there is a sentence spoken by Tiger Woods, after shooting a good round at the Master's Golf Tournament in which he otherwise did poorly. Woods said, "I just took what the golf course gave me." There we have a complex notion spoken with simple words and straight syntax. If, on the other hand, we are to find a contemporary equivalent of General Franks' murky sentences, we go not to the newspaper or the prose of most letter writers but to—well, here's a quotation: "The deconstruction, rather, annihilates the ground on which the building stands by showing that the text has already annihilated that ground, knowingly or unknowingly." This remark about Jacques Derrida's critical practice was written by the literary scholar-critic J. Hillis Miller. (See M. H. Abrams, "The Deconstructive Angel," in *Modern Criticism and Theory: A Reading,* edited by David Lodge, p. 272.)

I don't think either General Franks or Professor Miller was being deliberately obscure. I do think though that the habit of using language which can be understood by almost all reasonably intelligent speakers of the language regardless of their specialty is not important to them. They are each speaking either to or out of a smaller circle of specialists who will not only understand it, but do not mind that few people outside their circle will. It's as if they are saying, "Look, we are dealing with a subject that we understand and you don't. Leave the matter to us. Don't interfere with your ignorant questions, let alone your so-called contribution to the discussion."

There is another matter of great interest in General Franks' utterance. It may have something to do with what amounts to the ambience of the Bush family since the first President Bush left the softer precincts of Connecticut where his father, Preston, served as senator, to set up more or less on his own in the Texas oil business. There were no chauffeured limousines for his young children; his son, G. W. Bush, attended public schools, until family tradition, connections and money took over and sent him to Andover, and then, despite his mediocre grades, to Yale. The transmigrated Bush family was now identified with the town of Midland—we might call it the Bush equivalent of Saddam Hussein's Tikrit—the town where General Franks himself grew up and where George Bush found the woman he married, the woman who helped transform him from a drunken playboy who kept failing in business despite repeated and generous help from family connections into the public servant he has been for the last fifteen or so years. The young Bushes worship not in the Episcopal churches of the Bush family tradition but in the Methodist Church where I suspect the Franks family worshipped as well. I am a stranger to religious feelings, but the nexus of drink, transformation and Methodism struck me as I read my colleague Paul Hunter's brilliant book about the origins of the English novel in the eighteenth century. Here is Hunter on Methodism:

> The distinctive genius of Methodism was in discounting temporal continuity and emphasizing the possibility of an epiphanic moment that involved experience wholly new and without a basis in the individual's past—a moment that could, paradoxically, be shared with others in a community of believers so that individual, even ecstatic experience could become the basis for a new kind of spiritual communality . . . Gin and Methodism are opposites in the sense that gin drinkers succumb to their lonely feelings and celebrate them to oblivion, while Methodism "converts" these feelings into the basis for a group. The novel . . . uses loneliness as a basis for a fully historical exploration of self. If gin drinking is fatalistic and Methodism similarly evasive . . . the novel offers individuals . . . intellectual and spiritual companionship . . . (*Before Novels: The Cultural Contexts of Eighteenth-Century English Fiction*, pp. 133, 134)

I don't know if gin was the young Bush's drink of preference,[2] but in any event, he dropped it when he took to the pretty librarian and reader Laura, and found himself reborn in Christ and Methodism. (Laura's experience included her running over and killing a classmate in her senior year. Perhaps this furthered the introspection which has made her the country's Reader in Chief.) General Franks grew up in Midland, a year ahead of Laura in the same high school. He did poorly in school, joined the army, reformed and became a top student. He married a high school sweetheart on whom he is dependent to the point of uxoriousness (and criticism for allowing her to sit in on meetings she

---

2. Probably not, if Laura Bush's oft-quoted ultimatum to her suitor is taken literally: "It's either Jim Beam or me." This was pointed out to me by my friend Peter Kovler, whose grandfather owned the Jim Beam company.

was unauthorized to attend). His linguistic excursions were not confined to the remarks quoted above. As his friend General Leo Baxter said, playfully, "Tommy is not quiet about anything . . . he's very outgoing and very opinionated. In the course of a five minute discussion about how you're wrong and he's right, he'll use words that are and are not in the dictionary."

7

On November 4, two days after the 2004 presidential election, I'm supposed to read a piece of fiction to an audience at the University of Washington. My professorial sponsor, the writer David Shields, emails me that political feelings will be so high that a story may have a rough time getting through to it. I'm writing these few words on October 20 in the hope of bridging these political and esthetic passions. As the deciding game of the Red Sox–Yankee series will be played tonight, it occurs to me to throw in a few words about sporting passion as well.

Almost everyone is roused about candidates, public events and teams, sometimes, as in Nicholson Baker's recent novel *Checkpoint,* to the edge of murderousness. The emotions excited by works of art are also powerful but more difficult to describe because they reach into or even create new sections of mentality. Artists are emotional specialists. The feelings they manipulate are akin to those roused by everyday experience, but their works condense and intensify the emotional ups and downs of love, ambition, despair and hatred. The sequence of artistic events and their special languages and conventions exclude the static which surrounds almost every worldly event. After a good play or movie, a wonderful song or painting, a powerful poem or novel, there's a half-dazed transition back to the usual life of contingent events, haphazard sounds and sights.

Like political campaigns, baseball games aren't controlled by a single artist, but are organized by the conventions of the game. To that degree, they resemble those works of art which unfold in time. They also resemble works of art in that for most fans there is no serious financial or personal consequence of defeat. (I'm not talking about the expense of spirit or a lost bet.) The tension felt by baseball fans is released in bits by partial triumphs and defeats, a homer here, a botched double play there, but the powerful release comes at the end of the game, misery for losers, exaltation for winners. The release of triumph is brief even for the players who try to extend it by such shenanigans as spraying champagne over each other. The game can be revived and relished in memory, and is embodied in statistical history, but I don't think that such memory has the sustenance of a powerful work of art. Artworks deposit a felt intelligence which doesn't just extend but alters mentality. (Which isn't to say that victories and defeats aren't instructive and formative.) Political tensions can be endured for months, with only the temporary relief of a poll here, an endorsement there. The final release, the defeat of one candidate, the election of the other, also results in comparatively brief exaltation or somewhat more extended anger, a gnawing sourness which only the delayed revenge of the next campaign may assuage. However, the consequences of defeat and triumph affect the lives of millions, even billions, and for years. History, the record of such consequences, reveals how they are entangled in events which derail or even subvert what originally launched them. Games and art may have originated as organized relief, repose, consolation and compensation for these worldly consequences.

8

For seventy of my seventy-five years, I have worked in schools, for fifty-nine of these in universities. For most of these years, one of the great pleasures of my life has been reading. My library is small compared to Hitler's sixteen thousand volumes (see Timothy Ryback, "Hitler's Forgotten Library," *Atlantic Monthly*, May 2003) or the one Jefferson bequeathed to what became the Library of Congress,[3] but it is one of my resources of comfort, inspiration and nostalgia.

A couple of years ago, knowing that after my retirement from the university where I'd spent forty-six of my fifty-three teaching years, I was going to be moving up the hall to an office shared with other emeritus professors and that there would be no room for the books in my old office, I asked a local bookseller if he'd be interested in acquiring them. He spent a few hours in the office, then put aside a couple of hundred

---

3. Most of which was burned when the British set fire to the capital.

books he wanted to buy. I went through them, one by one, and decided that I was unable to part with any of them. I wrote him a letter of apology which he courteously said was worth the time he'd lost that morning; but my problem remained. Although I took most of those two hundred books home and bought another bookcase for them, there still remained the books for which there would be no room. With the help of my friend Jim Schiffer, who was chairman of the English Department at Northern Michigan University, I got in touch with their library, sent them a list of the books I could give them, found that they lacked many of them and that they could sell those which would be duplicates. They would be most grateful if I packed, sent, and donated the books. I said farewell to them, and later went up to the beautiful frozen shores of Lake Superior for a final farewell as they reposed in the University of Northern Michigan's handsome, if book-starved library.

9

The European Union debated Turkey's bid to join its August ranks. Frits Bolkstein, a Dutch member of the Union's Executive Committee, warned that Europe would be "Islamized," and the 1683 battle of Vienna against the Ottoman Turks would "have been in vain." In Amsterdam, three young Dutchmen of Turkish origins agreed that the country of their parents should not be allowed to join. "They will flood into Europe," said Akag Acikgoz, a nightclub bouncer. His fellow card player, Firat Hokmanoglu, said it didn't matter to him, one way or another. "I'm already here." In Turkey, meanwhile, Prime Minister Recep Tayyip Erdogan, who when mayor of Istanbul in 1999, was imprisoned for reciting a poem that included the line "the mosques are our barracks, the domes are our helmets," said that Turkey had made progress in the protection of expression and would not accept anything less than full membership in the European Union.[4]

---

4. *NY Times,* October 13, 2004. I'm revising this on October 12, 2006, hours after the Nobel Prize in Literature was awarded to the virtuoso Turkish novelist Orhan Pamuk, indicted by his country for claiming that it systematically ignored the Armenian genocide, the bloodiest stain on its national escutcheon.

Saddam Hussein arrived in Kirkuk a dozen years ago with sacks of silver to buy out—at a quarter of their value—the houses of Kurds some of whom he had driven to the border, some of whom his lieutenants would gas to death, the idea being to import Arabs from the south to "Arabicize" Kirkuk and the surrounding Kurdish villages and thus protect the nearby oil wells. Now Kurds are demanding that those Arabs— or their heirs—be sent back south and Kirkuk be once again Kurdicized. Otherwise they say that they'll secede from the forthcoming Iraqi state.[5] These are days when that portion of the West which is fighting in Afghanistan and Iraq is waging what its fiercer opponents are calling "another Crusade." So Osama bin Laden compared George Bush to Richard the Lionheart, Frederick Barbarossa and "Louis of France." Saddam Hussein compared himself to Saladin (who took Jerusalem in 1187), and George Bush was warned about not repeating his use of the word "crusade" in the days following the assaults of September 11, 2001.

Thibaut of Champagne extracted some of the 50,000 *livres* it took for his 1201 crusade from the Jewish community in Champagne whose wealth derived in part from money lending, that is, usury. Usury was forbidden to Christians because it sold time which belonged not to man but to God. (See Psalm 15—a righteous man is one who doesn't put out his money at interest—and Deuteronomy 23:19–20.) In 1096, the People's/Peasants' Crusade inflicted horrors on the Rhineland Jews. Fifty years later, during the Second Crusade, similar horrors were inflicted on their descendants.

Said Peter the Venerable, abbot of Cluny, "But why should we pursue the enemies of the Christian faith in far and distant lands while the vile blasphemers, far worse than any Saracens, namely the Jews, who are not far away from us, but who live in our midst, blaspheme, abuse and trample on Christ and the Christian sacraments so freely, insolently and with impunity." That same year, 1146, Bernard of Clairvaux said, "Is it not a far better triumph for the Church to convince

---

5. See *NY Times*, October 2, 2004, and George Packer, "The Next Iraqi War," *New Yorker*, October 10, 2004.

and convert the Jews than put them to the sword?" which helped end
their persecution.

11

For every set of McDonald's golden arches, a steeple, mosque bulb or
synagogue stands for a place where human beings can to greater or
lesser degree exchange their critical, analytic, logical sense for shortcut
help from the Great Fog of their Faith, the comfort of celestial embrace. The fanatics of Rapture or Revenge use such tradition to reinforce their fear of the ever faster fastness of modernity, the instanta-
neities of cyberspace, the terrifying theoretical reach into the infinitude
of universes, the darkness of dark energy and matter, the "illogic" of
quantum mechanics, as well as to the temptations of the naked gor-
geousness of models and actresses, the freedom which for millennia
had been reserved for kings. So the turtle in us shrinks back into the
shell of superstition.

Pages from a Journal: Afghanistan

❦

OCCASIONALLY, I REREAD A JOURNAL I've kept steadily, although not daily, for almost sixty years. Now and then, I publish an excerpt which relates to some contemporary happening, such as the death of someone with whom I've more or less briefly, but—for me—significantly talked. I publish here a few pages dealing with a visit to Afghanistan in 1973, decades before its bloody troubles became the main international event. Later in the collection are pages from the journal written in Rwanda thirteen years before the most explosive mass killing in the annals of genocide took place in June 1994. Some of the interest here is in my lack of clairvoyance, my misreading of what I heard and saw. Nothing would be more damaging to the nature of this book than to whitewash such errors.

September 2, 1973
Ariana Afghan flight 710
Over Dasht-i-Kavir, or do these brown bumps, lumps, cracks and yawns of earth belong to Afghanistan? We should soon be over Herat, where Genghis Khan killed all but forty people, and then Bamian, the Valley of Mourning, where he killed every person and every leaf. Will the stone Buddhas be visible?[1] Not one house or shed or road, only trickles, dried beds, canyons, sand. The moon couldn't look emptier. How did conquerors make it here? What did they use for water?

---

1. December 2006. There is talk now of somehow reconstructing the great sculptures the pure-hearted Taliban blew up.

September 2, 4:30 P.M.
Kabul, Hotel Yama

At the airport, the man checking passports is enough to scare tourists from the country. Brown suit, tie choking thick neck. The scare is the great cleft in his head. What hatchet did that? How did he survive? What part(s) of him didn't? The cranial gorge wasn't all he suffered. He picked up the passports with the pincer on his wrist, the thumb and two fingers which survived the—same or another?—assault. He wanted to know why I wasn't staying at a good hotel. (I'd had to write the name of mine—Yama—on the form.) In any event, I needed a visa. Last week, the king, Mohammed Zahir Shah, while abroad in Rome, had been deposed by one General Daoud, whose unamiable features are hugely spread over the wall. The visa-getting took but a minute and five dollars (the nightly price of my room at the Yama. No wonder Mr. Pincers-Cleft rebuked me for staying there.)

From airport to town, a Rangoon-like stretch of pavement merchants. A Thursday special?

Later:

Where God plays Rembrandt: the most astonishing faces: the beards, the noses, the wrinkles and colors incised by sun and—well, life. Plus Rembrandt turbans, though less gaudy. (Some of the fezzes and beanies are gaudy.) Faces like the countryside, bare, brown, rough with their own canyons, cliffs and trickles. Un-gaudy, formidable, secretive.

I walk from the hotel over the nervous little bridge to the American embassy to suggest to Mr. Peppers, the cultural attaché, that I interview General Daoud. Peppers is a Georgian, has a reddish beard and young kids. He says people are apprehensive since the takeover. The general is a prince, both cousin and son-in-law of the king who, ten years ago, deposed him as prime minister. "There are new ministers all the time. Twenty-eight-year-old artillery lieutenants—no one knows who they are." (He's surely thinking of the twenty-eight-year-old artillery lieutenant Signor Bonaparte.) When I remark about the landscape, he says, "It's not as empty as it looks. There's always a tribesman waiting to shoot you."

"I couldn't see anything *made* by a human, let alone a human. How could Genghis or Alexander or anyone have made it through here? And why bother?" Peppers shrugs. We ring up the deputy foreign minister's office. After a few moments and words I can't understand: "Can't reach him. I'll try later, get a message to you."

Beggars all over. The man who says "Allah" over and over and over. "Allah, Allah, Allah." A block from the Yama, there's a small pyramid of black cloth. Out of it sticks a grizzled hand, and every few seconds it emits a word, not Allah, but, I suppose, the equivalent of *baksheesh*. The smell? Goat-butter (in which the little ears of corn are cooked). Foetid—that's the word, the effluvia of decaying vegetables, plus faint whiffs of shit. A poverty smell.

The Yama smells of modesty, but is a cozy retreat. Pashas and sahibs come in massively with turbans, vests, coats, baggy trousers. Two young male friends meet and kiss happily.

I change money at the Shahraza Market: fifty-four instead of fifty-eight afghans to the dollar. A nervous little American with a face like Arthur Miller's points me to a picture of the new boss, General-Prince-King Daoud, one of those boss faces that such types probably receive when *coup d'etat* fever hits them. They all take what Alane tells me is a syong gong——"facing the light"—pose.[2] Peppers said everything here is a tribal compromise. "Okay, you take Thursdays, you can smuggle X, you Y, you can rob the trains."

I mail cards and letters at the post office, insurance for surer expedition. Nearby, a few girls in Western dress. Most women are swaddled in burkhas. On sidewalks, young people stare at movie posters or collections of small snapshots, sold or just displayed by sidewalk vendors. Now and then you see shoes and even nice legs sticking out of a burkha. Whoops! The cloth tent just rose. The Assumption of Tent.

No pornography visible. Books in a small shop are in Persian or its country cousin, Farsi. Peppers said that Afghanis resent being regarded as the provincial tail of Persia.

I'm uncomfortable in the tourist trough today. My cold hangs on, though I'm getting stronger, and now and then eager to go on. Next stop: Tashkent. The trip is more than half over: some regret. A few days ago I was ready to head home.

I like the hotel personnel, the kindly bellboy and *maitre d'* (if that concept reaches over these deserts). Outside my window, a dozen yards away, three pairs of men in turbans sit on a wall beside the ragged gar-

---

2. My wife, who has an M.A. in Chinese language and literature.

den of the mosque, its flowers protected by a single strand of barbed wire. Peddlers, bent under burdens, move up and down the garden paths. At the back door of the mosque there are huge logs. Is there a huge fireplace?

The Kabul River here is a miserable trickle. Up a bit is a stone bridge, nearby a little wooden one with a protective rope, none too protective for the awkward likes of me.

Later:

Back again. Across the river, sheep wandering. I go by the Spinyar, the German shop, and into the plaza where a couple of hundred men circle around wrestlers (*chajors*) in striped coats, baggy trousers and beanies. The referee's chest is bare, perhaps to show he's not carrying a weapon. The wrestlers circle each other, then, signaled by a raised arm, grapple, grabbing each other's coat and pants. It's apparently a draw; the referee breaks it up. They circle and start again. Quite dull, and there's no crowd noise. After ten minutes, two other guys go at it. I leave, passing half an acre of melon-eaters.

In the balcony of the James Hotel, Afghanis are drinking coffee. Loudly painted buses depart from the old city. Near the Hotel Kabul, two boys about nine are selling books from a stall. There are about thirty of them. I buy—what a surprise-a Katherine Anne Porter. Past the clothing bazaar is a taxi stand. I make an arrangement with a driver to visit the Kabul Gorge tomorrow morning.

The loudspeaker in Zarnegar Park might be giving the news of the day.

After supper: talk, somewhat inhibited by the soundtrack of the Indian film playing next door. I should probably have tried the family restaurant across the bridge: two men, pots, a sign nailed to the lamppost in the garden; two yards away, a griller of hot sweets. The griller is an old man with a white beard. Next to him is a little boy with karakul-curled black hair. The man has a shrouded, intelligent face. What's in his head? Songs, coins, prayers? (I just heard, then saw him counting coins.)

In the Yama dining room, a piggish-looking fellow in a white striped suit eats in silence with his sport-shirted companion. I eat a beefsteak with eggs, a salad and a Fanta: eighty-five afghanis. A dollar-forty, and it was a good steak. Now to bed to read Hartley's *The Hireling* (bought in Isfahan).

Finished *Hireling.* It ends with Lieutenant Franklin kissing Ledbetter's St. Christopher medal. I've been worrying about Chris[3] since Nick's letter saying he'd gone off to Weekapaug.

The mosque outside the window turns out to be Shah Timur's tomb, and though this Timur is surely a child of Babar, not Timur Lenk, I think of Tamerlane and Christopher Marlowe and the talk I gave in Sam Johnson's class on the name Christopher, and the way I used St. Christopher in *In Any Case,* dedicated to my Christopher.

The soundtrack of the Indian movie battered the night until eleven o'clock when the show let out. Judging from the racket of comments and ha-ha-ha's, the audience was appreciative. After that, sleep, until about 4 A.M. when the pious started tuning up for the muezzin's summons. Then gaggles of businessmen started what may have been a debate about the day's corn and pistachio prices. A largish segment of the local public decided it was a good time to stroll under this window. Then the door handle churned furiously.

"Who's there?" I yelled. This led to what I suppose was an argument in the hallway between the knob-turner and the Room Boy. The former must have won because seconds later a fist pounded the door.

Stern (viva voce): What the fuck are you doing? It's 4 A.M.!

Silence. I'd found the magic formula and slept until 6:15. I must have gotten used to the muezzin.

Breakfast. The manager comes over to tell me the story of last night's film. "Rich man is died from poison. Man is accused. Is come to prison. Father not know son. Son not know father. Son finds mouse poison for medicine. The three accuse the father of mouse poison. The father get out of prison. He get tape recorder, put under table. He tell men, 'You did the dying of the rich man.' They talk. He take tape recording to police. It is very good film."

STERN: In Farsi?
MANAGER: No, Urdu. I understand from school, but some understand from gesture. Film very good dancing. Very good music.

---

3. My eldest son. Nick is my youngest.

STERN (who has heard the music, shifts): Is it in color?
MANAGER: Very beautiful color. Very beautiful India places.
STERN: I must see it.

Nur Mohammed, the driver, shows up. I know he's Nur Mo-hammed because he shows me an envelope addressed to "Nur Mo-hammed (Taxi Driver)." It's from "my friend in Japan" and kept as a charm or an advertisement above the windshield. We head for Kabul Gorge, which is rugged and dramatic, but not as splendid as the canyons around Boulder. We stop at a roadside stall and buy a giant wa-termelon for nine afghanis which, cut with a knife, is sweet and thirst-quenching. Then we drive to Jalalabad, an extra treat. It's a long, two-hour, hot trip.

J-bad is not one of the stellar cities of the orient. There is somno-lent bustle, pavement, shops, a few cars, carts. Nur Mohammed steers me to one—his friend's?—stacked with cruddy ornaments. Even out of mercy, this light traveler doesn't buy anything.

Back we drive, stopping for lunch in the hills, a large restaurant shielded from the sun by mats on poles. It's full of diners, all male, all Afghan, who squat on the unmatted turf. Nur Mohammed removes his shoes and gets his hands washed by boys with copper ewers who walk up and down aisles. I get washed as well. Nur Mohammed sits in lotus position; my shoeless feet and legs stretch into the aisle. Food is good, all taken in by hand: stewed chicken, meatballs, some sort of peas, rice, salad (which I skip) and wonderful flat bread to mop up the gravy. Sixty-five afghanis for the two of us.

Back at the wheel, Nur Mohammed yawns. I offer to drive, he grins, shakes his head. At the Gorge, he runs into a friend driving two girls, one from Toronto, one from Manchester. They watch two boyfriends slide a thousand meters or so down the grassed slope, then get back in the car to be driven around to pick them up.

Back at the Yama, Nur Mohammed tells me that the price is not the agreed-upon eight dollars for the Gorge but twenty-five, "because we have visited Jalalabad." Thrilling Jalalabad. We agree on twenty dollars. Nur Mohammed recruits the hotel manager to go to the bank with him as he doesn't have the clout to cash traveler's checks. He arranges to take me to the airport tomorrow morning at nine o'clock for one hundred afghanis.

Bisyot (Farsi) = "very"; *hisht* is the name for the inverted thimble dwellings rising from the terraced land which you see outside Jalalabad. The old mud brick fortress is, I think, the tomb of the last king's father.

I eat dinner with Herr Sichel from Hamburg. I think he's here on business and, if I haven't misheard or misunderstood his German, has something to do with hospital supplies. A Pakistani big shot comes into the room barefoot and ill shaven. He informs us that he has many cars and houses but that, despite such wealth, he was pulled off the plane in Kabul without money. He had to borrow the t-shirt he's wearing. He went on about his Mercedes and his firm, Mir something-or-other, "fine goods," two outlets, Karachi and Lahore. As for politics, he says, "Bhutto is an idiot." Believing a man at the airport who said it was illegal, he left sixty quid in Karachi. All this is, I think, to make *la bella figura*, not to borrow money from Sichel or Stern.

September 8
Kabul Airport
I tried to buy a karakul hat in the market this morning. No one would accept and no one would cash a traveler's check before nine.

At the airport, confusion. Aeroflot has overbooked the flight. A Russian lady tells me, "They do this all the time." A German geographer from Marburg says that he has been working on the Afghan-Iranian border: "The Hillman project. Irrigation. Sanitation problems did it in. High temperatures. The water rose and brought soil to the surface. We couldn't work it out."

Names of some—of the overbooked—Tashkent passengers: Lomanka; Nishino; Ashraf Yodigary; Sekretaura; Karoua; Garacho; Giso; Eklers; Sultan Papal.

On to Tashkent.

Becoming a Writer: The Forties

In the early forties, when, at twelve or thirteen, I began writing poems and stories, I bought for a quarter what may have been the first Pocket Book, M. E. Speare's anthology of English poetry, a treasury of formal models from Wyatt to Yeats' "Lake Isle of Innisfree." For stories, I had the Woolcott *Reader*s and Bennett Cerf's *Bedside Books of American and British Stories.* My versions of these delighted my father, who'd long deluded himself about the prodigy he'd sired. My mother, the household Sancho Panza, refrained from diluting the pleasure we took in my semi-thefts.

Of course I'd been reading for years, Grimm, Andersen, the Arabian Nights, Albert Payson Terhune, Tom Swift and the Rover Boys, Altschuler's *The Shadow of the North, Little Men* and *Little Women,* endless Wodehouse and much else borrowed from the little—huge and beautiful thought I—public library at 82nd and Amsterdam on the way home from PS 9 on West End. Birthdays and Christmas too brought a book, one my mother had somehow intuited I wanted. When my allowance hit a dollar a week, I'd spend parts of Sunday with my friend Larry Goldsmith in the cut-rate bookstores on Broadway, sometimes hauling home like a spy with crucial blueprints a Modern Library Giant.

Broadway between 42nd and 52nd was familiar stamping ground. Dressed in our Sunday suits, ties, overcoats and caps, Larry and I identified, we thought, crooks, pugs, whores, runaways, undercover cops, what have you. On the crowded streets or in the Penny Arcade on, I think, 51st, we played games after seeing a movie and stage show at the Paramount, Roxy, Rivoli, Strand or Capitol, then ate a hot roast beef sandwich from the twirling spits of a see-all restaurant on 49th, half a block away from Jack Dempsey's Restaurant. Jack always sat with friends in the window booth and, if he saw us waving, waved back through the glass. One day we went inside, stood at his table, unbuttoned our jackets, pulled up our shirts and asked him to punch us. He tapped our bellies and signed menus across the picture of his old fighting self. (A grandson has mine. I don't know where Larry's is; he killed himself in 1954.)

In the mysterious progress of literary appetite, I moved in my Stuyvesant High School years (1940–44) from Wodehouse and *The Count of Monte Cristo* to *The Forsythe Saga, War and Peace, The Ring and the Book,* and, thanks to Will Durant's *The Story of Philosophy,* to *the World as Will and Idea* and *Beyond Good and Evil.* These books were not creations one could steal from or imitate, let alone rival, but were countries to which one had been granted citizenship.

My first non-family audience was a sophomore English class. One day, not long after Pearl Harbor, I read a story aloud from the front of the room; the boys listened, laughed, applauded. The teacher, Mr. Jesse Lowenthal, a thin, dour, elegant fellow who sported a handkerchief in the breast pocket of his blue suit, smiled little and laughed less, but that day said, solemnly, that the story was good. Our teachers were people of dignity and intellect; their words had scriptural weight. A key turned in the lock of a door I hadn't even noticed.

In those naïvely hierarchical days, there seemed to be only one door to Literature, not hundreds labeled "Jewish American Literature," "Black Literature," "Chinese American Literature," "Gay Literature." There was regional literature, but my literary peers at the University of North Carolina were contemptuous of it. Unaware how many precincts had never been heard from, we felt that the immense, if finite, riches of literature were in one great room. The only literary exclusion was ourselves, and that could be remedied. At Chapel Hill, the ghost of Thomas Wolfe walked the paths, but for the small band of writers who somehow found each other—and not in the one creative writing class—that path was adolescence; our southern writer was Faulkner, whom we read before Malcolm Cowley packaged him in one of the first Viking Portables.

I learned about him and much else from a fellow I met in the UNC Library. He'd leaned over a wonderful book I'd just discovered there, Louis Untermeyer's anthology of modern British and American poetry, and said something like, "Good stuff in that." Don Justice was this fellow's name, he was on his way to New York City from Miami at whose university he studied literature and music with Carl Ruggles. He was worldly, nineteen, three years, a thousand books and ten thousand thoughts beyond me, but with the generosity of the literary aristocrat, he welcomed me as peer and friend. I can't locate the first letter he wrote me days later from New York, but a few sentences from one he wrote a year or so later from Miami suggests the literary standard I'd failed to meet.

> The two poems you sent me I will be honest about. I did not like them . . . they show lack of organization, no feeling for form . . . uncontrolled meter, now and then an obvious rhyme, and quite often a banal or borrowed image; furthermore, no suggestion of a complete world-picture was there, no moral structure behind or beneath the surface of the poems which would serve to give them meaning and life . . . They seemed hurried and probably were, though I have the faith that you must on some things spend a great deal of time. At any rate, send me more of your work.

In 1946, Don came back to Chapel Hill for graduate work and met Jean Ross in our Renaissance Lit class. They'd marry the following year at her parents' farmhouse in western North Carolina where Jean, her sister and brothers grew up reading and writing for diversion. (They all became professional writers.) For a wedding present, I sent them Yvor Winters' *In Defense of Reason* about which, wrote Jean, they quarreled "unreasonably" on their honeymoon. Also in 1946, Edgar Bowers came back from the war in Germany to join us, Paul Ramsey, Burke Shipley and Ken Rothwell in a literary group which read and criticized each others' work. In the spring, we went over to a Greensboro literary festival where our favorite new writers, Robert Penn Warren, Robert Lowell and Peter Taylor (Jean's brother-in-law and Lowell's Kenyon roommate), appraised the poems and stories we'd submitted. Other submitting writers came from Vanderbilt, Grinnell, Harvard and Kenyon. (I particularly recall the Hecht brothers, Anthony and Roger.) We'd all read, liked or disliked the same books, the same writers, the same reviews.

There may have been a hundred or more literary quarterlies back then, but there were only a handful whose latest issues one could hardly wait to read: the *Kenyon, Partisan* and *Sewanee* reviews (the *Southern Review,* backed by Huey Long's pilfered dough, had stopped publishing a few years earlier) and, occasionally, *Accent* or one of the still smaller periodicals such as the *Western Review* which Don and I later (1952–54) helped Ray West edit in Iowa City when we were getting the doctorates which would help get us teaching jobs to support our families and writing. Today, there are a thousand reviews, most read by the few hundred friends and relatives of the editor, and there are also a million blogs to slake the critical and creative appetites of their million writers. Our common reading made for a community, perhaps a narrower one than we believed then, but one which gave our debates an intensity which was often absorbed into our own stories, novels, essays and poems.

The first story of mine accepted by other than a college magazine came with a letter from the poet John Crowe Ransom, editor of the *Kenyon Review.* My wife waved it from the window of our Iowa City attic as my whalish Hudson drove up after my morning teaching stint at Coe College. Fifty-three years ago now, and I'm not sure anything has topped that acceptance. (The joy was reinforced by the amazement, delight and—mostly subdued—envy of the other Workshop writers.)

In the fifties, when you published a story in one of the reviews, you'd get ten letters from New York editors telling you how much they liked it and asking if you had or were working on a novel they could read.[1] (If you didn't or weren't, you started work on one immediately.) Agents also wrote about the story, sometimes to let you know they'd be showing up on the campus where you and your writing peers studied or taught. So young, big-eyed Candida Donadio of Russell and Volkening showed up in Chicago to sign up Philip Roth and me. Large-circulation magazines like *Esquire* published pieces about the "red hot center" of literature in which, to your surprised delight, you found yourself, your friends, your agent and your publisher.

Since those days, I haven't had, perhaps haven't needed or even wanted, the sort of critical fellowship we had back then. I've had luck finding writer friends here or there to read and criticize my work. In the early days at the University of Chicago, where I came in 1955, I had the brilliant enthusiasm of Arthur Heiserman, a scholar-writer whose own ingenious and powerful fictions were seldom published although he was also in Candida's stable. In 1957, Saul Bellow, whom I'd first invited to

---

1. The first who wrote me was Joe Fox of Random House. Nora Ephron used his name for that of the book chain mogul in the movie *You've Got Mail.*

my Chicago writing class in 1956, began reading his work to me and criticizing mine. In 1962, he became a University of Chicago colleague. I also read the early work of my fellow instructor Philip Roth, although in those days I don't think he read mine. By then, though, one had not only editors but, when the books were published, critics. The intimacy of everything but what counted most—writing—was gone.

Individuality, Style and Other Forms of Identification

❦

I

A SLIGHTLY DIFFERENT VERSION of the following essay was given as the twelfth John Adams Lecture at San Diego State University on December 1, 2004. I've talked or read stories at this university several times over the last decades. I enjoy seeing old friends (Donald Shojai) and newer ones (Nick Genovese), eating lunch overlooking the ocean and flocks of seal-like swimmers in skintight black suits, breakfasting over the great S-curve of the harbor, the jaunty, uncertain skyline of the uncertain city, darts into the Luxembourg-size zoo, the haphazard spread of the university's lunar buildings, the thirty-five thousand students who work here every day and evening in the year but Christmas and New Year's Day. Perhaps it's the amiable spread which encouraged me to cover so much ground, but I print this revision because much that's here isn't elsewhere.

In the weeks after the suicidal attacks of 9/11, a handful of *NY Times* reporters wrote some eighteen hundred mini-biographies of those who'd died in New York, Washington, DC, and the Pennsylvania woods. Here is one which appeared with a dozen others on December 22, 2001:

> For the last eight years, Frank Koestner was a stock trader for Cantor Fitzgerald, leaving home at 6 a.m. and trying to leave his office by 7 p.m. At 48, there was never enough time for jogging or skiing or hiking or biking or whitewater rafting.
>
> Since his divorce two years ago, there was never enough time with his five year old daughter, Carolyn. He would spend alternate

weekends with her. In summer, they would go to a park or zoo or swim in a backyard pool he put in for her. In winter, they would shovel snow together, even if there had been only flurries, because she thought it was fun.

He was planning to marry Michelle Stabile on Oct. 28. During the week of Sept. 11 they were supposed to close on a three bedroom house in Massapequa Shores on Long Island. "He was articulate and educated and ethical," said Dominick Schook, his friend for 31 years. "He was the type of person where you could go away and leave a million dollars on the coffee table and when you got back there would be a million dollars plus interest."

Even those who read only a handful of these so-called "Portraits of Grief" believe that they helped relieve the sterility of numerical abstraction, more or less as the photographs and brief accounts of those who perished in the Holocaust relieved the faceless weight of a much larger enumeration.[1]

Two hundred words of ordinary prose cannot supply the pith of even a monotonous life.[2] Nonetheless, these two hundred words give most of us all we'll ever know of Frank Koestner, his active business life, his athleticism, his love for his daughter, the divorce from her mother, the imminence of a new life with Michelle Stabile in a three-bedroom house within commuting distance of his World Trade Center job, and finally, the most telling note, the tribute from his friend of thirty-one years, Dominick Schook.

Of course this Frank Koestner is not nearly as vivid or interesting as say, Josiah Crawley, the fanatically honest, impoverished clergyman invented by Anthony Trollope for his Barsetshire series of novels, nor as Anne Frank, the girl whose diary earlier transformed the Holocaust from abstraction to heartbreaking actuality. Yet, along with Koestner's photograph on the newspaper page, the two hundred words help condense a mist of historic brutality into a droplet of humanity.

---

1. October 2005. Recently a list of more than two hundred obituaries of "martyrs" has been posted on Islamist Internet sites. These mini-biographies serve the purposes of recruitment as well as celebration of individuality.

2. Jeffrey Rosen, in "The Naked Crowd" (in *spiked*), and the novelist Thomas Mallon (in *American Scholar*) claim that the biographies homogenized the portrayed dead. There are remarkable brief portraits in prose—as in the journals of good journal keepers—and quite a large number in poetry where condensation, obliquity and "musical" fusions of precision and extremity are part of the writer-reader contract. (I refer poetry readers to the wonderful books of Alane Rollings, especially *The Struggle to Adore* [1994], *The Logic of Opposites* [1998] and *To Be in This Number* [2004].)

Consider the video-biographies of the young human bombs sent by Hamas, al Aksa and Al-Fatah into the buses and streets of Israel. These were created not just to recruit successor suicides but to offer individuating human thermometers of the desperate fever gripping them. On the other hand, the videographs made in Iraq of the interrogation and beheading of non-combatants by hooded men were meant to terrorize and blackmail. The killers are hooded not just to veil their identity from pursuers but to say that none of them has a personal score to settle with their victims, whereas the unhooded victims, pleading for their lives and for what their captors want, call attention to the precious individuality about to be lost. Beheaded—the most dehumanizing and de-individualizing form of execution—they supposedly become exemplars of the inhumanity of that Great Satan who did not yield to the blackmail.

The Iraqi prisoners at Abu Ghraib prison were hooded by their American jailers to diminish their individuality and thus make it easier to humiliate and degrade them.

Another variation of the suppression of individuality was contained in the instructions to the September 11 hijacker-killers (found in the baggage of Mohammed Atta and two of his collaborators) telling them what to do in their final days, hours and even seconds. So they were to focus not on their individual lives and thoughts but on becoming martyrs. Their ablutions (shaving excess hair, applying cologne), the sharpening of their knives (to spare their victims), their prayers, their very thoughts on entering the taxi, the airplane and, finally, their targets were spelled out for them so that they did not have to exercise those choices which create and are the marks of individuality.[3]

This is a time when the ever-more-crowded earth is measured and

3. Although Horace's *Dulce et decorum est pro patria mori* can be called a Western equivalent of such stimuli to self-sacrifice, its poetic sweetness and propriety promote the individuality whose sacrifice it urges. Times of crisis tend to bring on annihilation of individuality. Following the September 11, 2001, attacks, there were mass arrests, sequestrations and legal deprivations some of which recent Supreme Court decisions (*Rasul v. Bush, Hamdi v. Rumsfeld, Rumsfeld v. Padilla*) halted, perhaps in the spirit of what Professor Woodrow Wilson wrote in 1889, namely that the chief function of the state is "to aid the individual to the fullest and best possible realization of his individuality, instead of merely to the full realization of his sociality" (*The State: Elements of Historical and Practical Politics*, p. 647). Sixty years before that, Tocqueville wrote that the American love of public monuments had to do with their sense of individual weakness and the state's grandeur (*Democracy in America*, part 2, pp. 56–57). This notion ascended—or descended—into "The individual is foolish but the species is wise" (Russell Kirk, *The Conservative Mind*), an idea cited when well-established individuals regard their less well-situated fellow citizens.

controlled by statistical instruments which ignore such marks. The more refined these classifying instruments become, the more important it may be to hear and tell these individuating stories. One of Bill Clinton's political charms was his awareness of this. At the dedication of his Little Rock Presidential Library on November 18, 2004, he said, "I grew up in the pre-television age, in a family of uneducated but smart, hardworking, caring storytellers. They taught me that everyone has a story. And that made politics intensely personal to me. It was about giving people better stories."

Few Westerners are content to be unstoried, to be identified only as members of a class, whether as insurance prospects, consumers of products or supporters of particular causes and candidates. Their story says, "Okay, I may vote like X, buy like Y, may be a member of the M class and the N interest group, the product of K, L and W, but I am also I, and to some degree unlike any other I. Even if there were an instrument which could convert the quadrillion fact-events which constitute this *Iness* into an I-clone, it would still not be I because conversion itself would be factored into it."

2

Here is an excerpt from a *New York Times* story dated March 31, 2004. Five times longer than Frank Koestner's, it deals not with someone known only to friends and family but to millions of cultured people. It begins:

> To most art lovers, a painting by Joan Miro is immediately recognizable as, well, a Miro. It probably shows cosmic, botanical, geometric or abstract lines or shapes floating against celestial blue, sandy yellow or earth brown background. It also probably exudes a mystical yet reassuring dreamy quality.

The sort of individuality this describes is that of an artistic style. The rest of the story deals with the life of Miro from his birth in Barcelona in April 1893 to his death ninety years later. We learn that he was eighteen before he became a full-time painter, that his initial inspiration was the primitive frescos in local Romanesque churches, his second that of the European avant-garde. After seeing the canvases of Braque and Picasso, Miro said he wanted to "break the guitar of Cubism," and to "murder painting" itself. He turned to sandpaper, tar, feathers, wire, string and nails. "I intend to destroy, destroy everything that exists in painting," he told a Spanish journalist in 1931. "I have utter contempt for painting. The only thing that interests me is the spirit itself, and I only use the customary artists' tools—brushes, canvas, paint—in order to get the best effects. I'm only interested in anonymous art, the kind that springs from the collective unconscious."[4]

Miro's work has become a recognizable part of the inner gallery of millions of educated people and, through its influence on design, part of the visual and psychological intelligence of even more people. To a lesser degree, so is his colorful career a part of many of us, part of that other gallery where Van Gogh's bandaged earlessness is not just an element of his late self-portraits but of the personality which created them.

3

In the same section of the March 31, 2004, edition of the *Times*, there is a story about the sale of a Vermeer painting, *Young Woman Seated at the Virginal.* Like several other Vermeer paintings, this one had been under the cloud of suspicious authenticity which formed after the forger Hans van Meegeren confessed to painting and selling seven so-called Vermeers to museums and collectors between 1937 and 1943. *Young Woman Seated at the Virginal* was examined by scholars and authenticated as one of the world's thirty-five true Vermeers. The crucial authentication was done by an analysis of the pigments which were of the rare and expensive sort which Vermeer and few other artists used. The most significant of these was the ultramarine made from ground-up lapis lazuli.

There is a literary equivalent of such physical authentication of style. It is the examination of filler or non-contextual words in a text. The use of these innocuous words is supposedly peculiar to every

---

4. It's worth remarking that the most striking individuals often champion the submersion of individuality.

writer. So the statisticians Mosteller and Wallace[5] were able to determine that Madison wrote all twelve Federalist papers whose authorship had been disputed.

In the last half century, we have grown accustomed to technical authentication of identity. In criminal investigations, fingerprint analysis has been supplemented, if not replaced, by that of DNA. Soon there will be genomic profiles of all of us, and who knows what micro and sub-microscopic individuation will follow that? The most remarkable I've seen comes from the biochemist Carolyn Bertozzi:

> . . . we have the tools to visualize chemical changes in the brain during the formation of a memory, the moment of first contact between a virus and its victim, the moment of conception . . . Proteins can be seen "breathing," DNA "relaxing." It turns out that individual molecules can have moods as different as those of individual human beings while retaining their molecular similarity.[6]

4

This sort of analysis may satisfy different sorts of interest in individuality or authenticity, but not esthetic hunger. For that, we look for sources of style which go beyond—or is it before?—breathing proteins and ground-up lapis lazuli. After all, we don't love paintings because of their pigmentation or people because of the whorls on their fingers or the patterns of their DNA It is what we call their character, their personality, their behavior, their look in action and repose which move us toward like and dislike, love and hate. In literature, the complexity of character arrives in the medium of narrative, a specially wrought language used in specially arranged sequences of scene, exposition and description. In court, the testimony of character witnesses softens, hardens or con-

5. *Inference and Disputed Authority: The Federalist,* 1964.
6. *Bulletin of the American Academy of Arts and Science* (Winter 2004): p. 4. After writing this paragraph, I attended a lecture by the Egyptologist Stephen Harvey, dealing with a wave of individuality in the eighteenth Dynasty (1400 B.C.). The notice of individually stamped bricks at Abydos and the individuality of certain El-Amarna painters testifies to the interest of recent scholars in "agency," i.e., individuality, although as biochemists and Egyptologists are uncovering it, many literary critics are intent on dismissing or annihilating it.

fuses the jury's view of the defendant. In a biography or novel, puzzling or "contradictory" behavior or "testimony" deepens a character's complexity. The greater the contradictions, the more interesting the character, at least if some sort of sense—perhaps only formal sense—is made of them.

A novel's success often has more to do with such arrangements than with its subject matter, although an author's treatment of such matters is of course a component of what we call his style.

5

The twentieth century grew increasingly thick with intimate biography and autobiography. The self-revelation of artists and writers in journals, autobiographies and interviews has more recently been augmented by such television programs as *American Masters* and by even more intimate videographies. Fascinating and valuable as these are, there are limits to their usefulness. Writing, composing or painting absorbs the artist in the process and limits his awareness of what he's doing, thus his reliability as critic of or guide to his own work.[7] He may know what he aimed at, but in the process of carrying out the aim, his unself-conscious energy has more often than not taken him to a very different place. I, for one, have been surprised, not always happily, by observations about my work made by readers and critics. I have not spotted themes they have seen or ways of developing the narrative which have pleased or displeased them. Writing, I've concentrated on bringing the narrative along in a certain direction, working up a variety of viewpoints while not straining the key point of view, or on such matters as alternating exposition with scene, comedy with pathos. Mostly I concentrate, or so I think, on the words of the sentence I'm writing. As writer, I'm able to talk about such matters, but until I become—after a few years, perhaps—more the reader of the book than its writer, I am probably a less reliable critic or appreciator of it than the average reader.

---

7. Philip Roth jokes about the lack of Intelligent Design in the composition of his novels.

I recently reread Anthony Trollope's 1866 novel, *The Last Chronicle of Barset,* the last of a series of books set in this invented county which began with a short novel called *The Warden,* a book I read more than fifty years ago. The remembrance itself is an acknowledgment of the Trollope style. I have read such dull Trollope novels as *Ayala's Angel* which, nonetheless, are clearly his. Style itself is no guarantee of worth, although the name "Trollope" on a book's spine, like that of any other well-established logo—Lexus, Gucci, Wheaties—is a promise of satisfaction, or, if you dislike Trollope or Wheaties, of dissatisfaction. In any case, there is inferior Trollope (as there is basically no inferior box of Wheaties). *Ayala's Angel,* although recognizably Trollope, is a Trollope in which analytic and narrative power is so weakened as to offer only the tricks and stratagems of Trollopian construction. Trollope himself writes about such degradation in his remarkable autobiography.

> That a man as he grows old should feel the labour of writing to be a fatigue is natural enough . . . there comes a time when he shuts his eyes and shuts his ears. To the novelist thus wearied there comes the demand for further novels. He does not know his own defect, and even if he did he does not wish to abandon his own profession . . . but he writes because he has to tell a story, not because he has a story to tell . . . [His] characters do not live and move, but are cut out of blocks and are propped against the wall. The incidents are arranged in certain lines—the arrangement being as palpable to the reader as it has been to the writer—but do not follow each other as results naturally demanded by previous action . . . The course of the tale is one piece of stiff mechanism . . . These, it may be said, are reflections which I, being an old novelist, might make useful to myself for discontinuing my work . . .[8]

Unfortunately, despite his unusually clear and modest self-regard, Trollope did not discontinue writing the demanded novels, and most of the late ones droop with the fatigue he describes.

The Last Chronicle of Barset's characters fit in the spectrum between

---

8. Anthony Trollope, *An Autobiography,* pp. 192–93. My own work stoppage was due to different things, a few of which I describe in "On a Writer's Endgame," *Dedalus* (Winter 2004).

those rational enough to see, tolerate and even welcome views and personalities different from their own and the resolute, stubborn, sometimes madly adamant who may hear and even understand other people and their viewpoints but whose convictions are cemented in self-certainty, sometimes, in their view, a God-inspired one. So Josiah Crawley, although uncertain about the provenience of a money order he has used to pay a bill, is as unshakably certain about his guilt in doing so as he is about his judgments of every person he knows. As surely self-convinced is the formidable wife of the Bishop of Barsetshire, Mrs. Proudie. The reader is set up for the collision of these two opposed certainties. Such collisions constitute the dramatic highlights of Trollope novels.[9] For Trollope readers, they spell out the Trollope of the novels.

This Trollope is only partly revealed in the *Autobiography*. There, for instance, one finds what isn't in the novels, such as the author's pleasure conjuring up and living among his creations, his pride in the workmanlike routines worked out to produce them and the money they've earned for him.

> I have published more than twice as much as Carlyle. I have also published considerably more than Voltaire, even including his letters. We are told that Varro . . . had written 480 volumes . . . I comfort myself by reflecting that the amount of manuscript described as a book in Varro's time was not much. (p. 301)

He *comforts himself*. Okay, most of us like being prolific, even of mischief, but Trollope is not just more naïvely frank about it than we are, he is, I think, a little batty about it. He makes a list of the forty-nine books published before he wrote the *Autobiography* (many more followed), including the money he was paid for each one. (The total comes to 68,939 pounds, 17 shillings and 5 pence, which I'd guess is the equivalent of 8 or 9 million 2004 dollars.)

The *Autobiography* also describes his full-time job at the post office, where he made important contributions to the delivery of mail not only

---

9. There are other, different pleasures in the novel. I particularly relish the interior monologue and conversation of the kind, moribund warden, Septimus Harding. Indeed, only in the novel's subplots about the painter Dalrymple or John Eames' long, fruitless courtship of Lily Dale do the author's narrative reins go limp, and one realizes that his obligation to fill the three volumes promised to his publisher has distended and thinned his narrative intelligence. Then, as Henry James put it, we may sense that the diligent author's eyes are wandering to the clock.

in Ireland and England but in some of the countries he was invited to visit. In addition to his double professional life, he rode to hounds two or three times a week, played whist at his clubs, read enormously in both English and Latin, traveled widely, ran for Parliament and, when defeated, wrote books about an MP. He loved wine and had a large cellar, loved books and owned at least five thousand volumes, had a long, apparently happy marriage and two sons, one of whom tended sheep in Australia. In short, he was the picture and probably the essence of the virtuous, intelligent, thoughtful, "liberal-conservative" (his term) Englishman of the upper middle class whom late twentieth-century viewers of *Upstairs, Downstairs* and the *Forsyte Saga* adored to watch, one well-dressed in fine broadcloth and full of opinions to which viewers could feel superior even while they longed for the world in which such opinions prevailed.[10]

Yet the personality and character of Anthony Trollope are not as clear, amusing or interesting as that of his invented characters. A mist of self-concealment hangs about the *Autobiography* as it does about even the frankest autobiographer. One wants to ask Trollope, "What was your wife like? How did your sons differ? Why did one go to Australia and become a sheepherder?" and a hundred other questions of the sort which would be absurd to put to Josiah Crawley, although that could be an amusing parlor game. A fictional existence needs but a tiny proportion of what constitutes a real life. Indeed, such characters as Crawley are purposely narrow and predictable, a source of our delight in them. They offer clarity seldom experienced in the murk and complexity of real life.[11]

---

10. Some of Trollope's world still exists, and not just in London buildings or Barsetshire-like villages. It has left enough grooves in habits of behavior and sentiment to make it a standard appealed to in domestic and public discussion, even though its notions of decorum and propriety are so distant from modern practice that they are regarded by many as absurd and useless as those of an isolated New Guinea village. Indeed, many Trollope readers now enter his world for the same sorts of pleasure they get reading about those remote villages, the sort of refuge foreignness offers. However, the essential situations and emotions Trollope describes, the growth of love and greed, the clash of interests, the agony of rejection and humiliation are recognizable parts of everyday life, and despite the contention of the young Henry James that Trollope writes for "minds unable to think," many of his treatments of them still ring true. James' eulogy of the recently dead Trollope was far more generous: "A race is fortunate when it has a good deal of the sort of imagination . . . that had fallen to the share of Anthony Trollope" (*Century Magazine,* July 1883).
11. This may be related to the well-known reluctance of infantrymen to shoot the enemies they've been—inadequately—taught to hate. Face to face, they sense the enemy as a fellow human being and will or cannot pull the trigger. See Don Baum, "The Price of Valor," *New Yorker,* July 12–19, 2004, pp. 44 ff.

Even if an autobiographer is as stable a character as Trollope seems to be, there is so much experience, so many millions of reactions to so many events, so much fantasizing, so many dreams, so much "uncharacteristic" thinking and behavior in his and every life that not even the longest biography could contain them.

We all have museums in which friends and relatives occupy certain niches, and public figures, that is, celebrities, occupy others, but these niches are of a different order from those in the museum where Raskolnikov and Hamlet, Leopold Bloom, Elizabeth Bennett and Charles Swann, Huck Finn, Emma Bovary, Moses Herzog and Josiah Crawley exist.[12] These fictional people have been honed and sharpened, rehoned and resharpened into a kind of perfection which not even the greatest saints, sages and heroes of real life touch. There is no revision in real life. Even if one makes up for what one has badly done, the make-up action exists alongside the "original." And even in the best of real life action, there is so much accompanying complexity, both ex- and interior, so much that reveals next to nothing, that it never approaches the comparative purity of fictional action where every thought, dream, opinion, exchange and interaction matters. The individuality of a living being may resemble that of an author's creation, but the creation is purer, clearer, as reflections in water, free of the bedazzlement and impurities of the atmosphere, are clearer and usually more beautiful than what they reflect. Finally, creations aren't mortal. Perhaps they're needed to soften mortality.

7

A word here about my sense of that part of my own nature which relates to my literary work. I am partial to terseness, if not dryness, and partial too to certain sorts of resolution and conclusion which involve a quiet, usually unexpressed sense of failure. Do I know why I am attracted to this sort of conclusion? No. Indeed, I don't want to know. All I can or am willing to say is that it feels right to me.

I don't intend my fiction to mirror, explain or transfigure my experience. I don't really know what I intend except to immerse myself in

---

12. Of course, the word "exist" has a different meaning for fictional and actual characters.

writing a story and, in the process, to discover its internal logic and power. I do not feel close to my completed and published work, although I believe that completing and publishing it has altered me in some way that constitutes preparation for future work, and perhaps to an expanded sense of self. I certainly don't believe that on my deathbed, I will, like Balzac, be calling out to my characters.

Some of the experience described in my own novels and stories is similar to what I've experienced, but my chief interest is not in its commemoration or defense (though there is some of that) but in the way it's transformed in fictional narrative. Even transcribing as precisely as I can feelings felt and experience had, I know that such transcription is a transformation which, under the pressure of narrative art, will become something further and further apart from what launched it.[13] I cannot, or at least won't, say that "My true autobiography is to be found in my fictions," although I believe that there is a part of me in them that can't be found elsewhere.

I do not want to parade a modesty I don't possess when I say that as far as I'm concerned, my own personality, my character, my individuality is of small interest, even to me. Less modestly, I believe that my best stories, novels, and essays may constitute a small addition to literary culture.

I conclude with the observation that the richness of a culture does in large part consist of the variety of individual ways of treating the active, sensate world and the internal consciousness and conscience. I also believe that the heightened, refined and intensified individuality manifested in the arts, crafts, and intellectual disciplines is the highest form of individuality which can be identified.

---

13. The unconscious plays a significant role in one's work. As one who regards himself as scrupulously rational, I yield to unconscious promptings with special deference. Forty-odd years ago, I dreamed that I was in a field being pelted by cabbage heads. In the explanatory part of the dream—and my dreams often include self-analytic components—I realized that the cabbage heads were certain large-breasted characters about whom till then I didn't realize I was writing. Furthermore, the analytic part of the dream informed me, these characters resembled my large-breasted mother. Waking, I resolved not to create such characters again, and I believe that I haven't.

Beazley's Goose

J. D. Beazley, the Professor of Classical Archaeology had a pet goose which he used to bring into college. When the goose died, and Owen, the senior tutor in classics, expressed his condolences in a tone of levity, Beazley rebuked him by saying, "Yes, Owen, Goosy is dead. There are many worse men alive."
—A. J. Ayer, *Part of My Life*

Unlike the poet's much loved Lucy,
Who "dwelt among untrodden ways,"
Professor B's beloved Goosey
Enjoyed two thousand Oxford days.

Many a lecture had been heard
Of Spartan and Hellenic things
Before the handsome white-plumed bird
Folded its puissant, idled wings.

"Consoled" the churlish classics' head,
"Sorry that you've lost your wife."
"Yes, Owen, Goosey's dead.
Many a villain still has life."

How I Think I Got to Think the Way I Think

THE ORIGINAL VERSION of the next essay was given as a talk to the History Section of the George Soros–backed Central European University in Budapest, on September 16, 2003. My friend Sorin Antohi, who presided over the lecture, suggested that the title include the word "ideology." I said that the notion of ideology went against the pragmatic American grain described and illustrated so well in Daniel Boorstin's three-volume history, *The Americans,* and in Daniel Bell's *The End of Ideology.* The ideologist enjoys the solution before he has the problem.

I

Everyone knows how much goes into why we think and feel as we do. Our body structure and state of health, the security or insecurity of our childhood, the relationship to those who raised us and their relationship to the changing world of their time, the experiences we have before, during and after schooling, the success and failure (ease and difficulty) of our working and emotional life, all this and much more, so much that despite the sophistication of the social sciences of classification—marketing surveyors, pollsters, insurance regulators—it's not simply a sentimental notion that every individual differs significantly from every other. Identical twins, raised in the same home, and educated alike, will have different preferences, habits, turns of phrase, and will frequently behave, think and feel differently. So of course not all thin, blue-eyed, thirty-year-old married Baptist sanitation workers in Chicago cheer for the same team, vote for the same candidate, buy the same sort of car, enjoy the same movies.

Yes, we are usefully bunched and classified, but almost all of us in the cultures of which I know something believe that the sanctity of human life has to do with the uniqueness of every person. Perhaps this is one reason we love personal stories of every sort, from gossip, jokes and anecdotes to novels, biographies, tragedies and epics.

My title promises my story, and I will offer some of it here, but the "I" that I am shies away from delivering much of what I know about myself. Perhaps reticence is not what an autobiographer should advertise, but it is indispensable for social relations, including family life, and even the frankest autobiographer refrains from publishing all he knows about himself if only to be sure that he'll have some friends left when it's published.

2

Fiction writers are freer to draw on what is otherwise repressed for they're protected by the understanding that they are inventing their depictions. I can tell you, though, that this fiction writer has been raked over the coals by some near and dear who believed that they were exploited and exposed in stories which the author thought had been skillfully transformed from originating actualities. My explanation for the hyper-sensitivity of such readers is that fiction is contagious: the reader catches it from the author and invents a story of his own out of the author's original one. This contagion is one source of fiction's power.

Here I don't write in the for me easier mode of fiction but set down more or less factually a few things which I believe influenced the way I think about social and political matters, the circumstances of my life, my parents' sympathies, my sometimes dim awareness of certain public events and developments and, finally, what I learned from participating in a public controversy. I better begin by saying that I am not what I regard as a person of strong, well-thought-out and -felt political views. I have never systematically formulated such views or until now considered their source. My opinions and choices are more easily moved than most by personal encounters, gossip, glimpses, gripes, even turns of phrase. Nonetheless, there is continuity in the way I think and feel about public matters. A social scientist could probably predict most of my votes. Still, the hope is that despite the paucity of self-revelation, this homegrown account will be of some interest, if only because its sort of public self-examination is not all that common.

3

In polls and surveys, I would be classified as an elderly American, New York City–raised professor and writer of comfortable, German Jewish middle-class background. Two of my great- and three of my grandparents emigrated to the United States (New York City) from Germany and Hungary; the fourth, my maternal grandmother, Rachel (nee Regina) Veit, was born in the city in 1860 and there married her first cousin Josef Veit, who'd come from Freiburg, Germany.

I myself have been married—I better say successively—to two white Anglo-Saxon Protestants, one a Connecticut Episcopalian skeptic, the other a Savannah, Georgia, Methodist one. Perhaps I know a bit more about the old WASP ruling class of the United States than I would have if I'd relied only on reading Edith Wharton and Louis Auchincloss or visiting places like Newport and Old Greenwich. I've spent far more time in zones of privilege than in slums, know more Nobel Prize winners than criminals, have more acquaintance with so-called celebrities (not all of them intellectuals) than with the wretched and downtrodden of the earth. Perhaps this is one reason that I sympathize more with the socially insulted and abused than with the privileged among whom I count myself.

As a university professor, I've helped educate some of the world's brightest young people, some of whom are now writers, doctors, entrepreneurs, journalists, filmmakers and public servants (or, for all I know, public enemies). I've lived abroad for several years, traveled a bit in the more civilized areas of the world, and for decades have tried to learn something about political and cultural, particularly literary, developments in the countries I've visited, lectured and taught in. The foreign experience has deepened a belief in the importance of political equality but also moderated my unhappiness about its absence as I understood a bit about very different standards of expectation and reward. Like most people I know, I can be roused to despair and fury by reading about or seeing on television distant human misery, tyranny, brutality, injustice and inequity.

I have what may be a deluded sense of good fortune: I know that I've suffered less physical, financial, social and domestic difficulty than most of mankind. It's hard to be sure of this because I also believe that my emotions are more labile, more up for grabs, than those of many people I've observed or know about. I do seem able to participate more readily in others' emotional situations than many others. It may be one reason I am a fiction writer. I also have a perhaps complementary streak of coldness which sees me through losses which might devastate others. This may be another reason I write fiction. A divorced man, I suffered guilt, bitterness, failure and betrayal. I was able to partially transfigure and thus ease the effect of these feelings by writing about them in novels. This form of relief and whatever praise or cash succeeded it has been an element of my life for more than half a century.

At the University of Chicago, I almost never suffered from bullying superiors or unjust assignments. At such a university, the belief that in some ways one has no superior is compensation for one's modest salary. Even awaiting tenure, I was not lorded over by those who voted for or against it. My "superiors" almost always made me feel that I was of them. (I know that this is not always the case.)

My private life has been marred but not scarred by violence and crime: over the years, a ten-year-old son was threatened with a gun by a drug addict, my wife was mugged and robbed, our house was burgled and three of our cars have been stolen. Again, writing about such events may have freed me from what might have permanently disturbed others.

To envy, jealousy and vengefulness, I am no stranger, but they have played a very small role in my life. I have tried to construct my days to avoid fearful situations and people. I know that I have a large tract of fearfulness in me but very seldom has fear dominated my life. As of this writing (January 9, 2007), I am not afraid of death, only of leaving a beloved wife without her thirty-eight-year-long companion. The days before my only serious surgery were fear-filled, and there were many days before and during my divorce proceedings when I was unable to control the anguish of no longer living in the same house with my young children. My writing has recorded some of this anguish and terror.

I have never been a soldier, never been in prison, never lived in a city being bombed, never been longer than three days without electricity and plumbing, have never lived under tyranny—except during brief lecturing or tourist visits—never been threatened by arrest because of my opinions, and never been restrained from expressing political sentiments (except before a 1979 appearance on a popular Argentina television program when I was asked by my U.S. State Department hosts not to mention *derechos humanos*). My psyche has itself been untouched by mental illness, although I have lived with a bipolar sufferer and shared some of the emotional drainage of her suffering.

In short, my life has been far less roiled by external events than most lives. The death of those dear to me I have usually been able to take in stride, although the last dozen years have become heavier and gloomier with such loss and the loss of the familiar, comforting world of which they were components.

4

I've usually lived among people deeply concerned with, and at times absorbed by public events, elections and civic matters. I grew up in a home where reading newspapers and magazines was taken for granted. Even before I myself read them, I was aware of their importance, partly as inexpensive diversions, partly as the chronicler-interpreters of events which counted. I was five years old when FDR and Adolf Hitler took office, and their importance was impressed on me. My father woke up my sister and me to listen to Roosevelt's "fireside chats," and although I may not have understood them, I sensed their importance. I understood nothing at all of the shortwave broadcasts of Hitler's speeches, but their bizarre semi-hysterical pitch accented my awareness of Hitler's hatred of people like me, my friends and family. Coming home one day from group play, I was told by my mother that we had a new maid who was German. In my never soft boy's voice, I said, "I thought we hated Germans." The maid left immediately. Every weekend, we went to the movies. The bill of fare included a ten-minute newsreel, an occasion for the audience to burst with cheers and boos as the famous figures—Roosevelt, Mussolini, Hitler, Lindbergh—appeared in their unambiguous roles.

My adult life has passed among particularly well-informed people whose professional lives almost demand an informed interest in political matters. My friends read the leading newspapers and news weeklies, and many of us read and sometimes write more or less specialized books on public affairs. There is seldom a lunch in which an article from the *Economist,* the *Wall Street Journal, New Republic* or *New York Times* is not discussed, and such discussion is soon augmented by an account of a new book someone has read or by an experience remembered. Some of my colleagues have worked in administrations as far back as the New Deal. Some have had important policy-making positions in Washington or are regarded as influential commentators. University of Chicago economists have been called the most influential single group of thinkers in the social-political world. Years ago, I used to lunch with one of the senior figures of the group, Friedrich von Hayek, and for a quarter of a century, my close friend and tennis partner Gary Becker has with his late mentors, Milton Friedman and George Stigler, been its leading member. The thinking of these economists is very different from that of almost all my English Department colleagues and from my own views as one who believes that government should level the economic and political playing field. Although I continue to argue with economist friends, my arguments are tempered by some understanding of their viewpoints.

I've had other colleagues who were active in the campaigns of Democratic candidates, and I myself briefly joined such presidential candidates as Robert Kennedy and George McGovern on campaign trips. These reinforced a long-held belief that most people holding public office were not—as I once thought—second-raters but people of exceptional energy, concern, knowledge and passion. For almost fifty years, I've published my form of political commentary. Sometimes the articles centered about meetings with such people as Chicago's Mayor Richard J. Daley or vignettes of friends who've held important Washington positions. Without participating directly in negotiations, I've learned a bit about the ambience, milieu and rhythm of public life. Every now and then, a new fact or ray of intelligence alters my thinking. So I remember arguing a budget matter with a director of the Office of Management and Budget (OMB) and hearing for the first time the word "trillion" used in connection with the American economy. (Getting used to ever-larger numbers seems to be a component of one's political maturation.) The point here is that even someone like me, who has spent most of his conscious life involved with writing, reading and teaching literature, has still spent an enormous amount of time thinking of and even being passionate about public affairs. Indeed, I can say that my passions, especially around the time of presidential elections, are fiercer about candidates and issues than they are or ever have been about anything else. During the Vietnam War, I could only get to sleep by inventing fantasies in which Presidents Johnson and Nixon were forced by me to end the war.

If hatred has been in my head during presidential elections, fear has seldom if ever been, at least not the fear which so many in the world experience as official power rubs up against their far less protected lives. A mite of such fear comes to comfortable people like myself as the ever more powerful conveyers of television news and documentary reportage bring the suffering of human beings into our bed and living rooms with the kind of force that dramatic tragedy brought to its small audiences in fifth-century Athens or sixteenth-century London. One's involvement in the disasters of others almost never has the redemptive and cathartic power which tragedy brings; what it does instead is deposit the need to change the terrible circumstances one has witnessed.

In my own case, the gap between this empathy and the passivity, indolence and careless avariciousness which follows it has become so familiar that I seldom even register it in my consciousness. Part of this consciousness is self-rebuke which, occasionally, results in my writing a check or a letter, signing a petition or even appearing on a forum, radio or television program. For several years, I wrote letters to the editor almost daily, and some minutes were cheered when a letter or, more rarely, an op-ed piece was printed in the *NY Times, Chicago Tribune, Los Angeles Times* or *Washington Post*.

5

I was born in the last month of Calvin Coolidge's presidency and spent my first years in those of Herbert Hoover's, but remember not one contemporary word from or about them. In the Depression which followed the crash of 1929, my family did not, as far as I can remember, suffer privation. As a moderately successful dentist, my father actually prospered, even morally, as he "carried" many patients who could no longer pay their bills. I was aware that when we moved in 1933 from 89th and Broadway to 84th and Central Park West we had somehow improved our social standing, aware too that my mother yearned to further improve it by moving to "the East Side."

My first sense of the political world has to do with the devotion of my parents to President Franklin Roosevelt. His "fireside chat" voice was authoritative, confident and familiar. Listening to it, my parents glowed.

My father's other passion was England (which he didn't visit till 1971, when he was eighty-four). One of his favorite patients was an English diplomat with bad teeth and a ready pocketbook. I've "inherited" his love of the King's English and even remember the pleasure I took in Edward the Eighth's broadcast abdication speech, although I understood next to nothing of what it meant. Even today, I am easily charmed by the understated manner and precise speech of English people and tend to overlook whatever snobbery, hypocrisy, moral cowardice and provincialism may lie beneath them. Age ten, at the Hunter Model School, I stood with classmates as the vice principal, silver-haired Miss Keith, "thanked God that Mr. Chamberlain has returned from Munich with peace in our time." During the newsreels, every audience at Loews 83rd and RKO 81st, my theaters, hissed the becapped, knickered, mustached, ranting Hitler and his huge-chinned Italian sidekick. The Spanish Civil War confused me. Accustomed to cheer for "rebels," I somehow knew I could not cheer for those led by General Franco. About history, I knew next to nothing: on a Maine camping trip, I saw a headline in a village store about the murder of Leon Trotsky and asked the counselor who he was. Decades later, I learned from my father's memoir that Trotsky's son had been his patient. (How small the world becomes, as Baudelaire's "Le Voyage" expresses so beautifully.)

With the help of that memoir, I can trace the source of some of my father's opinions. In 1904, at New York's DeWitt Clinton High School, his English teacher assigned him to debate the question "Are Labor Unions Detrimental to the Best Interests of the Country?" His research included trips to the sweatshops of the Lower East Side of Manhattan where his cousin, Dr. Carl Weisberger, practiced medicine. "I was appalled," he writes in the memoir, "by the filth, the terrible odor, the crowding of a hundred men and women in a space that would ordinarily hold twenty—one small window, one stinking toilet just big enough to squeeze in, the lack of air, the emaciated condition of the workers, rampant tuberculosis. I was sick at heart and asked Carl if all the factories were like that and was it possible in a supposedly enlightened society that this existed." (*Reminiscences of a Gentle Man,* by Henry George Stern. 1887–1979)

The dominant figure in my father's early life was his father, Adolph Stern, born in Flomans, Hungary, in 1849, orphaned at seventeen, married to Rosa Wildman (born in Eperia, Hungary, in 1852), who emigrated to the United States in the early 1880s and, after difficult years, prospered as a manufacturer of neckwear and accessories. My grandfather was a masterful personality, although for me he was just a dear old fellow who, in his long white nightshirt, slept and snored in my room one night every few months. As I wrote earlier, masterful as he was, he did not seem to influence my father's politics or electoral choices, let alone mine, but his rags-to-riches story was surely an element of my internal mythology.

He died in Palm Beach in 1938, a month before his ninetieth birthday. I have no memory of his ever speaking about Hitler or his Hungarian relatives. Indeed, I knew only one relative who had personally suffered from what came to be called the Holocaust and remember her chiefly because my mother employed her as a masseuse, and I associate her with the rare sight of my mother's naked body as she kneaded and pounded it.

During World War II, I began reading the family newspapers, the *New York Times* and the *New York Post*. I heard the words "Pearl Harbor" for the first time on December 7, 1941, from Harry, the bulky doorman at 239 Central Park West, who was to join the Signal Corps and take a famous picture of Benito Mussolini and Claretta Petacci hanging upside down in a Milanese piazzetta. (Unlike Benito, Harry returned to his job three years later.) With my parents, I listened every weeknight to the left wing radio commentators Johannes Steel, Gabriel Heater and George Hamilton Coombs. Age twelve, at Stuyvesant High School, I made my first black friend (the word we used then was "colored"), who revealed the anger he felt at treatment to which I'd been largely blind, although my sister and I once asked my father why he had no black patients and were dissatisfied with his embarrassed explanation that his patients would object if they found black people in his waiting room. Age sixteen, traveling to college on the Silver Meteor from New York to Raleigh, North Carolina, I watched in anger as colored passengers moved to all-colored coaches at Washington's Union Station. This absurdity fueled feelings given words by Bernard Shaw's preface to *Major Barbara* and John Strachey's *The Coming Struggle for Power*. At Chapel Hill, I joined the Carolina Political Union which held discussions of political topics every Sunday evening and invited well-known speakers to the campus. The one I remember best is the thirty-year-old John Kennedy, whose wartime heroism had been chronicled in the *Reader's Digest* magazine by John Hersey, but whom I then saw as the offspring of Joseph Kennedy, the isolationist sympathizer of the English Cliveden set. The two Communist members of the Political Union denounced me for political stupidity while others shrugged me off as a naïve, pesty artist type. I loudly advocated a 100 percent inheritance and a confiscatory income tax.

Two wartime summers, I worked on Vermont farms whose sons were fighting in Europe or the Pacific. It was the hardest physical labor I'd known, and I've never forgotten the effects of physical exhaustion on thinking and reading. During the summer of 1945, working as a messenger boy for a Wall Street bond house, I was thrilled when the atom bomb was dropped on Hiroshima, knowing that now I would not be drafted into the army. A few days later, the war ended, and I watched Wall Street fill with ticker tape while in the window of the gray stone fortress of the House of Morgan, an elderly gentleman slowly tore up pieces of paper which some of us decided were Japanese war bonds.

After college, I worked a year in an Evansville, Indiana, department store and then an Orlando, Florida, radio station. The jobs bored me silly but gave me precious experience of dull, tiring work and too, since I lived on thirty-five dollars a week, of the financial tightrope-walking whose perils dominate so many lives. I then came back to New York and worked six months for Paramount Films in Manhattan and Queens. The most instructive of many instructive days there occurred one day during which we played around with different musical backgrounds for newsreels, transforming an event—it was Tito's march into Trieste—from sinister invasion to operatic buffoonery.

In 1948, I headed for Harvard Graduate School. In 1949, turning twenty-one, I bought my first bottle of whiskey and cast my first vote (a lukewarm one for Harry Truman), but what counted evermore for me was literature, reading it, writing it, thinking about it, teaching it. I was mad to get to Europe, applied for and got a Fulbright Fellowship to teach at a college in Versailles where my closest friend was the son of a *pied noir,* an aristocrat whose sympathies—such as his dislike of Masons and, decades later, his vote for Le Pen—amazed and still amaze me. Another French friend persuaded a policeman that I was the son of the American ambassador, which got us past guards into a session of the French Parliament of which I chiefly remember bullet-headed Jacques Duclos conducting, like Toscanini, the jeers and cheers of the Communist deputies.

In France I met the American girl whom I married. The following year, I got a job as a teaching assistant at Heidelberg University. I supported my wife and the son born in the U.S. Army Hospital in Heidelberg by working as a code clerk in the Army's Staff Message Control. Even so humble a job made one an aristocrat with PX privileges and special scrip (money). I made German friends who'd served in Hitler's armies and been converted into democrats. I met German aristocrats filling out in ironic despair the denazification questionnaires (*Fragebogen*) passed out by the occupiers. Two such occupiers, my wife and I, went to Berlin in 1950 in a sealed train and watched Mayor Reuter and General Clay salute half a million Berliners who'd been sustained by an airlift when the Russians closed off the trains and autobahns. I traveled to Yugoslavia, Greece, Turkey, Syria, Lebanon, Jordan and Egypt, was the only Jew at the Western—Wailing—Wall when a Jordanian policeman told me to come with him to the police station. I went in terror only to be assured by a genial chief of police that if there were anything he could do for me to please let him know. These experiences and ten thousand others combined with reading Spengler's *Decline of the West* and the first eight volumes of Arnold Toynbee's *A Study of History* to form somewhat deeper historical views. The grip of the uniqueness of what I'd seen was tempered by the sense that there were historical sequences and cycles, that certain types of leader and certain forms of political organization recurred over and over. Still, like my somewhat naïve father, I believed that in many ways, and despite eruptions of technological brutality and tyrannies far worse than any heretofore recorded, the essential historical movement was progressive: increased longevity, deeper comfort and security, a more rational, scientific understanding of socio-political events, greater psychological sophistication, greater tolerance, gradually broadening political equality. Inequity, brutality, war, mendacious statesmen, tyrants and low-grade politics continue to depress me and center my politics, although I myself do next to nothing about them. In a narrower sense, I am a quasi-Rooseveltian liberal who believes as my parents did that government should repair social inequity as well as physical infrastructure. As I said above, this view has been modified by those University of Chicago economist and lawyer friends who spelled out the inefficiencies, waste and danger of so much government activity. (I'd worked for the government, and it was not difficult to understand the temptations of those who spend other people's money. On the other hand, I've known many able and scrupulously honest government workers, including a son and a son-in-law.)

Another autobiographical splinter: when my own economic situation improved, I began to feelingly understand how ownership of property and equities tended to soften, if not derail, one's views and even electoral choices. I have tried to counter such influence, but with less zeal than when I first became aware of it.

6

This rapid run-through has left out my—retrospective—awareness of the major socio-political shifts which more directly entered my life and helped alter my thinking and behavior. The most important of these came during the time of the so-called "student troubles" of the sixties and seventies. At Chicago, I was involved actively as well as emotionally, writing articles and poems published in the school newspaper, speaking and even chairing meetings, at one of which I encountered the linguistic sensitivity of the new feminism. The word "chairman" was the word challenged on grounds of gender partiality. "Not chairman" but "chairperson," called out a young woman. From those days, I became aware of the patriarchal roots and power structure behind many of the beliefs and deepest human relationships in my life. These too I have tried to counter.

I've also seen and felt the wonderful transformation of the American racial situation of my youth. This has been more striking to me than the anti-Semitism which, except for fossil pockets, largely disappeared in the United States during and after the war against Hitler. I'd say that half or more of my Jewish friends have married Protestants or Catholics. At least one married a Buddhist and became one himself.

The collapse of Fascism and Communism, the chief geopolitical transformations of the second half of the twentieth century, did not directly affect my feelings and behavior as much as the black, gay and women's movements which have been living parts of my experience and that of my students whose stories and poems reflect them.

7

THE *CHICAGO REVIEW* CONTROVERSY

In a long life, I've played a part in only one public controversy. Participation helped me understand something about the relationship of individuals to institutions and events, as well as to the way they're described in conversation, and in newspapers, periodicals and histories. It also helped me understand how my own feelings and prejudice helped create and define both the events and their reporting.

Almost fifty years old now, the controversy requires an historical context, the fragile situation of the University of Chicago shortly before I arrived to teach there.

By the autumn of 1953 enrollment in the University of Chicago College had sunk to less than 1,350 students. The entering class in that year—275 first-year and 39 transfer students—was less than half of what it had been twenty years earlier. The plight of the neighborhood, located in a police district that in 1952 had one of the highest crime rates in the City of Chicago, and the grimness of the budget had powerful negative consequences on the quality of the faculty. It is striking to read the list of the names of very distinguished senior faculty who left the university for appointments at other institutions throughout the 1950s; by the end of the decade many of its departments seemed near to demoralization. In response to both of these perceived crises, Lawrence Kimpton, the university president, formulated aggressive and even radical solutions. But in his own words to the Board of Trustees, he had "achieved a balanced budget by tightening up in terms of salaries, staff and activities, and that we actually ended up in serious danger of becoming a second-rate institution."

In September 1955, I came to the university as an instructor in the Department of English and American Language and Literature. The Southeast Chicago Commission, headed by the dynamic lawyer Julian Levi—brother of Edward, the law school dean and later president of the university and then, in 1974, President Gerald Ford's attorney general—had embarked on the "aggressive . . . radical" counter to the slummification of Hyde Park, hand-in-hand with the new mayor, Richard J. Daley. To me, Hyde Park looked fine, if somewhat dangerously exciting. It was packed with street drama: so, as my wife wheeled a baby carriage toward the grocery store, she was offered a pair of diamond earrings for a few dollars, the seller taking off like a cheetah at the sound of a police siren; less pastoral was my small son's witnessing a Capone-like assault on a neighbor's skull with a baseball bat. A story most told around the university concerned a couple awakened in their second-floor Drexel Avenue apartment by a burglar climbing in their window. "I told you we should never have left New Haven," cried the wife. "Shut up," said the burglar. But the wife was unable to and, while the burglar was going through the dresser drawers, again belabored her husband for dragging her away from the safe precincts of the East Coast. The burglar turned around, said if she didn't shut her yap, he'd do it for her. "Besides," he threw in. "You're living in this country's number-one place for smart people."

I was asked by Napier Wilt, dean of the Humanities Division, to chair a faculty committee set up to oversee the campus literary magazine, the *Chicago Review*. Student-edited, this journal printed work not by students but by writers and other intellectuals from all over the world. The first complaint I was asked to handle came from a member of the University of Chicago faculty, the sociologist David Riesman. He'd been asked by the editor of the *Review* to write a piece for it, had done so, then, months later, received a rude rejection letter. I explained what he already knew, the delight some students took thumbing their noses at distinguished professors, particularly ones like Riesman who'd appeared on the cover of *Time*. The main business of the Faculty Board, however, did not involve run-ins between sensitive professors and cock-of-the-walk student editors, but money. A year or two before I came, an enterprising student editor had promised advertisers that he was going to print ten thousand copies of the *Review*; then told the dean that since he had all these advertisers in hand, he should be allowed to print ten thousand copies. The printing was arranged. The *Review* sold its usual fifteen hundred copies, and the remaining eighty-five hundred reposed in the basement of the administration building. Dean Wilt paid the printer's bill with a groan and—since he knew he'd been taken by a clever entrepreneur—a twinkle. One such twinkle was enough. Thus the faculty committee, and thus another chore assigned to a young instructor.

The chore did not seem onerous. The committee met once a quarter, reviewed the *Review*'s finances, commented briefly on its contents and supervised the elections of new editors-in-chief. That was about it. I rather enjoyed being chairman of something. In 1958, I gathered from a few *Review* staff members that there'd been an editorial coup de main. Irving Rosenthal, the new editor-in-chief, a first-year graduate student, was a few years older than the undergraduate staff members. He seemed uninterested in their opinions about incoming manuscripts. I met with him a couple of times to discuss the complaints. He brushed them off as infantile whimpers. He also made it clear that he resented having to account for his editorial behavior to a faculty member not much older than he, and, in his view, not nearly as knowledgeable about what counted in contemporary literature. His resentment and superior air did not sit well with me. I disliked him from his first sneer. This was the ground bass of what became known as the *Chicago Review—Big Table* controversy.

Rosenthal knew the writers already well-known as the Beats, Allen Ginsberg, Gregory Corso, Gary Snyder, Lawrence Ferlinghetti, Jack Kerouac and the older man who'd first unlocked the box of their enthusiasms, William Burroughs. Rosenthal began publishing their work. Chapters of Burroughs' erratic, brilliant novel *Naked Lunch* appeared first in the *Review*. This was another sort of coup. Meanwhile complaints from the staff mounted: contrary to custom, submissions that they had discussed and in some cases voted to accept were ignored by Rosenthal, while manuscripts of the Beat writers were not even logged in, let alone discussed before acceptance. Once again I spoke to Rosenthal, telling him that one important function of the *Review* was the training of young editors. I asked him to please conform to the rules. Furious, he marched out of my office. It was the last time we were to meet one on one.

About this time, the *Chicago Daily News,* one of the city's four leading newspapers, had launched an investigation of Chicago's pornography scene. A columnist named Jack Mabley had come upon the issue of the *Review* that contained a chapter of *Naked Lunch* and poems of Ginsberg and others which celebrated the delights of gay sex in a vocabulary Mabley associated with locker rooms and bars. He got on a puritanical high horse, denounced the *Review* and the university which sponsored, or at least paid for and supervised it.

This column caught the attention of Monsignor John Egan, a priest whose Back of the Yards parish was the one into which the Hyde Park–Kenwood renewal project had "dumped"—that was the tone— the mostly black population which had been squeezed from the slumlorded three- and six-flats of Hyde Park. His diocesan paper seized upon the obscenities the university supposedly sponsored, and thus charted the priestly route to some Catholic members of the Chicago City Council, thence to Mayor Richard J. Daley, President Kimpton and the lowly instructor who headed the Faculty Committee.

Kimpton assembled the committee in his conference room. I remember being impressed by its size and by my presence in it. I was not though impressed by Kimpton's suggestion that we stop publishing the *Review.* We said that the *Review* had been and still was a reputable publication that brought the university honor. He then suggested that we simply not publish any more of the "obscene" writing that appeared in the issue which prompted the editorials. I said that anything that smacked of censorship would tarnish the university's reputation far more than anything called obscenity. It was our obligation to see that everything that had been accepted by the staff and the editor be published.

A day or two later, Kimpton's secretary asked me to come to his office, and I had my only face-to-face meeting with the university's president. A large, bespectacled, red-faced, charmingly forceful man, Kimpton treated me as an equal, talking with frankness about "our" problems. It seems that "our" problems were also Mayor Daley's. He had told Kimpton that for the forthcoming votes on issues which were important for the university's survival, he was encountering for the first time serious resistance from some Catholic members of the City Council who'd been told by their parish priests that on a matter of faith and morals it was the church, not the mayor, who should influence their vote. Said Kimpton, "The mayor is convinced that three or four institutions are crucial for the prosperity and standing of Chicago, and the University of Chicago is one of these. He's worked hand and glove with us to keep us here and keep us healthy." That's what was in back of the initial proposal to get rid of the *Review*. "What can we do?" he asked me. I was flattered to be asked that by the dignified, pleasantly humane man who led the institution for which I already had a familial affection. I reiterated the dangers of a university being—let alone being seen—as a censor and detailed the strategy of spreading out the work of the Beat writers in several issues, thus giving the church less of a target. "I imagine that it doesn't want to be thought of as the predatory mastodon it was in Galileo's time," said I, the fragment of erudition reminding Kimpton of the tradition we both lived to perpetuate. "Okay," said the decisive fellow. "We'll go with that."

"That," however, was sufficient to ignite what Rosenthal had already seen as an opportunity to make this a national issue. When he conceived the idea of raising money to start a new magazine in which to put what he now called the pieces "censored" by the university, I don't know. Nor do I remember when and do not know how the U.S. Post Office was brought in to challenge the mailing privileges of the *Review*. Whatever the dates or however the means, articles appeared in national publications. The one I remember best was by the poet and Dante translator John Ciardi. Appearing in the *Saturday Review*, it swallowed the Rosenthal censorship line, hook and sinker. I answered it and others in other publications. I was interviewed by and wrote letters to the student newspaper, the *Chicago Maroon*. There I was both called a tool of the administration and praised for keeping the *Review* from being censored and defending the cause of letters. (My favorite letter along this line was written by Robert Lucid, the son of a Wobbly labor organizer and the brother of a Catholic priest, thus no stranger to the vocabulary of persecution, censorship and martyrdom.)

I remember that part of me enjoyed the excitement; another part was repelled by what I believed were self-serving distortions, some of them my own. Another part was amused by them and even by this new public self of mine. I knew that to some degree it was the antipathy I had for Rosenthal which made me relish wielding power over him. I also knew that I'd been flattered to be a confidant of the university president. To some degree I knew that I was his tool, though one for what I believed to be the good of an institution I admired, even loved. I don't think I was worried about losing my job. For no good reason, I was self-confident and knew too little about the world to know that I could have been branded a no-goodnik and forced out of the profession I loved almost as much as I loved writing.

As this was going on, I read a book by Wayland Young called *The Montesi Affair*. It was about the enormous consequence of a misinterpretation. It seems that shortly after a young woman named Wilma Montesi drowned while swimming in the Adriatic not far from her home in Rome, some customers at a nearby bar overheard a discussion of the incident. The word for pigeon, "columba," was overheard, and they thought that it referred to the playboy son of Rome's police chief, Columba. Thus began a rumor that the police had something to do with Signorina Montesi's death. The rumor did what rumors do and soon took the form of a conspiracy to silence a young woman who'd learned about international drug smuggling among the rich and powerful of Italy and France. The newspapers fanned the rumor, agencies of government investigated it. As almost always happens in investigations, enough nastiness surfaced to keep the case alive. Government officials were brought in to testify before investigating judges; movie stars—I remember Alain Delon and Sophia Loren—added their beauteous celebrity to the flames, and before long the Demo-Christian government of Alcide de Gasperi, part of the political wall the West had erected against the growing Communist threat, was imperiled. Before the Italian part of the wall crumbled, investigators revealed the true story of Wilma Montesi, who, it seems, had had a particularly heavy menstrual period, had fainted from loss of blood and drowned. There was no connection whatsoever to Columba, father or son, and none to any international dope ring.

"The *Chicago Review–Big Table* controversy is my Montesi Affair," was my thought. I'd seen how a splinter could inflame a body, how a controversy in a literary magazine read by a few hundred people could reach into the heart of a great city and a two-thousand-year-old religion, and could endanger a university and the cause of free speech. And, as I said, I learned how my own disposition, my delight in being flattered and my dislike of another person, could play a role in these events.

Unlike most novels or plays, life frequently offers—if it does not largely consist of—anti-climaxes. Mine had to do with a downtown benefit which Rosenthal and the *Review*'s poetry editor, Paul Carroll, arranged to raise money for *Big Table,* the magazine which was to print the so-called censored material, Although I claimed that this was a form of theft, that this material was owned and would be printed by the *Chicago Review,* I accepted their invitation to read at the benefit and to have the story I read published in one of the few issues that constituted *Big Table*'s publishing history. Which was odder or more discordant, their invitation or my acceptance? Fifty years later, I can't explain either.

Pages from a Journal: Rwanda

◦❈◦

March 16, 2007

I just read a review of five books on Rwanda in the *New York Review of Books* ("Big Gamble in Rwanda," by Stephen Kinzer, March 29, 2007) which showed me once again how little I'd seen, how little I'd understood of the country in my three days there in the winter of 1981. The journal of those days printed here conveys some of what I saw and felt particularly about the remarkable "opera" in the village of Mbazi. The end note touches on the personal shock I experienced fifteen years later, but here I want to reflect on the gulf between what I experienced and interpreted back in 1981 and what I've learned here and there since, including what was learned from the review. So I had no idea that the genocidal monstrousness of 1981 had roots in the Belgian policy of dividing Hutu from Tutsi, measuring skulls and issuing identity cards which would, years later, be used by genocidaires as a guide to victims.

Elsewhere I'd read that these murderous villagers "approached their lethal assignment as they would 'a nine-to-five job.'" The French journalist Jean Hatzfeld reports in *Une Saison de Machettes* what one of the killers told him:

> Some offenders claim that we changed into wild animals, that we were blinded by ferocity . . . That is a trick to sidetrack the truth. I can say this: outside the marshes, our lives seemed quite ordinary. We sang on the paths . . . we had our choice amid abundance. We chatted about our good fortune, we soaped off our bloodstains in the basin, our noses enjoyed the aromas of full cooking pots. We rejoiced in the new life about to begin by feasting on veal. We were hot at night atop our wives, and we scolded our rowdy children. We sharpened our tools on whetting stones. We traded stories

about desperate Tutsi tricks. We made fun of every "Mercy!" cried by someone who'd been hunted down; we counted up and stashed away our goods.

I had no idea that the recent Rwanda story is more triumph than not, that under the stern presidency of Paul Kigame, this country, one of the most impoverished in the world when I was there, has more or less prospered. Perhaps none of this is relevant to the few journal pages which attempt to preserve some of what I saw and felt more than a quarter of a century ago. This note is supposed to call attention to what may be too obvious, the limitations of journal writing. Whatever vivacity a journal may have—mine does not have all that much—the journalist's ignorance of the context of what he sees compromises it.

March 24, 1981, 12:30
Kigali
In the house of Jeff Light, the political attaché doubling as cultural attaché. It overlooks Buta Butoro (the hill on which you don't build a house). Jeff's friend Teresa Stuart (plump, prettyish, thirtyish, an army brat, this her first post and she loves it) tells me of the three tones of Kinyarwanda which create much word play. (The class of professional poets is called Abu sizi.) I don't think she's Jeff's girl. In fact, I gathered he's very fond of Jennifer Newton [the Washington-based woman in charge of my tour]; but then, who isn't?

On the Air France flight from Nairobi, my seat-mates were an eighteen-year-old boy and a twelve-year-old boy, both missionary children who go to the Rift Valley Academy, founded in 1909 for such children. The older was born in and lives in Zaire. He speaks the Zairean version of Kinyarwanda and the "less polished" Swahili of Central Africa. Pointing to the map, he says, "I live under the 'I' in Zaire." His parents have been there twenty-three years and have endured two "evacuations," hiding their car under leaves in the bush. He'd helped raise a lion cub, is somewhat apprehensive about going to college, George Fox College in Oregon, another missionary school. The younger kid, Kirkpatrick, talked about the many thieves in Kigali.

100 francs = $1.10

Hotel Ibis. Butare

A one-story hotel with attached cottage rooms on the main street of this charming university town. We left Jeff's house about 1:40 after a good luncheon of Rwandan fish from Lake Tanganyika, string beans, avocado from Teresa's tree, papaya from Jeff's. He's from Hyde Park and South Shore, red-bearded, smallish, merry, bright, divorced, two kids in States. Very nice house; outside windows: cranes walking about or standing on one foot, their crests like tiaras.

Inside: interesting musical instruments and comfortable chairs. Like Bob LaGamma [CAO in Lome, Togo] and Tom Hart [CAO in Freetown, Sierra Leone], Jeff played tapes quite loudly throughout the meal. Is this part of their training? Does it mask the whirr of tapes recording conversation? Buta Butoro and other hills are like Switzerland or San Francisco. Rwanda has 5 million people, 120,000 in Kigali, 17,000 in Butare. Every inch is cultivated up and down the hillsides along *la route,* a muddy seventy-kms-long road lined with spectators and truck-pushers. Ambassador Melone, thin, white-haired, gap-toothed, very decent and intelligent, said it's one of the twenty-five poorest countries in the world. My room here is off to side of the cottages, overlooks a garden, hills, other small houses.

7:10 P.M. Back after a 1-hr-45-minute lecture and Q-and-A (in French) in the auditorium of the U. of Rwanda, a large, white two-story ex-convent. Butare was the intellectual center of both Rwanda and Burundi. The nuns prayed on the second floor while classes were held on the first (like the two tiers in a Renaissance painting, one for heavenly, one for earthly business). This university started in 1962. Small audience, thirty or thirty-five people, but full of debate, discussion, good questions. University buildings on hills are charming, one story, brick and stone, raised on piles, fitting into the green, flowering landscape; built by Canadians.

Landoald Ndasingua, my guide, works for USIA [the U.S. Information Agency, sponsor of my African speaking tour], is of a distinguished intellectual family, nephew of Abbe Kagame, the seventy-year-old historian and writer whom I'm to meet Thursday. He's married to Helene Pinsky of Montreal. They have two small kids. He's a Tutsi who'd been a professor here, has written on African literature, is crippled, has a pleasant, smiling face, long, toothy, eye-glassed. Told me much about Kinyarwanda poetry with its antique vocabulary, images, allegory and suggestiveness. Medad Nduwamungu spoke about Rwandan mockery, people driven to suicide by its wicked humor and biting criticism. Laurent Nkisi, the vice-dean, is a young, smallish fellow with glasses, a good sense of humor, very appreciative. Joseph Nsengimeno stood outside with me watching boys play basketball on the stone court as we talked of this and that. He asked the best question, made the strictest criticism and compared the lecture with "Orvieto Dominos" [a story] very intelligently.

Here, everyone asks about the condition of the road, *la route,* the country's lifeline. When it was cut, during the war, nothing went on, no one went out; if you did go out, you spent the whole day where you arrived. The German consulting firm miscalculated its completion. Rain mucks it up, trucks get stuck. The buses are open Datsun trucks, packed to the boards with passengers. I could make out only one real town en route here. Landoald said it was the market for the whole region. "You get everything there." As for the land, Laurent Nkisi said, "La terre n'est pas seulement cultivée, elle est humanisée." As for jobs, those lining the route are waiting to pull and push the trucks, buses and cars back on solid ground. Meanwhile, yellow caterpillars are flattening and firming it. Sisal plants (sisal is beaten, dried and turned into rope), pineapple, palms, flowering trees beautify the hills.

This hotel and its neighbor-competitor—the Hotel Faucon, down the little, nameless main street—are owned by father and son, Belgians (the dominant foreign group, twenty-five hundred of them in the country). Pink-cheeked, sixty-year-old père sits drinking and talking in the open lounge on the street side. Across the street, a boulangerie-patisserie and general alimentation, a Banque de Kigali, a Caltex service station, four or five other low buildings. Main business section is around the corner. In Kigali, more building on hills. There too was the five- or six-story ziggurat-shaped Presidency but the president, whom Bob Melone says is sensible and honest, refused to move to another hill.

Room: 1100 RF (Rwanda francs) a night: $12.0010:35

Back after an amusing dinner here at the Ibis: telepi, that good fish from Lake Tanganyika, a pate, good soup, pommes frites, salad, white wine, crepes with jelly and a liqueur. Ferdinand, the docent, very amusing, has the look and manner of the gawky, young wisecracker in U.S. sit-coms. Said he's often offended by American blacks whom he met in Canada. He said the dance in Mbazi village tomorrow is being staged for me. Says he and others can speak freely about foreign but not about Rwanda affairs—though they did: abolition of parliament, anger that the university is going to be split into two parts, Faculty of Letters and Pure Science going north. "Only eight hundred students in all. We haven't had a rector in two years. All politics." James Rumford, head of English, a linguist (Chinese and Persian), very smart, graduate of Irvine, like his wife who teaches at the theological seminary here. He talked of children learning old songs and poems around the fire from their parents, described some mnemonic devices and showed how the epithets enriched the lists of names, a la Homer. Above us: two stuffed ibises and basket-woven lampshades, horns, mounted heads, dim light. The Belgian owner, rosy-cheeked Campion, presides pleasantly over his table of whiskey drinkers and jokesters. Tom Banks, bald teacher from Ida, Ohio, said nothing, only laughed.

March 25.
Hotel Ibis. Butare, Rwanda.
7:00 A.M.
Drizzling. People walk to work while I eat papaya, pineapple, mangos, cheese omelet, rolls with real jam and butter, coffee. A charming place. In twenty-four hours one has the—surely false—sense that one's getting it all. At dinner last night, there was concern that the last be the best, Rwandan irony sprinkled over everything. Burundians are said to be less merry, more reserved. In breakfast room, sculpted panels, bas relief, Pisani-like, of a tree, a thatched hut, a torch, two stone pots of leaves, two framed batiks, buffalo horns, gauguinesque, five tables for four, five for two on sides, four for four in middle.

Landoald comes, says breakfast isn't eaten here. "It's the traditional agricultural day, up at five, work till noon, then a repast of *legumes de toutes sortes.*" After rest, socializing till the six o'clock meal. Almost no meat. He ate breakfast, this morning, cheese, two slices of pate, bread and comfiture. He knows family names back through the sixteenth century and in a couple of years, he'll start teaching them to his children. Other breakfasters: five male and one female; Europeans, Belgian probably.

Off with Landoald to Institute Nationale pour la Recherche Scientifique, the national museum. After that we'll see the vannerie (basket weaving) at Save and then the Watutsi dances at Mbazi.

1:35. Back at the Ibis after a wonderful morning including the most marvelous hour of the whole trip, the great Gesamtkunstwerk presented for me by the dancing-singing-poet-musicians of Mbazi under their Burgomester (yes), the blue-suited, eye-glassed little gentleman in back of the magnificent occasion. We pulled up in the four-wheel-drive Scoutmaster wagon after horrendous driving in the rutted muck to Save, then Mbazi. An hour late, the performers waiting for us. The Burgomester escorted us into the communal center in a courtyard; in front, my couch and chairs for Landoald, Jeff, Ferdinand, and Tom Banks. Under the timber-roofed stage were five huge drums and a large stringed—half-harp, half-guitar—instrument. We sit and boom, out come white-clad drummers and flute-like instrument blowers, then the corps de ballet, girls in long orange, red and green skirts and bare-armed tops, six singers followed by magnificently beaded, ankle-braceleted, yellow-wigged, spear-carrying, feather-crowned human rainbows, forming into chorus and soloists, singing, dancing, playing, one choir after another, each turn signaled by new rhythms, new instruments (calabash-like horns, lyres like striped butcher boards) and new, marvelous tones or melodies, another phase of terrific pounding (feet, drums), then apparently comic, satiric exchanges (townspeople grouped around the stage laughed, though God knows how often they'd seen the work), and perhaps praise songs, spears thrust out, a bit closer to us than was comfortable, but by now, I'm so carried away by it all, I don't recoil. There are interludes of incredible drumming, then playlets, characters exchanging insults or boasts. The beginning was clearly a song and dance of welcome, the end, a rousing gesticulating farewell. The Burgomester rose and spoke, and Ferdinand (who'd arranged the occasion) invited me to speak. I said, "Vous m'avez donees une des plus belles heures de ma vie," which was totally sincere and met with a burst of communal sweetness, applause, laughter, smiles, the ceremonies of farewell. "The hundred dollars I give now is but a minuscule token of gratitude for the gift of this communal art in which root, stem and flower of your culture appear in beautiful harmony. This is the exhilaration of great art and yet it seems to be the natural outgrowth of your village, your existence. Je vous remercie avec toute mon coeur." Their smiles and laughter were like that of flowers.

9:30, after a speech to 100–150 at the university. This after lunch with Peace Corps people at the Seventh Day Adventist restaurant across from the hotel. This morning, Landoald and I went first to the museum and saw the imzie (sp?), the amazing thatched round tent filled with mats and subtle divisions of space. Ten feet at the peak, the divisions made by scrolled mats. In the middle, a fireplace. The permeability of the straw keeps air in. Baskets contain clothes, etc. Bizarre that this can be a family home, but it is.

There's a section on the Ryangome rituals during which frontiers of behavior are crossed (as in the Venetian carnival). The initiators say and do anything, there are scatological and blasphemous outbursts, orgies. One enters the world where the soothsayer predicts success or failure by reading the entrails of chickens or the position of thrown pieces of wood. There is Igisora, a thirty-two-cup game with stones, a kind of war strategy game in which you block the advance of the opposing stones. (Landoald plays it.)

We leave to pick up Ferdinand, Jeff and Tom Banks and drive to Save (Sa-ve) through huge ruts of muck where cars are pushed. Around are groves of the indolently flamboyant green banana palms (source of the powerful banana beer, as well as potato-like food), the silver and dark green of the yellow-lined sisal plants. In the beautiful convent of Save we see these being cut, threaded, dyed and woven by the young— fifteen, looking like twelve—girls into baskets, rugs, plates, bags, plaques, marriage sticks (furred with monkey or cow tail). At a long table near the looms, girls worked the knots, each knowing the pattern by heart unlike the rug-making families in the dark Srinigar factory who each day are given a paper with the day's knot formulas. I bought a few things, said goodbye and went off on a slightly better road (only once did we have to lock wheels and use the four-wheel-drive) to Mbazi. Now to the Culture House of the university for a two-hour reception and then to Tom Banks' for dinner.

What a day, March 26.
Hotel Ibis. Butare.
Breakfasting, 7:05. Six Belgians, one being felicitated on his birthday. (Sixtieth?) Last night, a fine, lively reception at the Maison Culturelle

71

around the corner. Sixty–seventy people. Talked with batik-shirted vice-rector, a jolly, sportive fellow, about the mountain people of the world, their independence and ungovernability. Every comparison to Switzerland or for that matter to Kenya ends with the brute poverty of Rwanda, poor soil cultivated and recultivated into poorer soil, no minerals—"On cherche toujours." Then the students, one working on Twain as a cosmic dramatist, another on Faulkner. The problem is books, even reference books. There are a few in the American library in Kigali, next to none here. They pray fruitlessly for scholarships to the U.S. "They bring U.S. Fulbrights here." (Tom Banks. Joe Rumford.) Beside which, it's hard for a Rwandan to leave, too overwhelming. There is a hopelessness almost basic to the sweet, grateful temperament. The farewells have a kind of desperation in them. The hope is to see you again, but here, to ask you one more question, recalling something you said, asking if it is related to something in an essay by Richard Chase; if you run across it, could you possibly send it. Eight years ago, a professor in Zaire said something about the collective unconscious. Did I know where that could be researched?

Also here: director of the Institute for Research and my "old friends" from last night, the dean and vice-dean, then the visiting—from Kigali—director of culture from the Ministry of Education, a stiff fish in this academic water. There's also a very pretty girl with braided hair in a yellow dress, Annunziata, married to a Canadian. And Joseph, head of Romance Languages, a Tutsi, thin with sloping forehead. Tom Banks says the Tutsi are milk drinkers and develop high cholesterol levels. "I can't usually tell them [Hutu-Tutsi] apart. The identity cards identify them. No real trouble. There's the one language spoken by ten million people, in Burundi, Uganda and Zaire also. The president is a benevolent man, tries to play everything down. And the Central Committee—the director of research was just elected to it—consists of experts, not politicians."

There is beer, skewered mutton and meat pies. Then to Tom Banks and his wife Jerry's nice little university-supplied house for supper with Jeff (salmon loaf, beans, eggplant, soup, chocolate pie). Awfully good people, both tennis players, went to Ohio Northern (?). Jerry won the Kigali Open twice, the second while pregnant. She won tickets to Nice. He's compact, bald, looks like Wordsworth, from Clarksdale, Miss. She's pretty, firm, sweet. They love life here.

In the breakfast room: *Ca va, la route?*

Epouvantable. Onze heures. (This from the knit-capped man in eyeglasses whom I saw yesterday on the road to Save.)

11:10 A.M. Back in Kigali after a good ride on *la route,* two hrs, fifteen minutes. We passed an overturned bus and a Volkswagen in a ditch and the hill where Goondie's stomach burst. He is the Rwandan Gargantua (this from Landoald). In Kigali, passed President Juvenal Habyariman's small house.

6:35

Aboard Air Burundi out of Bujimbura

In Kigali, before we went to the ambassador's for lunch, Helene and Jeff talked about the awful housing situation. He's given fourteen thousand a year for housing. In Nairobi, officers are given eighty thousand a year. You pay five years in advance, so you put down five thousand, pay another five to a notary, pay thirty-five thousand to get it built (this borrowed from the bank), repay it in four years at $800 a month, and with luck, rent it out. Landoald earned $350 a month as a professor. A Tutsi, he never knew when the guillotine would fall. Where was their exit money? So he left Butare and what he loved (teaching oral poetry) and followed Helene into ICA.

Good lunch at Bob and Dominique Melone's. Their beautiful fourteen-year-old Sandra appeared briefly. Guests were three Rwandans including the meek director of culture met yesterday in Butare, and the papal nuncio, a fifty-year-old Irishman, literate and sophisticated, who's worked in Vatican diplomacy in Guatemala, Taiwan, fifteen years in Africa, two and a half in Rwanda. In Catholic countries the nuncio is dean of the diplomatic corps. Melone thinks he has a chance of becoming Secy. of State. Dominique (who kissed me goodbye *a la francaise*) says he saves their lives. Not a genius but he does read and know things. Landoald says that his abbe uncle wrote a book on missionaries ruining the local religion which is on the Index. The uncle makes mistakes when he says mass. He's huge, very fat, full of energy—"beaucoup comme vous"—is a diabetic with a drinking problem.

At the airport, a good talk with Jeff, then off to Nairobi.

Months later, back in Chicago, I collected books for the Rwanda university, packed and mailed them. A month later, I received a graceful letter of thanks. I didn't think much about the country till 1994 when, after the airplane crash which killed President Habyarimana and the president of Burundi, Hutu resentments, carefully planned and fanned, exploded into the systematic annihilation of eight hundred thousand Tutsi and sympathizing Hutu "cockroaches." Only Landoald had spoken to me about this racial rivalry. Most of the few other comments were essentially benign: "There's so much intermarriage, the physical differences have practically disappeared." I read Philip Gourevich's book on the terror, then, a few months later, watched his PBS film about it. A few minutes into the film, he said that Landoald and Helene had been decapitated.

Then and Now: The Chicago Literary Scene

❧

FIFTY YEARS AGO THIS SPRING [2005], I think it was the day Einstein died, I opened a letter, in the tiny Quaker Hills, Connecticut, post office, inviting me to interview for a job at the University of Chicago. I borrowed money for plane fare and a decent suit and flew to Midway Airport. (This was pre–O'Hare Chicago.) I taxied to what was to me a surprisingly handsome, Oxford-looking university and soon began a series of professorial interviews. I had lunch with another inquisitorial, professorial group which I felt was checking out my table manners, then was driven around the city by the chairman of the Committee on General Studies, Norman Maclean. Left hand on the wheel, right hand pointing to Frank Lloyd Wright houses and the lakeside pillar which is Stephen Douglas's tomb, he told me how close in every way the university was to the city—"Modern sociology was born out of the closeness"—how the 1909 Burnham *Plan for Chicago* saved the lakeshore from the fate of Cleveland, Duluth, Erie and other lakeside cities, what the sturdiest urban tree was—the locust—how the solitude of woods was half an hour from his office and how he wanted me to make committee students real writers. I was to be its first hired hand, as I was the first professional writer at the university since Thornton Wilder in the thirties. "And Wilder only saw writers after his literature classes." I was to be the committee's secretary and to teach courses in the novel and modern drama for the English Department.

A pretty full plate, one which helped turn off the first man offered the job, Donald Justice, who happened to be my oldest friend. Just before my invitation letter came, I'd heard from him that both the university and the city scared him and his wife, and that although he enjoyed Maclean, he thought he was a kook. "He goes on and on about Custer," not the usual subject of an English professor. Kooks were up my alley, and I liked everyone I'd met, especially Maclean.

I didn't learn for thirty years that he wanted to be my kind of writer. The only manuscripts he showed me were a speech on the late eighteenth-century "graveyard poets" and an unfinished manuscript on George Custer's transformation from an indolent West Pointer to the hero whose picture hung in every other American saloon. Maclean asked me to treat his manuscript as I, rather notoriously, treated student papers, so I marked it up with queries, arrows and exclamations of disgust. He thanked me, then, apparently, put it away for ever. (For years, I berated myself for that.)[1]

Back on that spring day, Chicago looked beautiful. Hyde Park was in bloom, the lake glittered with sails among the water purifying stations, and the skyline looked like a great three-master taking off into the blue. I'd spent 1954–55 at a small, pretty women's college in New London and, although I had good students and friends there, it felt like the sticks. Unlike the Justices, I'd been born and raised in a big city. To me, the countryside and its small towns were where you vacationed, not where you lived.

Chicago was clearly different from New York, its ethnic borders were distinct and counted politically; indeed, local politics were like Italy's, more theatrical than civic, the institutions—political, academic, religious, cultural and financial—were in close touch with each other. "You can know anybody you want to around here," said Maclean. The best-known Chicago cop, Jack Something-Or-Other, a hearty naif who went around ticketing aldermen, was the press's comic contrast to standard policemen such as the one who'd just stopped my friend Tom Higgins on Lake Shore Drive. Higgins was wearing the camel's hair overcoat a prodigal or hasty guest had left behind at the Del Prado hotel where Higgins worked nights as a bellhop. Days, he was finishing a master's in piano at Roosevelt U. Without looking at the cop, Higgins handed over his wallet, to which a five-dollar bill had been clipped. A beefy mitt reached inside the car, its fingers rubbed the fine camel's hair. "You're gettin' a little big for five, Higgins." Chicago. I loved it.

As for the university, I'd read an old issue of *Life Magazine* which showed rows of professors in academic garb under the headline "Is the

---

1. See "On a Writer's Endgame."

University of Chicago the World's Greatest?" Back in Connecticut, my colleague Paul Fussell and I leafed through the U. of C. catalogue noticing whole courses devoted to single works, one on E. M. Forster's *Passage to India,* another on Beethoven's C-sharp Minor Quartet. At Connecticut College, we covered six hundred years of English literature in a semester. "This," said Fussell, "is what I call a university." When I came for good, I learned that E. K. Brown's class on *A Passage to India* only got through two-thirds of it.

It took me a year to see that the Chicago literary scene wasn't all that great. There was a hazy notion that there was a tradition of urban writers going back as far as Mrs. Kinzie, the author of *Wau-bun;* the names Hamlin Garland, Theodore Dreiser, James Farrell and especially Nelson Algren were known, but largely the way stamp collectors know geography. I gave a Channel 11 lecture on Chicago writers directed by the twenty-year-old Bill Friedkin; I think only Maclean watched it.

I did have talented students. In my first class were the poets George Starbuck and David Ray, there was a good campus literary magazine, the *Chicago Review,* but few of my colleagues seemed to know or care what was going on in contemporary literature.

My second year, I asked Dean Napier Wilt for money to invite published writers to talk to my student writers. A burly, shrewd, Indiana romantic, Wilt loved the idea of real writers roaming the campus and dug up two thousand dollars, enough to bring four of them in for a week each to discuss their own and then students' work. With the first two grand, I invited Saul Bellow, my old Iowa teacher, Robert Lowell, Norman Mailer and John Berryman. They made a terrific literary splash, not only in the English Department, but in the whole university community and, for that matter, the city itself. Adlai Stevenson's ex-wife, Ellen, gave parties for them at her Lakeshore Drive brownstone—though when Berryman broke his leg there, she called me at 5:00 A.M. to say that she had his bar bills so there'd better be no attempt to sue her. There were interviews in newspapers and on the radio; people from all over town read the visitors' books and came to their public lectures. The next year, I invited Flannery O'Connor (whose blue eyes glared at me with bitterness when I picked her up at 3:00 A.M. at the Greyhound Station after her plane had been iced down in Louisville), Ralph Ellison, Howard Nemerov and Kingsley Amis. Local writers started coming out of the woodwork of urban silence. A South Side post office clerk trundled his handwritten novel over to Ellison. Even Algren, who for years had had Chicago's literary attention to himself, came around, and though he often got physically ill around writer peers and betters, he seemed to enjoy what was going on. I remember a dinner in a West Side Croatian restaurant when he and Lillian Hellman—a third-year visitor—were taken with each other, she with his sly macho tales of poker, cops and whores, he with her tales of the Spanish War and the Russian Front. When he characterized his onetime lover Simone de Beauvoir as "another deluded broad," the spell was broken. Hellman was a softie when it came to love.

When the two thousand decanal dollars no longer sufficed for four writers, the visitor number went down to three, then two, and finally one. Still, the university, and the city too, had gotten into the habit of seeing, hearing and reading the best active American writers. The bookstores stocked and sold their books, and young writers were ignited. (My fellow instructor Philip Roth has written about what meeting Bellow in and after my class meant to him.)

For twenty-five years, the university was a familiar stopover for writers. Ex-students, writers and non-writers, have written me for decades about their delight in these visitors. It was, I think, not only the excitement of having fine new books talked about by those who'd written them, but contact with personalities whose lives often involved at least the imaginative transgression of social and psychological borders.

In the last twenty-five years, authors don't have to be seduced by university dollars to come to Chicago. Part of their writing life is the promotional trip, planned by publishers and coordinated with such bookstores as 57th Street Books, radio and television programs and whatever groups sponsor their readings. If anything, there's a glut of such appearances, and although there are surely plenty of times when the mental flame passes from writer to audience, I'm not sure that there is anything like the concentrated creative excitement of those campus visits in the fifties, sixties and seventies.

How the Stories Changed

⌒∞⌒

THERE ARE MANY HANDLES on history. You can study changing styles of transportation, communication, jokes, songs, clothes, cuisine, curses or what have you. For half a century, my professional handle was the stories written by students at the University of Chicago.

Twice a year, I assembled a class of about a dozen writers out of the forty or so who submitted stories as a form of application to it. The class was a workshop—that is, a student would read aloud the story he'd written followed by comments on it by each of the other students, in turn followed by a general discussion moderated by me.

The changing subject matter of the stories over the years is the focus here, but a word should also be said about changes in literary style. Hemingway was alive in 1955, but for most students his style wasn't. (*The Old Man and the Sea* was more frequently parodied than imitated.) The Hemingway understatement implied stoic control of strong feeling. A good Hemingway story made clear that such feeling was underwritten by hands-on experience intelligently, bravely and deeply understood. In the 1940s and 1950s, the obliquity and solidity of this style turned into the impassive notations of Camus' *Stranger,* perhaps the single most influential fiction of its time. In American fiction, this impassivity turned into minimalism, an unaccented accretion of decisive remarks, gestures, events and situations that, though violent, were almost always quiet. Post-*Stranger,* French fiction was a systematically emotionless notation of objects, settings, human beings and events sometimes organized by a covert mythic pattern. Only a few American students followed this French mode, although in class we talked about its theoretical justification, the essays of Roland Barthes and Alain Robbe-Grillet. Over the years, the protagonists of the student stories changed from

Hemingway stoics to passive misfits and then, though less frequently, to barely described characters whose emotional reactions and interior development seemed beside the point.

Many student stories from 1955 to, say, 1990 were about coming out of sexual or other closets of social abnormality. The misery and joys of discovering, practicing and revealing to more or less unsympathetic relatives or friends one's homosexuality, criminality or emotional emptiness often made for very moving—and perhaps therapeutic—classes.

When parental divorce became common in the 1970s and 1980s, one sort of story dealt with the protagonists' puzzled resentment that their parents—sometimes grandparents—were leading second or third lives before they, the children or grandchildren, were launched on their first. It was as if there were a fixed portion of life-stuff, and the children were being robbed of theirs by those whose duty was to lead them to it. The children were sometimes burdened by the additional weight of parental requests to participate in the theft: so they were asked about the suitability of parental partners and/or served as best man or maid of honor at parental nuptials.

Variations in these stories dealt with the young protagonists' intellectual and erotic discoveries, usually at college, and failed attempts to interest, let alone absorb, their parents in them. Such failures either diminished or ratified the importance of the discoveries. In any case, whether the parents were sophisticated or naïve, well educated or not, the discoveries marked new levels of independence and insight.

American literature is rich in immigrant stories. The ones new in the 1970s and 1980s were about first-, second-, and, more rarely, third-generation Asian Americans. Earlier, the Indian-Pakistan political crises had initiated a literature whose most visible figure was Salman Rushdie. I had several Anglo-Indian students whose sometimes hilarious, sometimes touching stories described the conflict between those still immersed in their countries of origin and their ever-more Americanized children and grandchildren. From what to eat and wear, to whom and how to marry and raise children, the subject matter of these stories was mostly domestic compared, say, to the finest of Kipling's Anglo-Indian stories, Forster's *A Passage to India* or Paul Scott's *Staying Behind.* Few students had the imagination and almost none had the experience to deal with the politics of adultery or the clash of nostalgia and expulsion on a public stage. Instead they dealt, often splendidly, with exchanges over dining tables, conflicts about television programs and dating.

In the late 1960s and early 1970s, the stories by Asian American students tended to describe clashes between first and second generations. Sometimes these clashes emerged in class discussions, first-generation students criticizing second-generation students for willful erasure of the ancestral past. More powerful were the dramas of helter-skelter flight from Vietnam followed by complex resettlement in the United States. There were also some U.S. army veteran stories about the fields, jungles, rivers, battles, intrigues, miseries and horrors of the war and the more or less difficult return home—the sort of story Hemingway and other World War I veterans introduced into post–World War I literature. The story I remember best dates from the 1980s. It had to be rewritten over and over because of the writer's inexperience with English. (I'd come close to rejecting her for the class.) It had to do with a Vietnamese family who'd come in a great rush from Saigon, settled and prospered in a small Ohio town. When they assembled for dinner, one chair was always left empty: it was the mother's agonized reminder of the baby they'd had to leave behind in Saigon with her mother. The absence of this child was the heaviest presence in the growing years of the narrator's life. One day, news came that the grandmother had died and that the now twelve-year-old child was coming to Ohio to join the family. The end of the story concerned the mother's inability to handle this tremendous news. When the writer, a small, lovely Vietnamese girl, read it aloud, the class, after a silent moment, applauded—a rare occurrence.

More and more, the influence of television was seen in the stories: television programs were a lingua franca shorthand for appearance, style, occupation, whatever. So instead of "Who does he think he is, Hamlet [or Gable]?" one read, "Hey, Kojak, your lollipop's dripping."

In my last years as a professor of literature, the ubiquity and fluid power of the Internet and the ease and shorthand rhythms of email were altering narrative rhythms. These changes made for a speed of allusion that I think related to the increasing casualness of the relationships described in the stories. (Some of the most brilliant were on the verge of being surreal prose poems.)

What was also conspicuous was their global reach. I'd spent my student years trying to figure out ways to get to the Europe Fitzgerald and Hemingway had described. Many of my students had been born and raised abroad and almost all had traveled. What they hadn't seen with their own eyes, they'd seen in movies—movies that weren't filmed on Hollywood lots but on location around the world. (Cell phones, digital cameras, Blackberries and iPods had not yet transformed lives, so I can't report on their narrative expressions.)

In retrospect, what interests me is the changing depiction of constriction and resentment, ambition and liberation, by privileged, intelligent and ambitious young people in their late teens and early twenties.

More than most arts, literature depends on continuity as much as on change. Language itself is basically conservative, and the emotional repertory of human beings has not much altered. Many of the conflicts, quests, hierarchies, dreams and appetites depicted in the three-thousand-year-old *Iliad* can be recognized, if not experienced, today. Literature teachers describe the differences that different places and times account for in works and try to demonstrate their special narrative and poetic powers. Literary history—even an account of changes in student stories—may supply the historians of economic, social and political change with something between filigree and marrow.

II

❧

Posting

ONE REASON FOR DOING these blog posts was—see above—to try various ways of composing short pieces of this sort, but my blogging eye was never far off the actualities which engendered them. Blogs are getting increased attention, read by campaign workers and reporters, cited in newspapers and by TV commentators. That one collects them now is, I hope, a way of aligning them with the short pieces which writers since, say, the seventeenth-century character writers or essayists considered forms of mental play. They are closer, say, to diary entries than to the intricate and touching "try-outs" of a Montaigne, but the hope is that some will be enjoyed despite their ever-increasing distance from the news events which prompted them.

Open University Blog. *The New Republic*

⁕

Post 1

September 19, 2006
The difference between a veteran tennis player in a major tournament and a veteran journalist on serious assignment appears to be that the tennis player has to perform at least adequately or he'll be laughed or hooted off the court. I'm thinking of the final professional matches of Andre Agassi and contrasting them with (1) Mike Wallace's recent interview with President Ahmadinijad of Iran and (2) Brian Williams' end of August (2006) interview with President Bush. Wallace's stumbling, falsely jocular, ill-informed and even rude interrogation was in stark contrast to what was for me the totally unexpected knowledgeability, courtesy, intelligence and even charm of the Iranian president. I had thought of that ill-shaven little man as a nationalist thug, bellicose, ignorant, inflammatory, a loose cannon unmoored by good sense, manners or general decency, but he dealt with the ancient, hollow journalist with a skill and charm that made me realize that this well-educated (Ph.D. in civil engineering) man had not risen to his position by accident or by being someone's puppet. It's clear that he should be treated very seriously. To a degree then, Wallace's ignorance, vulgarity and, yes, stupidity accomplished more than a good interviewer would have. As for Brian Williams' patronizing "discussion" of George Bush's now celebrated summer reading, it would have helped if Williams had picked up Camus' *Stranger* and seen that it was not a work of philosophy but a novel. He could even have asked the president a question or two about the book, but, no, it was clear to any watcher that Williams knew next to nothing about it and was afraid of leaving the safe waters out of which

his other standard questions were drawn. (Later: Williams did better with Ahmadinijad than with Bush.)

Post 2
September 21, 2006

Why did we think that the world's presidents and prime ministers (many democratically elected) would conform to our notions of how they should perform? Thank God, the UN gives these supposed mountebanks and archvillains space for their theatrical self-presentations. According to Hugo Chavez, the American president speaks to the world "as if he owns it." As for the wily, tiny, haughty descendant of Darius (the entitlement about as merited as our president's descent from Washington—of whom, incidentally, he claims to have recently read three biographies), he had sufficient history to know that nations decline and fall as well as grow and prosper. Born decades after World War II, he asked why the world should still be governed by its victors. Iran is rich and getting oil-richer every minute, its scientists are savvy enough to produce nuclear fuel and—why not?—the nuclear weapons which the old dominators and their protégés have. Who are the U.S. and Britain to tell the new Iran what it should have?

Chavez and Ahmadinijad are first-rate performers. They didn't get elected because of their good looks or humble ways. It's time to stop talking about ignoring them or—as our good secretary of state said today—not "dignifying what they said with an answer." No, we needn't take their verbal assaults like whipped dogs, but what we do need to do is find ways of talking to the world which are neither patronizing nor officious.

Bush's address to the UN went from one country to another telling them how to behave, what pleased and what displeased us and what rewards they'd reap if they elected the right leaders to guide them along the democratic paths we ourselves know in their hearts they want to follow. Even if true, this domineering *tour d'horizon* will not help us get them there. It is not enough to esteem one's own aspirations, motivations and essential goodness. I think that doesn't even work in the president's church. It certainly doesn't work in the motley world he was addressing. (I'm assuming that the words were addressed to that world and not just to voters in the upcoming American election.) A bit more humility, even in rhetoric, Mr. President, Mr. Vice President, congressmen and diplomats. Try thinking of the dwellers on the axis of evil as if they were friends whom by accident one has sprayed with shotgun pellets. (We did after all aid the Venezuelans who tried to depose Chavez, and I assume that we are aiding those we hope might depose the shrewd little Iranian gentleman who parries the best that the American foreign policy wonks can throw at him.) Intelligent sympathy mixed with a *soupçon* of diplomatic humility will go a long way to the table at which one can get down to the nitty-gritty of national self-interest.

Post 3
September 28, 2006
Beautiful fall days here in Chicago, "regular" (gasoline) is down to $2.64 (60 cents lower than it was weeks ago), the Dow Jones is near its all-time high, our president assures us that his "Democrat" opponents are well-intentioned, patriotic Americans although "absolutely wrong." The day's news is salted with the usual quota of bizarre horrors (fetuses knifed from mothers' bodies, a Colorado school held hostage by a madman), the annual fires are devouring thousands of western acres, Baghdad's daily life is a sort of *auto-da-fé,* the pope explains and re-explains the old warnings of a Western king about Islam's bellicose proselytizing, Mozart's *Idomeneo* (heads of Buddha, Jesus and Mohammed carted on stage for God knows what reason) is canceled for fear angry Muslims will display the violence about which the pope talked, Cormac McCarthy publishes another beautifully written, if monotonous, book— about post-apocalyptic bleakness, ugly pre-electoral discoveries (such as Senator George Allan's racist collegiate vocabulary and uneasy jitter-bugging away from his Tunisian Jewish mother's ethnicity and his opponent Webb's befuddled animadversions on the inadequacy of women soldiers), the pro football season is in full swing, the baseball play-offs are almost here . . . what can the average American household complain about? Obesity? Lousy schools? Enormous medical and scholastic costs? A mendacious and hypocritical government that talks tough and takes few tough decisions ("Chicken 'n' Rice")? A governing class so aloof from the presidential rhetoric of total war against the islamo-fascists that almost none of its sons and daughters is inspired to actually enlist and fight in it? (Where are all the Bush family children, the nephews, nieces and daughters of our inspiring leader?) Oh say, can you see . . . ?

What a jangling medley the least complex of us is. When the medley is heard on the great speakers of public life, its discrepant elements become components of either tragedy or farce.

Take the gifted and attractive person who serves as our secretary of state. Child and grandchild of high-minded, accomplished people of exceptional dignity—grandfather and father Presbyterian ministers, mother a teacher of science, music and oratory—she grew up in Birmingham exceptionally alert to the racial fires from which her parents could not completely protect her. A friend reported frequent calls from Condoleeza about what Bull Connor had done that day. Of the church bombing which killed a young friend, she said, "I remember the bombing of that Sunday School at 16th Street Baptist Church in Birmingham in 1963. I did not see it happen, but I heard it happen, and I felt it happen, just a few blocks away at my father's church. It is a sound that I will never forget, that will forever reverberate in my ears. That bomb took the lives of four young girls, including my friend and playmate, Denise McNair. The crime was calculated to suck the hope out of young lives, bury their aspirations. But those fears were not propelled forward, those terrorists failed." (Commencement 2004, Vanderbilt University, May 13, 2004. One need not point out the use of the word "terrorists.")

Her father opposed such heroic Birmingham activists as the Reverend Fred Shuttleworth[1] and believed that by being and doing better than others, blacks would succeed. Condoleeza (*con dolcezza:* with sweetness) practiced ballet, figure skating and piano, intense insulation from the terror of the street.

In 1967, her father accepted a teaching and administrative post at the U. of Denver, where after graduating from St. Mary's, his only child graduated cum laude, Phi Beta Kappa. After taking an M.A. at Notre Dame, she returned for a Ph.D. at Denver, her teacher in foreign policy being the Czech immigrant Josef Korbel, the father of Madeleine Albright. Condi became a sort of second daughter to him. (At Denver, she is said to have dated the pro football player Rick Upchurch.)

Her involvement in the world of foreign politics began as an advi-

---

1. A charming man, whom I met in the early sixties. He said, "How I used to love planes. Now, every time I hear one, I look up and say, 'Thank God I'm not on that one.'"

sor in Jimmy Carter's State Department. Carter's foreign policy was supposedly the chief reason she became a Republican. She held important advisory posts in the G. H. W Bush administration, and by the time she was established as a professor at Stanford in 1981, she'd already served on some of the many boards—some connected with the difficult schools of East Palo Alto, others in business, others in government—which mark a prominent career. She co-authored a book on Germany with Philip Zelikow, another on Russia with Alexander Dallin, then was chosen by one of the great university presidents of the twentieth century, Gerhard Casper, to be provost of Stanford. Here reports of her success are mixed, partly because as provost, she served as a lightning rod for the discontents simmering in every university.

For six years now, as the confidante, friend, advisor, tutor and secretary of state to George W. Bush, she has revealed both her disciplined, hard-working, knowledgeable intelligence and what might be called an overly deferential, if not servile allegiance to his messianically defined policies. More independent in her present role than as national security advisor, it is not clear how much her intelligence has subtilized, let alone altered them. Her charm, her sheer delight in the elegance of power (has there been so well-dressed, coiffed and bejewelled a woman of power since Marie Antoinette?), her complex devotion to the president and his family fused in a conscience deeply formed by racial insult and injury, make for the kind of character she has read about in the pages of her favorite Dostoievski. Will her own story, far from over, be written in the key of tragicomic subservience or of liberated independence?[2]

Post 5
October 2, 2006
How wonderful if everything was governed by Intelligent Design, and if we were intelligent enough to figure out the design. As far as the universe is concerned, my guess is that we have about the same sense of its

---

2. January 12, 2007. Appearing before the Senate Foreign Relations Committee a couple of days ago, she was confronted by another chink in her solidity. Barbara Boxer, California's showy junior senator, said that because her own children were too old and her grandchild too young to fight in Iraq and because Ms. Rice was childless, neither of them was qualified to send other people's children to war. Appearing on the Fox network the next day, Rice said that she thought that "single women" had come further than that sort of remark suggested. Rice has endured years of intrusive interrogation and learned how to handle it gracefully, but it cannot be easy to have millions of people staring at you while you do so.

"design" or its "designer" that a worm has of a Chevrolet. As for matters closer to home, the human record is not all that great. Thus predictions about the outcome of events or of major policy decisions are seldom right. One of the country's most celebrated non-astrologist prognosticators, Henry Kissinger, frequently broadcasts teutonic ponderosities about the future, usually in such labyrinthine formulations that few attend to them.[3] So his assessment of the U.S. "failure" in Vietnam doesn't have much to do with the amiable prosperity of today's Vietnam. So what about less gifted predictors who now foresee "unimaginable" chaos in an American-abandoned Iraq?

Every parent worries about leaving little children with a babysitter the first times he goes out to dinner or a movie. Oh yes, it turns out that there was much crying, some of it desperate, but then things turned out quite well. The children quickly learned to adapt to parental absence.

Okay, in Iraq there might be even greater eruptions of torture and killing if the Americans took off, but how long would or even could that go on? Isn't it as likely that these intelligent people, used now to having an independent voice, would move toward social contracts and a less deadly existence?

Perhaps the worst decisions of our present and recent leaders—Cheney, Rumsfeld and Colin Powell—occurred after Gulf War I. Saddam Hussein was left in power. Why? James Baker said that Saddam would have been difficult to find, and that the effort would have required a war wider than the one mandated by the UN. How about the Iraqi generals asking General Schwarzkopf if they could keep their weapons? Sure, he said, and those weapons soon mowed down the Shiites in the marshes whom we'd pledged to assist. The draft of the peace treaty which Schwarzkopf submitted to the State and Defense departments came back unmarked by suggestion or corrective. A decade later, this carelessness led to Gulf War II, the foulest quagmire since Vietnam.

Intelligent Design? Tell it to the marines.

Post 6

October 4, 2006

A friend (my wise brother-in-law, Arthur Karlin) writes in response to my last *NR* post:

---

3. Exceptions, according to Bob Woodward's most recent book, are the president and vice president.

Who says Bush et al. want to "win their War on TERRORRRRR" or their war against Iraq? I think that they would prefer the latter to be at a lower level, just to justify the permanent U.S. bases astride the oil supplies but not so intense as to give traction to the bleeding-heart liberals and the traitorous wing of the Protestant clergy. These wars or, in their Goebbels-speak, THE WAR, will keep them in power long enough to fill the Supreme Court with Thomases and Scalitos and to eliminate all legal restraint on their power to do whatever they want to whomever they want, whenever they want, and if you cry you will get worse! Things are getting worse daily. Who would think that we are all wondering whether or not the Supreme Court will allow stand the latest corrosive bill on detainees, the power of the President, and of anyone he delegates, to designate anyone (citizen or otherwise) an Enemy Combatant, and the gutting of habeas corpus. It is past time to offer calm analysis of the misconceptions of this gang. I think it is we who are subject to the misconception that they are just misguided.

This powerful indictment supposes a machiavellian intelligence in those who govern the country, an intelligence which would involve a high-level conspiracy just south of treason. Some of the cast of this political melodrama are on stage: the insouciant, often contemptuous vice president, the gray eminence Karl Rove, the churlish gamester[4] president."

All right, back in the early nineties, Paul Wolfowitz, student of the international policy realist Albert Wohlstetter, saw the possibility of destabilizing the totalitarian regimes which controlled the oil which controlled American industry by setting up a democratic regime in Iraq. Over the years, he was able to persuade those who'd been stained by the essential failure of Gulf War I to back this idea. One can still make a good theoretical case for such an enterprise, but real realists, knowing what usually happens to the best-laid plans of men, saw that we'd be where we are now, bleeding away in Mesopotamia while thousands around us die and millions everywhere hate us.

---

4. An article in a recent *Vanity Fair* quotes boyhood friends of the president remembering such things as his changing the rules of games if he were behind in them. "If we were playing one on one to eleven and he was behind, he'd insist we play till 15." He was also well-known as the riskiest player of the international warfare game Risk.

Post 7

When the Republican congressman Mark Foley of Florida was found to have made compromising sexual suggestions to young male congressional pages and subsequently resigned his office, the rhyme of his name with "holy" led to this use of the famous hymn "Holy, holy, holy / Lord God Almighty."

A DEMOCRAT'S HYMN

Foley, Foley, Foley! Congressman Almighty!
Early in October our song doth rise to thee.
Foley, Foley, Foley! Lascivious and lusty,
In three-legged government, a fourth empowered thee.

Foley, Foley, Foley! All Democrats adore thee.
Casting our votes upon thy smarmy sea,
Pages and cherubim harken oft to thee
Which wert, and art, and evermore shall be.

Foley, Foley, Foley! Though the darkness hide thee,
Thy sick pathetic self we still manage to see,
Oh tragic, tragic Foley (a misspelled folly),
Why wert thou so clumsy in thy impurity?

Foley, Foley, Foley, Congressman almighty.
Lust shall stain thy name on earth and sky and sea;
Foley, Foley, Foley, lascivious, loony, lusty,
A filthy trinity.

Post 8
October 25, 2006

I've just heard President Bush's not ineloquent description of the war that the rational, peace-loving people of the world are waging against the evil murderers who hate liberty, democracy and peace. He speaks of this as a war very different from but comparable in importance to the war against fascism which concluded the year before he was born. I was alive and aware during that war, and as far as quality of national life goes, that did not resemble the life we are leading now. Like almost every boy in my class, I did such things as collect and roll tin foil into supposedly usable balls and when in the country, had a "victory garden" where I raised a few radishes. My mother rolled bandages down at the Red Cross. My uncles were either in war-related businesses (the silk business which was involved in parachute making) or volunteering their time at the Office of Price Administration. Uniforms were everywhere, the trains were packed with soldiers, the stations thick with heartrending farewells. Everyone you knew was connected with the war: Your cousins were fighting in North Africa, Sicily, the Pacific; your friends' older brothers were mailing the thin blue wartime V-letters back home. Every civilian adult had a ration book with points for red meat, butter, gasoline and silk—later nylon—stockings. Almost everyone followed the day's battleground events, charted the progress or retreats on the map, knew the casualty figures, cheered and booed the political leaders in the newsreels.

Today, the war is something in the papers and the television news or the occasional presidential speech and the responses to it. Few are in uniform. I know no one fighting in Iraq or Afghanistan. In World War II, President Roosevelt's sons were in the army. And eighteen-year-old G. H. W. Bush volunteered as a pilot, postponing his life at Yale. Is there anyone in his son's large family serving in the military? Have none of them been persuaded by his eloquence and force to volunteer in the great cause he espouses?

As for the rest of us? Yes, we were aroused on that amazing September day when the two great towers disintegrated before our eyes, and for a few days afterward, we digested a new turn in the life of the nation, but now? Weariness, disgust, frustration, fury, boredom.

Post 9
October 26, 2006
One of the enrichments of a teacher's life is the reaction of his former students to his post-class activities and utterances. In response to my contrast of the "War on Terror" to World War II, my fine former student, Mary Scriver, emailed me from Montana:

> . . . the war of my childhood was something like yours: relatives overseas, ship yards running 24 hours a day, Victory gardens (my mother's garden was generous), saving fat, tinfoil and soap.
>
> The present war is evidently NOTHING like yours. Every

small town has displays with photos of dozens of local kids who are serving in Iraq or Afghanistan. Every death is marked with long stories in the newspapers. The Blackfeet send every soldier, male and female, off to war with an eagle feather and honor songs and welcome each back with a small parade through town. In Great Falls, where Malmstrom Air Force Base is located and the families of the soldiers work around town, clerks have piano wire nerves drawn taut by worry. On the way to Great Falls we pass missile siloes—one is just over the hill from my town and they say that if fired, the backwash from the rocket might set the town on fire. If it is nuclear-armed and goes wrong, I won't know about it. I won't even be pink mist, as are enemies in Iraq when hit by heavy fire.

No one is bored. We are very weary. We worry about the economy and about law enforcement since so many of our best people have been called up in the Reserve. Yet I would wager that fewer than twenty Montanans were ever in the World Trade Towers when they existed.

I have been lucky enough to have taught some distinguished reporters (Seymour Hersh, David Brooks, Mike Taiibi), but unprofessional reporters such as Mary Scriver rank equally high as alert, intelligent and sensitive observers and critics. Her description of the Terror War in Montana should be placed beside my characterization of that War in Hyde Park, Chicago, neither contradicting the other.

Post 10
November 3, 2006
The election is next Tuesday, feelings are agitated, anger becomes fury, disappointment misery, temperate criticism raging indictment. Hertzberg, a brilliant observer, wonders (in the *New Yorker*) if Bush is the worst of the forty-three presidents or, at least, of the sixteen two-termers. Thomas Friedman lashes the administration's incompetence and the viciousness of the smoke with which they try to screen it. Karl Rove is seen as a vendor of political cancer.

Those who sympathize with these viewpoints—as I, in part, do—fear that not enough voters will share them next Tuesday. If the Democrats don't take control of at least the House, many will be heartsick and enraged at the U.S. electorate, but the country will go on more or less as it has ("Call that going, call that on"), a top-heavy giant, trying to tread delicately on the world scene. (The image is of the elephants dancing in frilly skirts to Ponchielli's "Dance of the Hours" in *Fantasia*.) Long-range thinkers will reflect on comparisons to sixteenth-century Spain beginning its long slide down the chute, China and India playing the roles that England and the U.S. played in the next centuries. More dire prognosticators will see the infuriated Moslem world in the successor role.

Here in Illinois, the races are peppered with slander. Democratic congressional candidate Tammy Duckworth, who lost both legs in the Iraq War, is confronted by an opponent of full-fledged stem cell research who advertises with wife and children claiming that Tammy will not only raise everyone's taxes at least two thousand dollars a year but will tax the dead (the "death tax," Republican name for the "inheritance tax"). [She lost in a close race.] Todd Stroger, the unaccomplished son of the stroke-hammered ex–head of the Cook County Board, is invoking Bush as his opponent instead of Tony Peraita, a self-made Republican millionaire who might just swim through the Democratic wave here to victory. [He didn't.] A decent Democratic governor is opposed by a decent Republican opponent but should pull through. [He did. It wasn't close. And so Illinois was treated to two years more of Rod Blagojevich's shenanigans.]

Post 11
November 13, 2006, 1:54 P.M.
Cass Sunstein's graceful post on the graciousness of President Bush and Senator Santorum bespeaks the enlightened political climate sometimes called "Jeffersonian." (Well, he was less vituperative than Adams and Hamilton.) Today the president dedicated the Martin Luther King memorial site under the smiling sun, acknowledging "my predecessor . . . and fourth brother," Bill Clinton, who was sitting a few yards down the platform.

For some perverse reason, memory kicked up one of the first jokes I remember hearing: a Jew walks down a back street in 1938 Berlin and is confronted by Hitler who, infuriated at the sight of this noxious being, pulls out his revolver, forces him to his knees and orders him to eat the horse turds in the street. The Jew gets down on his knees, eats and then, enraged, knocks the gun from Hitler's hand and says, "Now you eat." Hitler eats, the Jew flings the gun away, runs all the way home where, opening the door, he calls out, "Momma, Momma, guess who I just had lunch with?"

Post 12
November 17, 2006
I didn't know Milton Friedman well but yesterday, reading of his death, I felt that special grief which means the loss of another part of one's life. Death, like a novelist, assembles the contacts and associations one has had with the dead person and then makes some sense out of what had been more or less incidental encounters. To my surprise, my assemblage is fairly large, much too large to recount in this post. In addition to these encounters, there are many stories heard from colleagues and friends, friends who were Milton's colleagues, intimates, students and collaborators. As for shared beliefs, my own were far from many of his, but, persuaded by his columns, talk, TV programs and by the first chapters of *Capitalism and Freedom*,[5] I modified some of them.

In October 1976 when he and another U. of Chicago faculty member, Saul Bellow, won Nobel Prizes, some remarks of mine about Jews reinvigorating American notions of individuality were quoted in the *Chicago Tribune*. Friedman sent me a letter "across campus" asking whether I thought he should give his acceptance talk in Yiddish. A year or so later, I encountered him in the elevator of Steinhenge, the high-rise on Dorchester where he and Bellow lived. [It was financed by the Stein of Stein Rowe Farnham.] In shirt sleeves, he stood by a hamper of laundry he was taking to the cellar. I asked him about some downward turn the economy had taken. His response: "How do you feel?" I was carrying the manuscript of *Humboldt's Gift,* Bellow's great, not quite finished novel. I held it up and said, "I feel fine," and, waving the manuscript, "I'm looking forward to reading this." "There, you see," he said, the intimation being that high-level production and consumption were going on, no room for pessimism.

At his ninetieth-birthday party in a Chicago hotel, I heard George Shultz say that of all the people he'd known, he believed that Milton was the most influential, and then, after listing the occasions when Milton's economic predictions had correctly flown in the face of events, sang—

---

5. Which in 1962 was not reviewed—according to Milton—by any leading publication.

"Although tone-deaf Milton won't recognize it"—a lyric whose refrain went "And no theory's good without a fact." Milton's marvelous grin shone even more.[6]

The tiny economist was apparently sharp till his last hours, hungry, as always, for intellectual debate (he debated cabbies on the way to O'Hare where a plane would take him to debates with Margaret Thatcher), and though I doubt that he believed it would happen, perhaps he's already questioning the layout of his new quarters with St. Peter.

Post 13
November 18, 2006

Every now and then, a remarkable person breaks out of a social prison, and spends her liberation returning like Socrates to the dark cave to redeem as many of the still-manacled as he or she can. In recent times, many of these redeemers have been women, for in much of the dark world, women still bear the heaviest chains.

Today's *NY Times* tells the story of the tiny Kenyan marathon champion Tegla Loroupe. Tegla learned to run on the dry hills of northwest Kenya so that she would not be late for school after the morning chores which her father piled on her. Against his will and that of the contemptuous, domineering cruelty of his male peers, Tegla not only went to school but began entering and winning races. Supported by her sister Albina, she went on to win the NYC marathons in 1994 and 1995. She won the last one days after Albina died from undiagnosed hemorrhaging. "There was no hospital within miles," said Tegla, who now is helping to build one. She has set up a Peace Academy to encourage the warriors of her tribe, the Pokot, to exchange their guns for top-notch athletic training, and she wants to help Pokot girls, brought up as she was to think they are worthless, to know that they are capable of living full lives. Her marathon winnings have gone into these great causes, and thirty-three-year-old Tegla devotes herself to the difficult task of raising funds for them.

The same edition of the *Times* reports that Willem de Kooning's painting of a woman (*Woman III*) with huge, machine-filled breasts, im-

---

6. At the table, I asked Rose Friedman how her brother, Aaron Director, was doing. She said, "He's awful. There's nothing wrong with him, but he just sits around and does nothing." "How old is Aaron now, Rose?" "He's 101," she said.

mense shoulders, claw-like hands and a cruel, sly face has been sold to a hedge fund billionaire for $137.5 million dollars.

Post 14
November 24, 2006

While Americans filled cars, trains, planes, buses and streets en route to celebrate Thanksgiving with parents, grandparents and friends, several thousand miles away a new wrinkle in family relations degraded the human story. Fatimah Omar Mahmud al-Najar, a sexagenarian mother of nine, grandmother of forty, dressed for the occasion in white headscarf, green bandanna and a belt of explosives, detonated the belt, killing herself and wounding two Israeli soldiers, perhaps including the one who, believing the old woman was acting oddly, threw a "stun grenade" her way. On Hamas television, Fatimah Omar's martyr video showed her wide-eyed and open mouthed, holding an M-16 automatic rifle in her strong hands, her expression half puzzled, half fearfully eager.

This grandfather of five, who relishes every moment he spends with his grandchildren, read this *New York Times* report with horror even when its final paragraph supplied what constituted the explanation of Fatimah Omar's final act: Fathima al-Najar, her oldest daughter, said that her son had been killed by Israelis, that her mother's house had been destroyed, and that another grandson was in a wheelchair with an amputated leg. "She and I went to the mosque," she told reporters. "We were looking for martyrdom."

Post 15
November 29, 2006

In part to escape the continuous, if secondhand assault by the murder machines of Iraq and Darfur, one diverts oneself as one can, some with the marital and maternal adventures of rock stars, or, as some like me, with literary doings. So this morning, repelled by the opaque, un-, no, anti-English translations of Rilke by J. B. Leishman cited in John Banville's review of Rilke's correspondence with Lou Andreas-Salome in the *New York Review of Books,* I wrote what is I hope a fairly clear and accurate translation of the wonderful poem Rilke managed to write two weeks before an agonizing and untreated ("I want my own death, not a doctor's") leukemia killed him.

Come, you, you the last I recognize,
incurable pain within the web of flesh.
As my mind burned, you see that I burned
in you, the wood that long resisted
the flame you feed. Now I nourish you and burn in you.
My mildness becomes in your fury
a fury out of hell, not here.
Totally pure, totally unplanned, free of the future,
I climb on the tangled pyre of suffering,
certain of never getting anything back
for this heart whose reserves are gone.

Am I still the one who, unrecognized, burns?
I bring no memories here.

Life, life. To be outside it
While I burn.
       No one knows me.

Here is Rilke's original German.

Komm du, du letzter, den ich anerkenne,
heilloser Schmerz im leiblichen Geweb:
wie ich im Geiste brannte, sieh, ich brenne
in dir; das Holz hat lange widerstrebt,
der Flamme, die du loderst, zuzustimmen,
nun aber nähr' ich dich und brenn in dir.
Mein hiesig Mildsein wird in deinem Grimmen
ein Grimm der Hölle nicht von hier.
Ganz rein, ganz planlos frei von Zukunft stieg
ich auf des Leidens wirren Scheiterhaufen,
so sicher nirgend Künftiges zu kaufen
um dieses Herz, darin der Vorrat schwieg.
Bin ich es noch, der da unkenntlich brennt?
Erinnerungen reiß ich nicht herein.
O Leben, Leben: Draußensein.
Und ich in Lohe. Niemand der mich kennt.

The long-awaited Baker-Hamilton report is out, introduced at a news conference presided over by James Baker with his familiar mix of self-deprecation ("we has-beens") and aristo impatience (telling a reporter he could answer his question but "as it's answered in the *Report* it would be a waste of time") and the co-chair, Lee Hamilton, the icon of gravitas. Seven other committee members were there as well, some like Alan Simpson, so enamored of his own cleverness and wit you wondered how he could have ever given up the senatorial stage. Of the three others who spoke at the conference, only William Perry was usefully and modestly informative.

As for the *Report* itself, it begins with a description of the present situation of U.S.-occupied Iraq which contains nothing of novelty to TV news watchers or readers of the *New Republic*, but does offer some detailed recommendations, starting with the "milestones" suggested by Prime Minister Al-Maliki: so, by the end of 2006 or early 2007, the approval of the Provincial Election, Petroleum and de-Baathification Laws and the Central Bank of Iraq's raising interest rates to 20 percent and appreciating the dinar 10 percent.

The committee's recommendations deal with training the army (embedding well-trained and exceptionally able American officers in Iraqi units), using the FBI to help train the police, calling for a regional congress and otherwise engaging Iraq's neighbors in diplomacy, detailing problems in oil production, technical and monetary assistance, working on such trouble spots as Kirkuk, calling for the appointment of American supervisors of the suggested reforms, arguing against such suggestions as dividing the country into three more or less independent units, and, in short, dealing sensibly with the problems discussed ad nauseam in hundreds of newspapers, magazines, cable news shows and blogs.

Appendices offer maps, lists of the many people interviewed, presidents and prime ministers on down to professors and one-star generals, and biographies of the committee members in which one learns that Hamilton is in the Indiana Basketball Hall of Fame and the names of his five grandchildren (but not the names of anyone else's), and that Eagleburger's three sons are all named (a la George Foreman)

Lawrence. The one familiarity in this section is referring to Clever Simpson as "Al."

A classic government report, one which the administration could partly follow without being derailed from its "course." Oh yes, it is advised to fuse its "supplemental" fund requests with the rest of its budgetary needs, but outside of the acknowledgment that things are not going well over there, there is little in the way of criticism.

Post 16
December 7, 2006

I just read (in a fine *New Yorker* profile) that Jasper Johns praised Marcel Duchamps for inserting doubt into the air of the art world. I then watched the joint Bush-Blair press conference and wondered why the American president so sharply banishes it from at least his public self. Was it all those years of playing second fiddle to his father and his more scholarly, younger, taller brother, Jeb? Was it the years of business failure and the thousands of nights drowning the self-doubt they engendered in booze? Was it the discovery in his Bible Study class that there was an absolute verity and his rebirth—midwifed by AA—in accepting it that banished doubt from his being?

If it weren't for the Great Doubter, Abraham Lincoln, one might think that self-doubt was an impeachable offense. In any event, President George W. Bush spoke with the intensity and conviction which one sees in knights jousting for their beloved or in ideological ignoramuses screaming in the street.

Side by side with Tony Blair, his polished Tweedledee, whose civil tones suggested that he was capable of doubting, the president vaulted the strictures of the Baker-Hamilton Study Group to drive home to us doubters the latest version of the course first offered to him in his post-9/11 epiphany. It will take more than another three thousand American deaths, another twenty thousand broken American bodies and minds, another hundred thousand Iraqi deaths and a broken Iraqi generation, and even a delegation of senior Republican legislators to the Oval Office to derail this doubt-free president from "the course." And of course, who knows, not this doubter, if in the trickery of History, the one-horse shay that is President George W. Bush may turn out to be "right."

Mourning Becomes the Media
a short play

Scene 1. The Puce Room of the White House. Light coming through rose-colored window glass beautifies the reflections bouncing off the handsome silver tea service. The First Lady, simply and expensively dressed in tweed skirt and green silk blouse, pours tea for her visitor, Colleen Dowdy, the columnist.

COLLEEN DOWDY: It's always reassuring to see you, Mrs. B. How do you remain so calm and self-assured?

FIRST LADY: Why wouldn't I be calm? Look around.

CD: It is lovely, here, Mrs. B., but I'm thinking about life outside. I believe you do get outside.

FL: Every Tuesday. Under cover. What about "outside"?

CD: Well, for one thing, your husband was repudiated in the November election.

FL: I didn't realize he was on the ballot.

CD: You have me there, ma'am. He's been recently called "the worst of all forty-three American presidents" by a panel of historians.

FL: The one discussing the Holocaust in Teheran?

CD (*laughing*): No, ma'am. Then there is the little matter of Iraq, which your good husband decided was a perfect place down which to flush the blood and treasure of the U.S.

FL: And to think I've been misled into thinking Saddam Hussein and the UN had something to do with that.

CD: I did hear Saddam interviewed on television, ma'am, but I don't recall him suggesting that we invade his country.

FL: No, he adopted the Hitler strategy, just do whatever awful thing you want to do until someone finally does something about it. Incidentally, Colleen, I've actually been to Iraq.

CD: In the Green Zone?

FL: It isn't very green. I did speak to soldiers. They seemed to think they were defending the rest of us.

CD: I don't think you'd find that sentiment as common today. Even our generals are saying that things are getting worse every day. It was bad under Saddam, but most people managed to get on with decent lives.

FL: Would you like him back in his palaces?

CD: I like him where he is. But it doesn't change the fact that today, people are terrified when their children leave the house to go to school.

FL: Look here, Colleen, I know that things aren't good in Baghdad, though there are still people in parts of it, outside the Green Zone, who smile and play and eat their dinner. But what about the rest of the country? Why aren't you and your colleagues writing about all the schools which have been built, all the town councils which make decisions which used to be made by Saddam? Most of the country is functioning, but you media people focus on disaster, on bombs, on blood, on the dying and those in pain, not on the living, the prosperous, the happy.

CD: Mrs. B., isn't that like saying, "You're concentrating on the bullet in the man's brain, instead of on his strong legs and arms, his gleaming white teeth"?

FL: I don't think it is. Your business is selling papers; disaster sells papers.

CD: Mrs. B, you and I wouldn't live there for all the money in the world, would we?

FL: I do like it here, Colleen.

CD: I too. Do you know any young man or woman, perhaps friends of your daughters or members of your husband's large family, who is fighting in Iraq?

FL: Senator McCain's and Senator Webb's sons, for one, though I don't know them personally. Several congressmen have children fighting in Iraq. We have an army of wonderful volunteers who choose to fight for their country and accept the terrible risk of dying for it.

CD: They are brave men and women doing what your husband and his generals tell them to do. And that's my point. Do you think they are doing the right thing? Now, not three years ago. Now when even your husband says that we're losing the war.

FL: We weren't winning World War II in 1941 or 1942, not even in '43. Anyway, it is the Iraqis themselves who are going to win the war. We are there to train them.

CD: How is it that it takes the Iraqi government so long to train its army and police when it seems to take the insurgents next to no time at all to train their recruits?

FL: It is easier to destroy than defend, and if you don't care at all about any life, including your own, you don't need much training. How much training do you need to strap explosives on your body and blow yourself up in a market?

CD: I'd think you have to be in a certain frame of mind.

FL: I agree to that. Just as you need to be in a certain frame of mind to write what you write. Have a little more tea, then we can take a stroll in the Rose Garden with Barney. It is a beautiful day.

Curtain

Post 18

December 28, 2006

I just read (in the *Weekly Standard*) a foolish piece by a writer many of whose essays I greatly admire, Joseph Epstein (who, as Myron J. Epstein, was a student of mine more than four decades ago). It talks of George W. Bush as a believer and then assesses Truman and the presidents who followed him as believers or non-believers (though not just in divinity). No factual basis, psychological analysis or anything other than the assessor's assertive chutzpah supports the contentions. Epstein asserts that all great presidents were believers, although belief does not suffice to make a president great. The greatest president of all, Lincoln was, of course, a believer—in the American Union.

One could challenge each of Epstein's assessments, and on this day after Gerald Ford's death, one is tempted to rebut his dismissal of Ford as a decent, dull unbeliever, but belief is so much more complicated than his essay makes out, that it would be the equivalent of wrestling a scarecrow. My very intelligent late friend Edward Levi, Ford's attorney general, told me that he was astonished by Ford's knowledge of every cabinet member's business and his remarkable awareness of what the cabinet member was going to say about it. Until I read Ford's marvelous eulogy of Levi (one that only the eulogist himself could have written), I thought that Levi might have been under the spell so many academics experience when they come into contact with important political figures. (It resembles that dazzlement which overcomes many in the company of movie stars.)

If one examines himself, something Epstein used to do in his best *American Scholar* essays, one may find, as I do, that what one believes in is less powerful a force than that disposition which is made up of loyalties and affinities, some of which one may be embarrassed to mention, certain fears, ditto, certain passions including instinctive dislikes, ditto. All right, George W. Bush was reborn in midlife, he attends a Methodist church one of whose central articles is a belief in the epiphanic experience, and on September 12 as cameras watched him stride back to the White House, a small, isolated figure in a shirt whose collar was loose, making him seem even smaller than usual, he was undergoing what he himself seems to have regarded as an epiphany, one which had to do with his presidential mission. This equivalent of conviction may well preclude his altering his course in Iraq.

I am now listening to Richard Goode playing Mozart's Piano Concerto No. 9 in E-flat Major (K. 271). I ask myself "Was Mozart a believer?" and respond "It's beside the point." Mozart was responding to things deeper than belief, his sense of consonance and dissonant surprise, his feeling for linear and harmonic progress, his broad, deep knowledge of what can go on between the pianoforte and an orchestra in the scope of a concerto, to, indeed, the intellectual excitement which these create.

Post 19
December 31, 2006

> *Saddam and Jerry*
> The buzzard never says it is to blame.
> The panther wouldn't know what scruples mean.
> When the piranha strikes it feels no shame.
> If snakes had hands, they'd feel their hands were clean . . .
> On this third planet of the sun
> Among the signs of bestiality
> A clear conscience is Number One.
> —Wislawa Szymborska, "In Praise of Feeling Bad about Yourself"

In the Anteroom of the Eternal sit two former heads of state. One had died in his sleep a couple of nights earlier; the other had just been hanged by a rope of yellow hemp after cursing one of the masked Shiite guards who had cursed him for ruining his life and country, then, with the thick rope on his bescarfed neck, cursed Americans, Persians, spies and traitors. Both men seemed to have died with their consciences clear as a newborn's or, to pick one of Szymborska's examples, as a piranha's.

Their careers, so different in some ways, had interesting similarities. Both were raised in the sticks; both had been deserted by their biological fathers, the Iraqi's six months before he was born, the American's at the age of two; both early found supportive males, the American his mother's second husband, whose name he took, the Iraqi his uncle who initiated him into political militancy. Both studied law, the American at Yale, the Iraqi at Cairo University; both had military training and were successful, the Iraqi as soldier, the American as naval officer. In politics, each made his initial reputation as party reconciler and peacemaker, the Iraqi in the Ba'ath party, the American in the Republican. Both attained ultimate power in irregular ways, the American by presidential appointment, the Iraqi by coup d'etat.

Both were large, good-looking, physically and mentally strong, both were considered charming, both had roots in small towns which they adopted as their hometowns and where they will be buried.

Many of the many differences between them can be traced to the cultures which formed them. In combative and dangerous Iraq, the Iraqi became increasingly isolated, fearful, aggressive, paranoid and megalomaniacal; in the much less stressful American political scene, the American stayed famously down to earth, eschewing the paraphernalia, let alone the monuments of grandeur, for which the Iraqi increasingly hungered.

The American died in his nineties, admired even by those who'd opposed him politically from left or right; the Iraqi died on the edge of three score and ten after being hunted down, discovered and pulled out of a bolt hole like a filthy rodent, then imprisoned and finally tried in a public trial during which he seemed to reforge the defiance and arrogance of his dictatorial years, traits which saw him through to his final conscious seconds.

Awaiting their Ultimate Assessment and Assignment, they exchange a few words.

SADDAM HUSSEIN: I envy the serenity and ease of your career, and wonder if, born and raised where you were, I'd have had one like it.

GERALD FORD: I've never been much at counterfactuals. Maybe it was my football training which made me face only what was facing me.

SH: But you say you had training, and that means preparation.

GF: Right, but when it came down to what counted, there wasn't time for what-might-have-beens.

SH: I understand that well. Much of my life consisted in making life and death decisions on the spur of the moment.

GF: But as a dictator, you created the situations. And until the last couple, you were doing all right.

SH: You have no idea. When Americans quarrel, it's like children; a parent says a few words, maybe slaps someone, and that's it. Iraqis have nothing better to do than quarrel and quarrel to the death. You're not a parent, you're a policeman, a dog keeper, the head of an asylum. Words don't work. A slap isn't enough. You have to be tough and act tougher. You don't come out smelling like a rose. Gerry Ford would look more like Mussolini than FDR—and look how even he, a cripple, was cursed as a dictator.

GF: So basically, you're soft as lambswool. In the U.S., you'd be Gerry Ford.

SH (*laughs*): Well, maybe Tom DeLay, your Hammer.

GF: Elections do tend to bank the fires. Even as a congressman in a safe district, you have to mollify a lot of different interests. It's tedious, and I would have gotten out in '74, if Nixon hadn't disintegrated.

SH: Nixon has Iraqi characteristics. We have great liars, great complainers and moaners. I could have worked with him, though he'd have had to be killed.

GF: We killed him slowly, with kindness.

SH: Your pardoning him.

GF: I did feel for him—he was such a confused person, smart as hell except about himself. I covered it by saying that he sucked up the country's energy, became its agenda. We have an indolent and voracious press. They can only manage one story at a time, and Nixon would have been the story, but I did feel for him. He was like a broken-mirror version of what I could have become.

SH: We're more alike than headline readers will ever know.

GF: Heads of state. We both know what that requires, you in your state, me in mine.

A voice is heard: Gerry, come on in now. We have a few things to
talk over.

Ford rises, shakes hands with Saddam and says: Good luck to
you. Maybe we'll see each other.

SH: Never can tell who'll be looking up at whom?

GF: I'll try not to act over-confident. (*Goes inside. A rumble is heard,
then, after a pause, the infernal music from Don Giovanni. Saddam
shakes his head, smiles, straightens the yellow hemp around his neck and
prepares for his own final interview.*)

Blackout

Post 20

January 1, 2007

It's said that one reason the U.S. is out of its depth in Iraq and
Afghanistan is our ignorance of tribalism, yet we have our own forms
of tribalism, so it shouldn't be so difficult to understand theirs.

In the waning hours of 2006, I watched my beloved—yes, beloved,
if also hated—Chicago Bears humiliate themselves in a cascade of ineptitude and self-destructiveness the like of which we've not seen in
what has been largely a triumphant season. Their opponent, the classic
foe of their long history, was the Green Bay Packers, playing as well as
they have in their poor season in what was probably the final game in
the long career of their thirty-seven-year-old quarterback, Brett Favre.
As usual, I watched the game behind closed doors and allowed myself
to vent strong feelings of disgust, despair, fury and, occasionally, exul-
tation. My good wife, understanding that the cries coming from the
closed doors were heard only during these hours of communion with
the Bears, added to her chapter on the idiocy of the American male.

Five years earlier, we'd flown to her father's hometown, Hattiesburg, Mississippi, for a family wedding. The post-wedding dinner was
given in the local convention center, which was wildly decorated and
filled with tables devoted to the appetites of the two or three hundred
guests. After I'd fed myself and drunk some champagne, I went into an
adjacent room where it seemed that a goodly proportion of the male
guests were cheering and moaning as they watched a football game between the University of Southern Mississippi and a southern rival.
Tuxedo jackets were off, black bow ties were hanging loose on the

bestudded white dress shirts of the perspiring cheerers. It occurred to me that USM, a local institution of which till then I'd never heard, was the focus of a profound identification which went pretty much to the core of those watching the game. It was at this institution that Brett Favre first came to the notice of those who drafted him to play for the Atlanta Falcons, from whom he was purchased by the team of which for more than a decade and a half he'd been the great star.

USM was the tribe of the whole region around Hattiesburg and perhaps for a good part of the state. To a somewhat lesser degree, the Chicago Bears are my tribe. At least for some hours, my emotional life is in their hands and my sense of fulfillment or depletion depends on what happens in Soldier Field a few miles away from my room.

After the game which Favre and his team won in a decisive way, the grizzled, good-looking (in the manner of the just-deceased Gerald Ford, who'd once been offered a tryout by the Packers), not ineloquent quarterback was interviewed by one of the ignorant and vulgar tootsies who are now part of the athletic package offered by the networks. She was probing for the "big story." "Was this the great quarterback's last game?" and, if so, "How did he feel?" Favre choked up. "This is very tough," he said, and went on to say how much he loved his teammates and how much he loved the game. She had her story, though in her jackal-like way, kept at him till he got out of her grasp and made his way to the locker room. My own parochial feeling for my soundly defeated team had broadened and deepened by now, so that I felt for and with this old enemy. My tribalism had been extended by emotional alliance which now included the memory of the wedding festivities in the town where one is shown Favre's house.[7]

No need here to go over the familiar ground of the sedentary American man's involvement with professional or college teams. It involves forms of expression our everyday life denies us. We can hate openly, we can join thrillingly with others of all sorts and classes for a common end. It involves the lingua franca which enables us to talk with a cabbie, a grocery clerk, and with our colleagues on a Monday morning before our serious professional discussions. It's tribal glue.

---

7. Brett Favre was eased out of Green Bay, played for the Jets, and, in 2009, retired from them to play for the Vikings. One senses he'd like to end on the field, a sort of Custer.

Post 22

January 9, 2007

Was it six and a half years ago that a smartass newsman flunked Candidate G. W. Bush on ignorance of world leaders' names and countries?

Which Western leader today would be able to pronounce, let alone memorize, some of the names of today's world leaders? A few might manage the new UN secretary general, Ban Ki-Moon of South Korea, but his deputy-secretary designate, Asha-Rose Mtengeti-Migiro of Tanzania, will surely take more getting used to than that of the under-secretary designate, Alicia Barcena Ibarra of Mexico. It's when we call the roll of ambassadors and foreign ministers that the new nominal orchestra is apparent: Dumisani S. Kumalo of South Africa manages to trip off this American tongue, but the deputy prime minister of Turkmenistan, Gurbanguly Berdymukhammedov, doesn't. Jeno C. A. Staehelin (Switzerland) is on the border of the manageable, but Vijay Lunhianandan (India) requires a special visa.

Read the *NY Times'* world news columns fifty years ago, and the average American has little trouble with names; today's columns make a road pocked with sink holes.

Now that 46 percent of the Berkeley freshman class is of Asian background, it is not unlikely that a name quiz given to U.S. presidential candidates in 2040 might be full of such mouth-stoppers as Bill Jones and John Reilly. Or will the transnational flow of information have made all the world's names as straightforward and euphonious as Lee and Rockefeller are for most of us?

Post 23

January 11, 2007

Last night, standing in front of bookcases (History), wearing a dark blue suit (Seriousness) and a light blue tie (Hope), a handkerchief barely visible in a breast pocket (Limited Hope), President Bush spoke soberly, without a single one of his self-betraying smirks, for twenty minutes about his "new" strategy for "winning" the war in Iraq. The central proposal was to bring in five brigades (16,000) of American soldiers to join eighteen brigades (74,000) of Iraqi soldiers plus an unspecified number of Iraqi police to bring order and security to the nine districts of Baghdad, the center of the thirty-mile zone in which 90 percent of the country's violence erupts. U.S. soldiers will be "embedded" with Iraqi units, and one coalition brigade will be affixed to every Iraqi division. Soldiers will remain in the areas they've tranquilized, insurgents will be hunted down, the Iraqi government will use the ten billion dollars it has pledged to reconstruction projects to employ its idled citizens and increase the security and confidence indispensable to the burgeoning, if imperfect democracy whose birth was perhaps over-optimistically celebrated a year ago. The Iraqi government will work out such difficulties as the equitable sharing of oil revenues and the reintegration of those—Sunnis—deprived of civic roles in the de-Baathification program. Americans must steel themselves to the bloody slaughter with which the enemies of peace and democracy will smear our TV screens this coming year. The Iraqi government must know that if it does not fulfill its responsibilities during this same year, the American people will lose confidence in and withdraw support from it. Iran and Syria are put on notice that their efforts to reinforce the insurgents and terrorists will be interdicted. (A naval strike force has been assigned to the region.) Saudi Arabia, Egypt, Jordan and the Gulf States will be reminded what dangers a defeated Iraq will bring to them. Secretary Rice, the reminder, leaves for the region Friday. She will appoint a reconstruction chief to work alongside a new Iraqi reconstruction chief and two deputies. May the Author of Liberty bless us all.

Speaking for the new Democratic majority, Senator Durbin of Illinois said that the Iraqi horse had already left the barn, and the new lock-up system was expensive and useless. Republican senators (Smith, Hagel, Collins), editorial writers and other commentators described, sometimes passionately, the inadequacies of the presidential plan, complained of presidential "fog" (the *NY Times*) and said that it was time for the U.S. to begin withdrawing its troops. Implied was denial of the presidential depiction of the "unimaginable" horrors which would follow such withdrawal: the exposure of a wimpish America betraying its allies; the galvanized recruitment of murderers; the creation of a Taliban-like, oil-rich haven-state from which attacks on the U.S. could be planned in security and leisure.

Shaken and uncertain, although enduring no personal sacrifice, physically secure, indeed comfortable, I reached for my copy of Yeats' poems and read:

Hearts with one purpose alone
Through summer and winter seem
Enchanted to a stone
To trouble the living stream . . .
Too long a sacrifice can
make a stone of the heart . . .

Post 24
January 15, 2007
Ahmadinijad is visiting Chavez in Venezuela and will go on to Equador
and Bolivia mortaring the alliance of those who resist the domination
of those who won the hot war of 1939–45 and the Cold War which
ended forty-four years later. There are agreements to buy each other's
goods and products (cars, tankers) and to fuse their oil interests so as to
squeeze the United States and other dominator countries which depend
on it.

The little Iranian is a wide-ranging visitor and an interestingly in-
clusive host. Anyone who furthers his drive to remap the world his way
is welcomed with smiles and hugs. During the recent Teheran Holocaust Conference of such renowned historians as the Klu Kluxer David
Duke, he was photographed with Rabbi Yisroel Dovid Weiss, assistant
director of Neturer Karta ("Guardian of the City"), an American group
which believes as he does that the Holocaust has been exploited (or invented!) to underwrite Israel. (The rabbi's group believes that a legitimate Israel will come into being only when the Messiah arrives.) Rabbi
Weiss had indeed lost much of his family to whatever phenomenon Ahmadinijad substitutes for the Holocaust, but this shared interest in the
illegitimacy of Israel was enough to bring them together. (In October
2004, Rabbi Weiss arrived in France to bring flowers to the dying Yassir
Arafat.)

Meanwhile, Bush and Company were appearing on American networks in their non-accusing, all-understanding, steady-as-a-rock,
Daddy-knows-best mode to stem the negative reaction to their "new
Iraq strategy." Scott Pelley of *60 Minutes* was invited to Camp David and
on the presidential helicopter, the president treated him to his special
tour of the city about which he'd just read a book. He was photographed emerging from a meeting with the relatives of soldiers killed
in Iraq and to Pelley "seemed a different man," shaken as anyone not

made of stone would be. His softness of heart was further underlined when he told Pelley that although someone had showed him the film of Saddam Hussein's hanging, he did not watch nor want to watch him going through the trap door.

Before the NFL playoff games, CNN showed a powerful documentary called *Combat Hospital.* It dealt with a MASH unit in Iraq. No Robert Altman–*MASH* wisecracking here, only as much humanity as could be packed into an hour, young American military doctors and nurses immersed in the desperate, brilliant work of repairing or failing to repair the terrible wounds of those brought in—American soldiers, Iraqi insurgents, bystanding children–bleeding, screaming, dying. Shaking, my wife and I drove down to a gallery on Dearborn Street to lose ourselves in the last five years' work of the seventy-seven-year-old American painter Vera Klement, gorgeous expressions of a great visual mentality that stands for that flowering of civilized life for which all, I suppose, Bush and Ahmadinijad, Chavez, Rabbi Weiss, the late Arafat and, more surely, the MASH doctors and the makers of their documentary alike, ultimately aim.

Post 25
January 17, 2007

A friend, visiting from Washington, DC, yesterday, remembered hearing President Bush talking to a small group about four years ago. "It was frightening," he said. "He couldn't finish a sentence. Aides tried to throw him words, he didn't—couldn't!—pick them up. He seemed dyslexic. I almost felt sorry for him. I certainly felt sorry for the country."

Practice, practice, practice gets you to Carnegie Hall, and Bush, like an NFL quarterback, has had lots of practice talk since then. Interviewed by Jim Lehrer two days ago, he was fluent. His syntax didn't falter, his word choice was excellent, he was in verbal command of his intentions, and only once or twice did a response perish in the verbal desert of uncertainty. One such had to do with unequal war sacrifice. Bush's quavering response suggested that American anxiety about Iraq constituted a kind of tax, and thus a sacrifice. Otherwise, he was on the solid ground of presidential self-confidence. His well-practiced thesis: everyone agrees we can't fail, therefore, I chose, after much conferring and thinking, the best means of succeeding. If anyone has a better one, speak up. Our fine generals suggested the proper troop level and defined the mission. They and I were wrong not to send in more troops after the bombing of the Samarra mosque, but at that time we were hamstrung by our Iraqi partner. Now the Iraqis have assured us that together, our soldiers can go into any Baghdad neighborhood, chase out and hunt down its murderous disturbers, then leave sufficient force behind to insure that those living there will enjoy a peaceful existence. Reconstruction projects employing Iraqis will be launched, and newly energized and enfranchised citizens will be evermore grateful to the government which has brought them this fine new life. In time, Americans can leave Iraq to the Iraqis. If we left now, extremists on both sides would kill each other at a much greater rate, al Qaeda would grow amidst the turmoil, oil revenues would give it power to launch murderous, perhaps atomic attacks at us, and generations of Americans would face problems far worse than those we face now.

Lehrer tried to find cracks in the presidential façade. The new, literate Bush (now reading—at Professor Kissinger's suggestion—Horne's account of the French collapse in Algeria) was as uncrackable, confident and courteous as Louis Quatorze.

Lehrer did not explore either *apres moi, le deluge* or *le deluge, c'est moi.*

Post 26

January 19, 2007

The most telling way to convey my time of life is to say that my oldest son will be fifty-six years old tomorrow. One of life's props is the formation of "temporal chords," parallels or "rhymes" in time and space, and the ways to record, express and make sense of them. At my age, they are "found" everywhere. The latest for me is the day's *University of Chicago Chronicle* whose two lead stories deal with (1) the discovery of the remains of a fierce battle which destroyed the town of Hamoukar in Syria about fifty-five hundred years ago and (2) the award of the year's University of Chicago alumni medal to James Watson who, in the April 1953 issue of *Nature,* announced that he and Francis Crick had figured out the structure of the "copying mechanism for the genetic material." The common theme here is the repetitiveness—the sustenance—of the human condition, its bio-chemical mechanism and the brutal debris which testify to it.

It's clear to most of us that our daily life and decision-making can't be chained to the past but those of us lucky enough to have the leisure to learn about and reflect on it find that its most bitter and painful stings are less painful if they are placed in the perspective of repetition and comparison. (This may be small consolation to those bleeding from today's wounds.)

Does this ease diminish our responsibility to act in the present? Perhaps not, but it is often the actuality for those of my age who "have been there," have "seen it all," "done it all," "heard it all," have read "*tous les livres.*"

I testify here that this is not the case for this citizen, who, although his hatred may be less fierce and his suffering less intense, finds himself far more than ever before in the past grieving over those he does not know, the twenty-year-old soldier whose life ends in a tangle of steel and blood on an Iraqi road or the beautiful black-eyed Iraqi twelve-year-old whose house and body have been exploded by an ideology-maddened neighbor who should have been doing what for years he'd habitually done, embraced her with love.

Post 28

February 6, 2007

It was 9 degrees below zero when I woke this morning, minus 26 degrees wind chill. Neither of our old cars would start, it was not worth trying to get a cab to an appointment. Two days ago, in the heavy rains of Miami, our Bears were unable to adjust to Peyton Manning's short passes and the runs of a pair of Indianapolis Colts; our boyish quarterback, Rex Grossman, kept tripping over his own feet and under-throwing receivers.

A friend, watching the game on French television from midnight to 4:00 A.M, wrote that he'd never seen a game buried under so much pedagogy. "It eased the pain of the loss."

Is such salve a component of all pedagogy? If so, then it may be a component of the heavy-breathing semantic senatorial struggles over non-binding resolutions opposing the "surge" of American troops into the streets of Baghdad and Anbar province.

In Damascus, the somewhat worn, still lovely Diane Sawyer interrogated the restrained, intelligent, very tall, very thin president of Syria, Bashar al-Assad, the ex-ophthalmologist whose sometimes giggly puzzlement about the inflexible, poorly informed, head-in-the-sand non-diplomacy of the United States did not obliterate the memory of such statements as the one he made in May 2001, greeting Pope John Paul II, that the Jews tried "to kill the principles of all religions with the same mentality in which they betrayed Jesus Christ and the Prophet Mohammed." With Rex Grossman–like boyishness and sincerity, Bashar assured Sawyer that Syria had nothing to do with the killing of President Hariri of Lebanon or with the financing of Hezbollah, whose leader lives comfortably in Damascus not all that far away from where the forty-two-year-old president and his lovely, British-schooled, Sunni, ex–Morgan Stanley employee wife, Asthma' al Akhrae, live with their three children.

Perhaps international conferences should be held under the auspices of such charming interrogators as Diane Sawyer, who seems to bring out the most rational and well-meaning responses from heads of state.

However, this isn't the way either the world of international diplomacy or that of professional football works. There it is nearly always raining or 25 degrees below zero, people are almost always marshaling their power to inflict maximum harm on their opponents and too much of the time they're tripping over their own feet.

Post 29

February 15, 2007

It's warming up here in Chicago: the wind chill temperature is up to 12 degrees below zero. I'm supposed to be in Sacramento, giving a reading, then a seminar at the state university there. The flight was canceled, and since my Sacramento-based son called to say that he and my grandson had flu, I did not spend time working out a route there via Phoenix or Denver. (This week's *New Yorker* cartoon features one suit telling another, "Long term, I worry about global warming. Short term, I worry about freezing my ass off.") I'm delighted to be home, though I'll miss reading and talking to students (and my son and grandson). Retired from teaching five years ago, I miss discussion with the intelligent, energetic young (though not reading their term papers), and despite the secure warmth of home, feel both regret and guilt at not being in Sacramento.

It was in Sacramento that the marvelous photograph accompanying Paul Krugman's *New York Review of Books* essay on Milton Friedman (a "hatchet job" was the to me surprisingly unjust judgment of a distinguished Friedman-follower) was taken. It shows an enormous, huge-shouldered, full-toothed, grinning Arnold Schwarzenegger patting what might be a growth out of his rib cage but turns out to be the somewhat sadly smiling homunculus, Friedman, whose PBS series *Free to Choose* had, years ago, converted the body builder–movie star to the values which procured him the backing of one of Friedman's greatest admirers, George Shultz, and subsequently that of those serious thinker-doers who were no small part of his political triumph.

Some of the world's greatest triumphs involve unlikely protagonists, sometimes revealing surprising gifts, at others triumphing not despite but because of their flaws and deficiencies. Here is the delightful Lord Macaulay on James Boswell and his Johnson biography:

> If he had not been a great fool, he would never have been a great writer. Without all the qualities which made him the jest and torment of those among whom he lived, without the officiousness, the inquisitiveness, the effrontery, the toad-eating, the insensibility to all reproof, he never could have produced so excellent a book. He was a slave, proud of his servitude, a Paul Pry, convinced that his own curiosity and garrulity were virtues, an unsafe companion who never scrupled to replay the most liberal hospitality by the basest violation of confidence, a man without delicacy, without shame, without sense enough to know when he was hurting the feelings of others or when he was exposing himself to derision; and because he was all this, he has, in an important department of literature, immeasurably surpassed such writers as Tacitus, Clarendon, Alfieri, and his own idol, Johnson.

If I were employed to write a biography of our current president, I would brood long on these sentences and see if the gaucherie, shallowness, inelegance, evasiveness and downright mendacity of my subject not only didn't stand in the way of his following what he regards as his noble course but insulated him from those who daily assailed it and strengthened what he regarded as his version of the heroic, Churchillian, Lincolnesque pursuit of a god-given mission. In a nice warm house, with a good dinner waiting in the wings, this doesn't seem to be so difficult a job.

Post 30
February 16, 2007
In certain movies of the thirties and forties, one motif was "Let's Put On a Show," and sure enough, the local adolescents, the best-known of whom

were Mickey Rooney and Judy Garland, were soon singing and dancing up a storm before the hearty appreciation of their peers and elders.

The intellectual equivalent of this phenomenon in my lifetime has been "Let's Start a Magazine." I myself have been involved in various publications of varied worth which have lasted anywhere from one issue to a dozen. Perhaps the best-known was *Noble Savage,* edited by Saul Bellow, Keith Botsford and Jack Ludwig. It contained the earliest published prose of Pynchon and Coover as well as pieces by such Bellow friends as Ellison and A. Miller, but lasted less than two years or six issues.

Once in a blue moon, one of these ventures is a durable success. The most distinguished, mentioned by several OU contributors, is the *New York Review of Books,* which rose from the void of a New York newspaper strike with the help of the Robert Lowell circle and the editorial smarts of Robert Silvers and the Epsteins, Jason and his then-wife, Barbara. A less far-reaching but very important periodical, *Critical Inquiry,* was started in the sixties by the late Shelley Sacks at the University of Chicago and continued on its advanced level by Tom Mitchell. But the successes are few. What begins with the familiar ache of intelligent people that their important work has failed to be recognized, written about or in some dire cases even noticed ends when the ache is somehow lessened and the energy and time required to put out the periodical are regarded as less important than their next work. (A very few console themselves with the history of such books as *The Interpretation of Dreams*—whose eight hundred copies were finally sold out in ten years—or *Capitalism and Freedom,* whose publication wasn't greeted with a single review.)

Jeffery Herf's intelligent plea for a new publication which would consist largely of reviews of important scholarship makes plenty of sense and undoubtedly fills a need that isn't temporary or transient. Franklin Foer's suggestion that the OU columns are themselves a place where such reviews could appear is also excellent, although it means the displacement of the original notion of the Open University. My own notion is that a new periodical requires the slaking of more than this need for reviews of scholarly books. I suggest that it include surveys of foreign publications. T. S. Eliot's *Criterion*—circulation about eight hundred—the U. of Oklahoma's *World Literature* and several other periodicals have done this.

At this writing, I favor the Foer notion that OU contributors extend their reach beyond the thematic centers which have dominated these columns to include mini-reviews (such as the one cited, Empson's surprising assessment of *The Bridge of San Luis Rey*) which might at least alert readers to the significance of works of which they'd otherwise have no knowledge.

Post 31
February 23, 2007

I used to think that Kafka's wonderful story "Hunger Artist" revealed the tragic crushing of high art by the creeping glacier of entertainment. After all, its poor artist was displaced from his solo stage in the center of town to a sideshow in the circus where, finally, unwatched by anyone, he starved not to perfection but miserable death.

Now, following the apotheosis of the one-time Texas beauty turned ludicrous fortune-hunter and, finally, burned-out addict, Anna Nicole Smith (her "true" name a more humble Texas monicker), I read "Hunger Artist" in a new way. The need of a country like the post–Marshall Plan United States for tragi-farce is enormous. To confront nothing but the savagery, corruption, selfishness, vulgarity or sheer murderousness of so many of our greatest public and private enterprises would plunge most of us into stupefaction or nervous collapse. Somehow or other, when confrontation with Middle Eastern bloodiness, African starvation, disease and organized murder, or the American chasm between haves and have-nots becomes too much to take, our wonderful media throw up on the shore of the national consciousness an Anna Nicole Smith, a Britney Spears, an O. J. Simpson, an Elian Gonzales, and around each of these decipher an intrigue peopled by the usually invisible dramatis personae who make up most of our population. Which of us could have come up with Anna's mother, Virgie, the plump, peroxided grieving mater dolorosa who hadn't seen her addled daughter in ten years, the parade of Anna's pimps and lovers, the Kentucky photographer-reporter, the worshipful parasite-lawyer, the vasectomied Carolina land baron, the ninety-year-old German prince, hitched for fifty-two years to another world-class character, Zsa-Zsa Gabor, who refused to let the old fellow adopt Anna's motherless five-year-old so that she could be a real princess? Who could have conjured up the ex-Bronx-born cabbie turned lawyer, turned judge, spewing the caramelized gunk of his half-baked sentimentality and illiteracy over his courtroom as if touched with the divinity of a mad Narcissus and then, so moved by his own bathetic view of the matter, sobbed as he read out his decision? How wonderful that millions and millions of us could convert revulsion into laughter as these marvelous humans quarreled about the final resting place of the "remains" of the poor Texas floozie who in death achieved the celebrity she'd so long pursued? We didn't need to think about eighteen-year-old boys learning how to walk with their new mechanical legs in hospital room–battlegrounds, didn't need to see five-year-old Iraqi children bleeding to death in their parents' arms, didn't have to contemplate American sages debating the latest profundity of men and women campaigning for the American presidency. We were, at least for a few hours, saved. You would have understood, Franz, *nicht wahr?*

Post 32
March 7, 2007
Hard to think that an American jury would convict a well-spoken, clean-featured, polite little fellow called "Scooter." Who next, Tom Sawyer?

Sure enough, a juror, minutes after the verdicts were handed over, said the jurors liked Scooter and wondered why it was he, rather than, say, Karl Rove, in the courtroom. Little Scooter looked to them like "a fall guy."

As they were arriving at their verdict, Jean Baudrillard, one of the most famous "postmodern gurus," died in Paris, age seventy-seven. For M Baudrillard, "l'affaire Libby" would have been another "simulacrum," an event or series of events so thick with reports about itself that any underlying actuality would have been displaced. For him, after all, *The Gulf War Did Not Take Place* (the wonderful title taken from Jean Giradoux's play, *La Guerre de Troie N'Aura Pas Lieu*); it was a sequence of violent, "hyperreal" events which simulated the old, genuine wars of cause, purpose, clear beginnings and conclusions.

Scooter, a man of letters, might well, yesterday, have felt himself in what Baudrillard called "a desert of the real." Eleven years earlier, he'd published a novel, *The Apprentice,* about a group of Japanese caught in a 1903 blizzard during a smallpox epidemic. (Libby had once been so insistent about universal vaccination that his friends called him "Germ Boy.") Its blurb talks of the novel's "bestiality and paedophilia" and boasts that it is "packed with sexual perversion, dwelling on prepubescent girls and their training as prostitutes." Some of its unhappy readers were disgusted by scenes of bears "coupling" with these little girls. (One reader suggested that when Bush pardons Scooter for his indicted crimes he include his crime against literature.) Although no reader wondered if the novel were autobiographical, I wonder now if such a sanguinary imagination might have something to do with the ease of concocting bloody wars fought by others.

Irve Lewis Libby was known as Scooter after his investment banker father noticed him scurrying around the cradle. His later moves took him through Andover, Yale and Columbia Law School, a much smoother career than that of his old companion in simulacra arms, Dick Cheney. (Scooter graduated magna cum laude from Yale; Cheney was thrown out of it.) It was in New Haven that Scooter came under the influence of one of his professors, Paul Wolfowitz, who would later draw him from prosperous legal work (Marc Rich, Clinton's notorious pardonee, was one of his clients) first to the State and then to the Defense Department. There, with Wolfowitz, Feith and Cheney, Scooter helped work up plans for the democratic transformation of the Middle East and the recreation of what another of last week's losses, Arthur Schlesinger Jr., decried as the imperial presidency.

Baudrillard delighted in a story by Jorge Luis Borges about the huge map of an empire which continued to decay as the map became larger and larger, soon displacing the empire it originally charted. With the conviction of the first of this band of simulacra brothers (Scooter was known as "Cheney's Cheney"), one wonders if the tattered record of their grandiose plans will be what survives the chaos and destruction those plans engineered.

Post 33
March 9, 2007
Old fellows trained as I was, disposed as I am, hope to stumble on transfiguring expressions of contemporary difficulties in literature. So, yesterday, reading Shakespeare's *Troilus and Cressida,* I was more alert to the characterization of its famously protracted war than to the erotic swings of Cressida and her predecessor, Helen. Sure enough, in Act 1, Scene 3, King Agamemnon describes a familiar situation to what amounts to his cabinet:

The ample proposition that hope makes
In all designs begun on earth below
Fails in the promisd largeness: checks and disasters
Grow in the veins of actions highest reard,
As knots, by the conflux of meeting sap,
Infects the sound pine and diverts his grain
Tortive and errant from his course of growth.
[Sounds a bit like our leader, doesnt it?]
Nor, princes, is it matter new to us
That we come short of our suppose so far
That after seven years siege yet Troys walls stand,
Sith every action that hath gone before
Whereof we have record, trial did draw
Bias and thwart, not answering the aim

The king goes on to explain the failure as God's attempt to test the "persistive constancy" in men, the fineness of which metal is not found when things are going well so that the distinction between the bold and coward / The wise and fool, the artist and unread / The hard and soft is lost." Agamemnon is not the first caudillo to see the virtues of war. We can praise our chief for avoiding that sentiment. (He and his vice-chief certainly knew that the Vietnam War wouldn't be good for them.) It is probably the word "distinction" which leads to Prince Ulysses' amazing speech about the terrible consequences of failure to distinguish the proper order of things. It begins with a failure to acknowledge leadership (with perhaps a hint of what seems our problem, the failure of the leadership):

The specialty of rule hath been neglected,
And look how many Grecian tents do stand
Hollow upon this plain
When that the general is not like the hive
To whom the foragers shall all repair,
What honey is expected?
O, when degree is shakd,
Which is the ladder of all high designs,
The enterprise is sick

Marvelous lines about the universal consequence of disorder follow, but although one can see in our own factions and disorder enough to warrant reading the play for some sort of guidance, the Greek solution—to draw the Trojan ace, Hector, into single combat with their sulking ace, Achilles—does not do us much good. (Osama bin Laden is sulking in some Waziristan care and it's George W. Bush who is the most conspicuous object of our dismay and wrath.)

> Take but degree away, untune that string,
> And hark what discord follows. Each thing melts
> In mere oppugnancy; the unbounded waters
> Should lift their bosoms higher than the shores,
> And make a sop of all this solid globe

Oops. Take your eye off Shakespeare for a moment, and he's off on another aggravation.

Nonetheless, he's a grand read, which is sufficient emollient for the nonce.

Post 34
March 20, 2007

Intellectual metabolism rates vary far more than physical ones. Some people understand more from glimpsing a street incident than others from years of living in a cauldron. A book read by a Shakespeare or a Lincoln may yield them more than what accrues to most of us reading through a library. To Joshua Speed, a friend who marveled at Lincoln's memory, Lincoln said, "You're mistaken—I am slow to learn and slow to forget that which I've learned—My mind is like a piece of steel, very hard to scratch any thing on it and almost impossible after you get it there to rub it out." This reader sometimes forgets page 231 when he's on page 235.

To assay the experience of presidential candidates is not a simple matter of calculating the number of years in this job or that one, the length or frequency of their marriages, the number or distinction of their academic degrees. These are important and should be known and considered, but my guess, say, is that Barack Obama's boyhood years in an Indonesian school might be the equivalent of years of anthropological or ambassadorial presence in Jakarta, that his years at the racially mixed private school in Hawaii count for understanding of racial peace and strife as much or more than five years work at the NAACP, that his years of community work on Chicago's South Side, his subsequent terms in the Illinois and United States Senate, his lecturing at the U. of Chicago Law School close to such men as Cass Sunstein, Richard Posner, Douglas Baird and Richard Epstein have taught him more about dealing with varieties of intellect than a dozen years of diplomatic intercourse in the capitals of Europe, Asia and Africa.

I cannot gauge his patience, tolerance, equanimity or charm (although my one encounter with him at a South Side block party brought evidence of exceptional charm), but he has already met tests for these in his weeks of campaigning. As for administrative experience, he has far less than George W. Bush, Dick Cheney, Donald Rumsfeld and a million other people, but then consider their bitter harvests.

Post 35
March 21, 2007

> *New York Times:*
> BAGHDAD, March 20—Insurgents detonated a bomb in a car with two children in it after using the children as decoys to get through a military checkpoint in Baghdad, an American general said Tuesday.
>
> Speaking at a news briefing at the Pentagon, Maj. Gen. Michael Barbaro, deputy director for regional operations at the Joint Staff, said American soldiers had stopped the car at the checkpoint but had allowed it to pass after seeing the two children in the back seat.
>
> "Children in the back seat lower suspicion," he said, according to a transcript. "We let it move through. They parked the vehicle. The adults run out and detonate it with the children in back."

Every day we think it can't get worse. Last week, it was blasted American soldiers, their head wounds and traumas unrecognized, discharged from first-rate initial treatment to the swamps of paperwork, the discomfort and filth of halfway houses. This week, George Packer's "Betrayed" *(New Yorker,* March 27, 2007) tells of the abandonment of brave Iraqi interpreters, hunted down, tortured and killed by their Iraqi neighbors and now ignored, abandoned and betrayed by the American authorities for whom they were indispensable.

And always threats, bombs, torture, beheadings, bodies on garbage heaps eaten by dogs, explosions at weddings, in markets, schools, mosques, networks devouring, recording, broadcasting the views and sounds of burning and exploded flesh, anguish, mourning, desolation, despair.

Like sufferers from incurable, agonizing cancers, like addicts in the filth, stench, helpless hatred of self, parents, the world and all in it, we say, "It can't get worse."

"Kill, kill, kill, kill, kill," said mad old King Lear. "All's cheerless, dark and deadly," said his faithful Kent, and Cordelia, young historian of catastrophe, "We are not the first / Who with best means, have endured the worst."

But the *Lear* line that comes as I try to imagine the two children blown up in the suicide car (what age? whose were they? what did they think? what did their parents and grandparents think?) is from Edgar:

The worst is not
So long as we can say, "This is the worst."

Post 36
March 29, 2007

Three years ago, my wife and I spent about five weeks in Hyderabad (Andra Pradesh) lecturing on English and American literature to the well-trained students of Osmenia University. After ten days of some discomfort at the lodge adjacent to the excellent American Studies Library, we lived in a good hotel and commuted by taxi or by the chauffeur-driven car of the head of the department. How much of the town we saw is hard to know, but we did go around a good deal and saw, heard and smelled enough to fill our minds for quite a while. Among the thousands of things we didn't see or, till the *Lehrer News Report* a couple of nights ago, know anything about was the existence there of seventeen transition home-schools for five thousand young girls brutalized into the world of childhood prostitution. These schools, called "eternal flames," or Prajwala, were founded and are run by a heroic and brilliant thirty-four-year-old woman, Dr. Sunitha Krishnan, who herself had been raped at fifteen and beaten many times before and since.

By chance, I'd just read a story of Hemingway called "The Denunciation" which celebrates in his inimitable way a very different sort of heroism and gallantry. Its center is the wonderful Madrid bar Chicote, which for years served martinis made with the finest yellow gin and whose waiters were famously cheerful, friendly and helpful. The time is 1938 and to the astonishment of the narrator, into the bar walks one of its former patrons, now a flyer for Franco. The narrator recalls what a wonderful pigeon shot the man was and the day that despite his own poor shooting, he won every peseta the man had. The man was a wonderful sport. That he should now come into this bar where waiters have lost sons to the Franco forces amazes him. A waiter tells the narrator he wishes to denounce the man to the Seguridad. The narrator gives him the number of a friend there, and when he leaves the bar, the agents are already driving up to effect the capture. He asks himself why the old pigeon shooter returned to Chicote's and decides that he just couldn't imagine coming to Madrid without coming to this best of all bars. The narrator calls his friend at Seguridad and asks him to tell the man that the narrator denounced him. He does not want him to go to his death thinking poorly of Chicote's waiters.

Hemingway notions of gallantry and heroism have not entirely disappeared. The sexual hierarchy which was an unspoken ingredient of it still exists. The savaged, tyrannized eight- and ten-year-old girls in the Prajwala schools can be seen as its ugliest extrapolation. I myself know several brilliant and charming septuagenarians whose vitality can only be sustained or renewed by women forty and fifty years their junior. For almost forty years, I myself have lived happily with a woman more than twenty years younger than I am. I am not going to pin a medal on my chest nor do more than joke with my friends about their latest conquest, but I am delighted that more and more thinking and caring people realize the gallantry and grandeur of such people as Dr. Sunitha Krishnan.

Post 37
April 3, 2007
The sixteen comments on my thirty-sixth *NR* post inspire the sort of explanation writers like me hope they never have to give. One commentator said it was the worst of all the *NR* blogs he'd read.

Several commentators made little or no sense of the connection between the post's two sections, one a brief account of the fine work done for abused Indian girls by Dr. Sunitha Krishnan, the second a summary of a Hemingway story I happened to read after watching the *Lehrer* hour presentation of Dr. Krishnan's work. My posts try to juxtapose current events with each other or with historical or literary "events." The hope is that the "friction" will rouse a pleasurable insight or two. Sometimes the connections are too fragile or distant from each other. That seems to have been the case in the thirty-sixth blog.

My point there was this: Hemingway's brilliant short story described one of the subtle reactions of a person to an ugly event. Hemingway extended the range of human consciousness and behavior as many fine writers do and have done. The notions of honor, bravery, gallantry and heroism which the best of Hemingway adds to our cultural, psychological, and literary palettes have for decades now been largely ignored, if not scorned, mocked and parodied. The Hemingway world is often regarded as antediluvian and irrelevant.

I do not regard it that way, but after I hear about and see some of the marvelous work of people like Dr. Krishnan, I am glad that thoughtful people today respond to and celebrate her sort of gallantry, honor and heroism in a way that was very rarely the case when Hemingway published his story (although there are gallant and heroic women in his stories and novels). After Florence Nightingale's pioneering nineteenth-century career, a new world of caring and bravery opened up for thousands of young women, but for decades Nightingale herself was often regarded as the semi-fanatic of Lytton Strachey's famous portrait of her in *Eminent Victorians*. No one who counts today will regard Dr. Krishnan as a fanatic or as anything but a wonderfully brave, inventive, patient and heroic person.

The pleasure I get from the *NR* Open University blogs is the variety of the bloggers' interests, techniques, procedures and even expressive power. I've hoped that my somewhat eccentric posts have a small place in these pages.

Post 38

April 10, 2007

I have just listened to the Chaconne of Bach's second partita, a piece played by the violinist Joshua Bell in a Washington, DC, Metro station back in January while a *Washington Post* reporter watched sixteen-hundred-odd people hurry by on their way to work, only four or five pausing to take in a smidgen of one of mankind's greatest creations.

I begin with this human-all-too-human (Nietzsche) anecdote as I write about Don Imus, the sixty-six-year-old self-exhibiting radio performer, who, last Friday, slid along one of the worst of his many talk lines, as he mouthed one of the pathetic, self-boosting clichés of the wounded, black male about accomplished, beautiful, brilliant or otherwise successful black women whom the male wants to denigrate. Imus, following the low lead of his complexly semi-racist producer, Bernard McGirk, laughingly said that the triumphant Rutgers U. women's basketball team looked like "nappy-headed hos."

Protests, soon spearheaded by the usual spear carriers, Jesse Jackson and Al Sharpton, called for Imus to be permanently denied the publicly financed airways.

For the last two years, somewhat to my own surprise, I wake at 5:00 or 5:30 A.M. and make my way through the dim corridor to the day's activity via the Imus program. Too much of it consists of Imus's daily report about his health and mood or about his recent, unexciting doings; another chunk consists of his selling some of the Imus products— household cleansers, Salsa—the profits of which go to a New Mexico ranch which he and his deeply decent wife, Deirdre, run for "kids with cancer." Another chunk boosts other worthy causes he champions or the books of his guests. Perhaps the most brilliant and original part of the three-hour-long show consists of well-written and delivered aria-like spiels by the actor Rob Bartlett or McGirk as they imitate such figures as Cardinal Egan, Bill Clinton, Alberto Gonzales, Jerry Falwell or Dr. Phil. Imus himself is frequently the target of these spiels and laughs along with others as his body, his marriage, his complaints and his activities are mocked, ridiculed and damned.

Like millions of others, I have grown almost addicted to these shenanigans, jokes, ploys and characters. Imus's opinions, the most Philistine of which annoy me no end, often at least rhyme with my own. He was one of the first public personalities to be outraged by the Iraq War, and he doesn't hesitate to call President Bush and Vice President Cheney war criminals and imbeciles. Meanwhile he champions an odd array of political and other favorites, Rick Santorum, Joe Biden, Joe Lieberman and Harold Ford, the military analyst Jack Jacobs, Howard Fineman, Evan Thomas and Jonathan Alter of *Newsweek,* the reporting staff of NBC, Brian Williams on down, and many country musicians, a few of whose songs I, surprisingly, enjoy.

Occasionally I get tired of the program—it is very repetitive and an hour of it five days a week more than suffices. Imus' endless strip tease ultimately reveals what a peeled onion does. His many sensible, often impassioned views are often subverted by his mercurial character which is what happened last Wednesday in the remarks for which he will be suspended for two weeks. Nonetheless, I want to make the record here by saying that he is one of the few genuinely interesting people who fill the airwaves of the country, that he ultimately stands for many good things and that as far as a mere listener can tell, he is a better human being than many of those who rush to get him permanently off the air. Which does not mean that he should not pay the price—suspension and a permanently soiled reputation—for these years of public self-exhibition and idling self-indulgence which have made him rich, influential, powerful and the object of jealously, envy and hatred.

Post 39
April 12, 2007
For me, the writing of these posts helps fill the gap left in my life when I stopped regular teaching at the end of 2001. Most of my life, I walked to and from class thinking about what we'd be—or had been—discussing and where next I could fit in ideas generated during the familiar, beloved walks. In good classes, these ideas would be tested, combated, approved or found irrelevant to the day's subject, poems of Rilke, Borges and Pound, *Swann's Way,* plays of Beckett, Joyce's *Ulysses,* the archaeological-anthropological components of modernism, object-subject complexities in twentieth-century poetry. I miss these classes, but at least the blogs allow me to find what at least to me are interesting ways of reacting to the news or to what still pops into an old head.

For chasers, I sometimes read the comments. Some of these seem to me the reactions of people who should be blogging on their own. Some are thoughtful and intelligent. A few simply express dislike of me, my style and points of view. Since I have been publishing stories, novels, essays and even a few plays, libretti and poems for almost sixty years and have been reviewed seriously for more than half a century, I am somewhat inured to misunderstanding or its reverse, sympathetic comprehension. A problem now is to pare off old callus and try to understand the commentators. Why for instance did an early response to Don Imus's ugly remark about the Rutgers women's basketball team draw thirty comments whereas a post on the depth of Senator Obama's experience drew but a handful? And what about these posts makes one commentator desire my Imusian disappearance? I wonder what this person is like, what he does and how he lives. (The novelist part of me is not dead.)

In today's paper, I read of Kurt Vonnegut's death. His books have not meant much to me, but I respect him, his work and his life, and believe that his influence—one thousand times greater than my own—was not only benign but significantly creative. He is another part of the almost daily disappearance which even more than physical difficulty saddens the life of the elderly. But life pours in and while one can, one keeps up with it: so my wonderful twenty-one-year-old granddaughter emails yesterday that she's won a Fulbright research grant to Morocco. (I've just read with pride and profit her 112-page bachelor's thesis comparing the coverage of last summer's Hezbollah-Israeli War by Al Jazeera and CNN.) My pride is undershot with worry as I read about terrorism in Casablanca and Algiers. Last night, I read *Legends of Glory,* Harry Mark Petrakis's moving novella about the death of a twenty-one-year-old man in Iraq and the effect it has on his Medal of Honor–winning grandfather.

The bloody disintegration of Iraq doesn't stop; nor does the flow of theft and hatred, injustice and betrayal, inequity and overwhelming cruelty (Darfur) which composes so much—too much?—of what we take in, we being the leisured, comfortable, semi-idling old academics who occasionally try to earn a place in the world by blogging on the Open University.

Post 40

April 17, 2007

I flew back to Chicago yesterday after a weekend in Sacramento where on Friday I gave a reading at the California State University there and spent the rest of the fifty-odd hours with my youngest son, his wife and my four-and-a-half-year-old grandson. In its way, a perfect weekend. Moving around was always a stimulus to write, and though more and more the moving is difficult, apparently that's still the case.

I probably could write twenty-five thousand words on the Sacramento hours, but I'll just zero in on a few things. The first came yesterday in the plane. My seat-mate was a fifty-two-year-old woman, small, dark, good-featured, energetic, high-spirited, her fingers and neck festooned with silver necklaces and rings. She's lived in Sacramento for years, has a daughter, perhaps a second husband, and was going to Washington, DC, to deal with federal funding of child welfare cases. Like her seat-mate, a woman of about the same age, she took a thick paperback book of popular fiction from her bag, but within a minute the books were laid aside, the women talked with each other about their homes, their families, their origins, their hometowns, their children and husbands. Often, peals of laughter burst from them. From being their eavesdropper, I became their admirer, the admiration almost generic, the object of it the way in which two fluent women of—and this was my perhaps overly snobbish judgment—limited education and culture were able not only to sustain a constant exchange of views about many things but actually to begin what might become a real friendship. (They copied down each other's names and addresses. May I add that they were extremely courteous and friendly to me?)

As for Sacramento, I learned a bit about the university from a twenty-four-year-old fellow behind me in the Super-Shuttle from the airport. He told me that he was a third-year student majoring in kinesiology and about to take a few courses in radiology after which he hoped to get a job in sports medicine. He'd been a "street kid" in southwest LA. One evening he and his friends were jumped by a gang. He was stabbed six times, the blade just missing his lungs, heart and kidneys. He woke in a hospital where for weeks he was cared for by doctors whom he then decided were models. "Otherwise I'd probably just be hanging around the street," he said. "I came up here to get away from things down there." "So in a way, your life was saved twice," I said. "That's right." "Did they ever get the guy who stabbed you?" "No. The detective spent about ten minutes with me. Never saw him again." We said goodbye wishing each other lots of luck.

Two hours later, I was in a small auditorium, reading to about forty people, most of them writers in the class of Doug Rice, my host, a few others people who'd read something I'd written. It was, I thought, an especially attentive and responsive audience. After the reading itself—the story was about a Chicago bus driver on his fiftieth birthday which his wife has ignored—there were intelligent comments and questions. My chief point here is that one can never tell where in this country of a thousand—or is it sixteen hundred?—institutions of more or less higher learning one will find people of exceptional sensitivity and intelligence. My heart is hardened against people—including friends and relatives—who care so deeply about seeing themselves or their children in but a very few schools in the northeastern U.S.A. that they grind ease and happiness out of thousands of their hours.

My son, a California deputy attorney general, had recently seen the Supreme Court in a 5-4 decision (Justice Kennedy the swing vote) sustain everything that he and his fellow attorneys around the country had, somewhat to their delighted surprise, wanted in their "global warming" case (*Massachusetts v. E.P.A.*). Eighty-six-year-old Justice Stevens (whom my late friend Edward Levi had brought to the attention of President Ford) had written the majority opinion while dissents were written by the chief justice (who, months before, had welcomed my son to the court with exceptional kindness) and by Justice Scalia (whom Levi had also admired and whose daughter Ann had been, thirty-odd years ago, a good friend of my son at the U. of Chicago Laboratory School. Her recent arrest for driving under the influence had saddened but not surprised him: "She was the first alcoholic I'd met; she used to take the IC down to a bar before class so she could get through the day"). My son married a charming, able, sober woman who is director of development in an agency which deals with water problems. They have a wonderful, non-stop, fun-loving, generous little boy with whom I played games, read books, talked and hugged for much of the next two days, a "bonding" which I contrasted to that of mine with my own paternal grandfather whom I loved but with whom I had to stop playing games because he could not stand to lose even to the grandson he clearly loved.

This was my fifth or sixth visit to Sacramento, a town which does not resemble what Joan Didion, from a line of old Sacramentarians, wrote about in some wonderful essays. It seems to me a scattering of unkempt green oases between giant malls filled with giant stores. At times, the American River, where, my son tells me, salmon swim and spawn, pops up under a bridge. There are numerous coffee houses where we passed good hours, inexpensive restaurants where we ate outside in the delicious evening air, and blocks of state buildings near the famous capitol, looking as deserted as those in de Chirico's paintings.

Post 41
April 23, 2007
A week ago today, an anguished, humiliated, infuriated paranoid named Seung-Hui Cho burst from his self-made cocoon of silence to wreak

vengeance on the world of those whom he believed had insulted, injured, abused and ignored him. Following in the wake of the two Columbine high school students whose resentment and hunger for recognition had led to slaughtering their fellow students, Cho armed himself to the teeth—how easy to do this in our manly country—and slaughtered more people than had ever before been slaughtered on an American college campus. Hours before his end, he mailed to NBC his crude version of *Mein Kampf*, pictures of himself in fighting form—with two guns a la Billy the Kid and Rambo, with an eighteen-hundred-word testament which has not yet been released by the police, and rather powerfully phrased and uttered words about his hatred for those who strutted in wealth and inflicted on him unbearable wounds.

This was one of these "events out of nowhere" which suddenly become the center of national and even international discussion and debate, occasions to discuss many matters of importance to a country and the world: the predictability and possible prevention of such occurrences, the nature of a society where such gun-inflicted private slaughter is greater than the total of all war-related deaths, the hunger of the media and its audience for such murderous attractions—"everything in modern life comes down to entertainment," our modern equivalent of Mallarme's "everything ends up in a book"—and wondering if media display gratifies the ambition of the killer and leads to the creation of more killers.

That President and Mrs. Bush came quickly to condole with the students and faculty of Virginia Tech when they had been rather conspicuously absent from the funerals of soldiers for whose deaths he, at least, had been indirectly responsible led such commentators as Frank Rich to point out the ugly political calculus behind every presidential move and word.

There are a million handles to this hot pan, from, say, the Yiddish proverb about a fool throwing a stone in the water and twelve wise men analyzing the rings it makes to a belief that events of this sort reveal the warp and woof of the society in which they occur.

As for me, among the many reactions was a confirmation of my long-held belief that people reveal their true selves less in vino than in what they write, and that such alert writing instructors as Nikki Giovanni and Lucinda Roy spotted the danger in the poems Cho submitted to them, and that their warnings to people supposedly responsible in the administration should have been taken much more seriously than they apparently were. It may be that from now on such signs of dangerous disturbance will be acted upon.

Another reflection came as I listened to some of Franz Schubert's wonderful songs in the *Schwanengesang*. Written a year before his death at thirty-one to lyrics by such equally young men as Heinrich Heine and Ludwig Rellstab, some of these songs promulgate the desperate romantic behavior which 177 years later broke out in the distorted viciousness of the young Korean American. Here, for instance, is the English of some lines of the Schubert-Rellstab "Lebsensmut" ("Life Courage"):

> The bold leap—dare to take it.
> He who holds back will never win
> Luck changes very fast.
> Yours is the moment.
> He who never tries the leap
> Never enjoys the sweet fruit . . .
> Bravely embrace death
> When it comes to summon you . . .
> Death's brotherhood
> Opens life's prison.

I doubt that the little song had ever entered the cauldron of Seung-Hui Cho's mind either to tamp its heat or to translate its boldness into mass murder, but that it is one of a billion components of the world in which he acted is not without interest.

Post 42
April 26, 2007

A word about one of the more interesting U.S. senators, Lindsey Graham, particularly about his reiterated defense of the Bush-McCain policy in Iraq. The defense is that Iraq needs more time to become a functioning democratic state. "It took our country thirteen years to become such a state," says the boyish, little (five-foot-seven), somewhat feline senior senator from South Carolina. Thirteen years? I suppose that these are the years between the Declaration of Independence and the election of George Washington. Yes, it wasn't an easy time, but was it an analogous time? For most of those years, the states were fighting a war against the world's most powerful state. Who or what in Iraq is the equivalent of England the enemy? The world's most powerful state today is on the side of the Iraqi government. Or is that the trouble? Would Iraq do better on its own as the incipient American democracy did in the eighteenth century? Who knows if an unbolstered Iraq might not see brilliant Iraqi patriots on the order of Adams and Jefferson, Jay and Hamilton rise up on all sides to deal with the raging terror?

Senator Graham is and apparently prides himself on being an independent thinker (although his party-line votes have been tabulated at the 90 percent level). Even when displaying a nasty sanctimoniousness when presenting the House's impeachment case against President Clinton, he voted against the most troublesome of the indictments, the president's lying in the Paula Jones civil suit, on the grounds that lying in sexual matters was more or less conventional. His experience as a military judge led him to work with Senator Levin to slow the careening Bush-Gonzalez–John Woo drive to bypass the Geneva Conventions. His gratitude for the Social Security payments he as a twenty-two-year-old law school student and his thirteen-year-old sister received after the death of their parents (who ran a small bar near a textile factory) diverted him from the drive toward privatization. His memory of textile workers coming into the bar like ghosts, covered with cotton, every other one of them missing a finger, seems to have given him a John Edwards–like streak of understanding and sympathy for workers. (Like Edwards, he was a successful malpractice attorney.)

Graham is one of the most frequent talk show guests. Partly it's his fluency and charming accent, partly the independence which doesn't always give the expected response; partly it's his availability as a bachelor, he seems free of the demands of home life. His influence, therefore, is considerable, which makes it more troublesome when he reiterates such weak comparisons as Iraq in 2007 and the almost-country of 1789.

Post 43

May 1, 2007

A bit too much beef on George Tenet. A bit too much of everything, gestures, words, passion, too many professions of devotion to the men and women of CIA, to his own unremitting labor, his day-and-night brooding about al Qaeda. How this beefy, expressive gentleman has worried about what more he could have done, how prevented 9/11, how capture bin Laden and Zawahiri. God knows he tried: he put the warning of imminent, bloody al Qaeda deeds into Condi Rice's hands weeks and weeks before 9/11, and what did she do but turn it over not to the president but to her deputy? Instead of up and at 'em, it was down and forgotten. Sure he saw the president every day but he couldn't tell him directly about the danger: "That isn't the way Washington works." Our Paul Revere is a decorous and deferential fellow who, unlike the villains he tracks, doesn't break the rules. Shall he go behind Condi's back, upsetting her and the president by telling him that the fuses are lit and about to set off the TNT? Georgie Porgie may have kissed the girls and made them cry. Not our Georgie.

What did *they* do to our George *(they* being not Osama and Company but those in the White House who leaked his slam dunk remark to Bob Woodward.)? They threw him overboard, they turned him into a *bouc emissaire,* they claimed his decontextualized remark was enough to launch the one thousand ships and burn the topless towers of . . . oops, Baghdad!!

Baghdad?

Where did that come from, this agenda before the Agenda? Our George had run into Itchy-Richie Perle emerging from the White House on September 12 and Richie had told him it was on to Baghdad.[8] "I'm Greek and Greeks love conspiracies," said our George, but how this happened he will not explain in such terms. "There never was a serious meeting about it that I know."

It's years later now, and Uncle Dick Cheney shouldn't still be attributing the war decision to our George's slam-dunk remark. "That's dishonorable," says an angry George. So he writes his insider book, and italicizes yet another heap of careless, arrogant, lethal stupidities for the bumbling, stumbling record of G. W. Bush of Midland, Texas, and R. Cheney of Casper, Wyoming.

---

8. I have extrapolated the remarks Tenet quotes in his book, *At The Center of the Storm.* Perle denies making such remarks in a letter Tim Russert read on *Meet the Press* (May 6, 2007). He adds that he was out of the country on September 12. Tenet responds that he may have gotten the date wrong but that Perle spoke as he did and not only to him (Tenet) but to Robert Novak and the president. "Who shall decide when [retrofitters] disagree / And honest casuists doubt like you and me?"

Post 44

May 3, 2007

Why is it that the U.S. has not been struck by al Qaeda or an al Qaeda group since 9/11? Have we so disrupted its chains of command and operation that it hasn't had enough time, intelligence, equipment, money and concentrated willpower to prepare and execute a theatrically damaging act? Or is a friend of mine right in saying that it got everything it needed from the 9/11 attacks, the refocusing , if not transfiguring of the country, indeed the world, on terror and what lies behind it (the power of the dispossessed, the ignored, the insulted, brutalized and exploited to grip the world with novel claws of assault)?

That such terrorism became complicated by certain versions of Islam in rejecting the vulgarity, materialism, sensuality, monopolizing and faith-killing speed of modernity evokes the Huntington notion of a "clash of civilizations," and perhaps another One Hundred Year War. Has there been enough restraint in the Moslem and Christian worlds to hold off such a world threat? Perhaps more than a sensation-hungry media has allowed to surface. Let's hope that the human force of parenthood and peace-needy village-and-town-hood has shunted to the sidelines the publicized heroics of hatred, martyrdom and blood sacrifice (mostly other people's blood, other people's sacrifice) and kept what's already horrible from becoming far more horrible.

I've been reading a wonderful, oddly prescient book about terrorism, Don De Lillo's *MAO II* (1991). It's full of the madness of crowds and crowd behavior as opposed to the semi-maniacal reclusiveness of artists—particularly writers of the sort which used to knead and shape the mentality of the world as terrorists with their noise and mindless bloodiness do today. Here are a few of the more explicit sentences: "When you inflict punishment on someone who is not guilty, when you fill rooms with innocent victims, you begin to empty the world of meaning and erect a separate mental state, the mind consuming what's outside itself, replacing real things with ploys and fictions." The novel does not have the psychological genius and tragi-farcical narrative drive that the greatest of all terrorist books, Dostoievski's *The Devils (The Possessed)* (1872), has, but to a puzzled questioner like me, it does have insights which serve at least temporarily as answers.[9]

---

9. Commentators on the post cited other DeLillo books as guides to the world of terrorist conspiracy, this as the latest book, *Falling Man,* was coming into the stores.

"The killing of an innocent human child is incompatible with going into communion in the body of Christ," said Pope Benedict XVI thirty-odd thousand feet in the air en route to Brazil, the country with more Roman Catholics than any other. I would love to hear the learned and benevolent pope's views on the death of a thirty-week-old fetus in a tornado of the sort that just annihilated a small Kansas town, but I guess that God does not need to go into communion in the body of His Son.

In any event, the pope began his first papal trip to South America with the kind of learned bravado that prefaced his trip to Turkey last year when he quoted a medieval king on the murderous bellicosity of Islamic proselyting.

It is now thirty-four years since Justice Blackmun, after a summer's reading of technical and philosophical literature, penned the famous majority opinion in *Roe v. Wade*. A dozen years before that, I had my only personal involvement with abortion. For various reasons, my then wife, about nine weeks pregnant, decided that it would not be good to have another child and that we should seek an abortion. We consulted her gynecologist and obstetrician who said that there was no physical reason that she could not have a child and that ruled out having it done at our university hospital. That ended our quest. It was a relief to me. I hated the idea of abortion but said nothing to my wife as I felt that child-bearing was her realm and that my own job was to support her in any rational decision she made about it. This was part of the viewpoint that the best decisions are made by those directly implicated in them although I granted that many decisions had to be made by people whose involvement was indirect. (You did not have to have had someone in your family murdered nor did you have to be a murderer, to decide the fate of one.) Perhaps not so incidentally, my wife and I both lived to have decades of joy from the son that was born and indeed from his son born thirty-six years after *Roe v. Wade*.

It was sometime in the early 1980s that a student in my "Writing of Fiction" class wrote a brilliant story about a college girl who gets an abortion. The surgery was described in excruciating detail from the point of view of the young woman, and the psychological aftermath was also depicted with empathetic power. It was a rule in the class that we never question the actuality which might or might not lie behind the fiction we read, but no one in the class doubted for a moment that the author had herself undergone the experience she had so harrowingly described. We had all read "Hills Like White Elephants," the brilliant Hemingway story about a man trying to persuade his girlfriend that aborting their baby would be a trivial matter that would only deepen their relationship, and most of us agreed that, all in all, our classmate's story, if not as subtly reinforced by staging (the Hemingway story takes place at a small train station while the couple waits for a train) nor as overwhelmingly powerful at its climax (the girl begging the man to "please, please, please, please, please stop talking"), was as moving and effective.

Surely not every abortion nor decision to abort follows the kind of emotional debate behind the writing of these two stories and the anguished puzzlement, frustration and—in my case—relief of my personal encounter, but, again, surely, many more engage the intellectual and spiritual depth of those who seek and get or refuse them. Although as Justices White and Rehnquist, the *Roe v. Wade* dissenters, argued, there is no constitutional "right of privacy," if there is a derivative right, what better exists therein than the decision to abort or not to abort. For Brazilians, privacy may not be an issue, but President Luis de Silva, one of a huge family whose lives were narrowed—and expanded?—by each other's existence and who himself fathered a child out of wedlock, will surely discuss with the pope his awareness of the state's interest in the lives of young women and, as he told the press, in the recognition of them as complete human beings. Neither will persuade the other about legal or religious penalties and rights, and this debate will go on and on.

Post 46
May 13, 2007
In his wonderful post about the theme of personal authenticity through acceptance of one's blackness in *Radio Golf,* the last of the late August Wilson's remarkable ten-play cycle, John McWhorter writes:

> As much as I have loved so many of Wilson's plays, I do not accept that the life I lead is unreal, inauthentic, or broken. Our vegetable garden is authentic, and I do not water my cucumbers because I wish I was white. My life is authentic. It is authentic to me . . . the racial identity [Wilson] is suggesting is based on feeling ever conflicted, deeply different, with roots in a far off land in an-

other time. That might float some people's boats, but I am more interested in feeling whole right here and now. History is important—but not so much that, as Faulkner had it, the past isn't even past. August Wilson was, no questions asked, real. I wish that in his parting message to the world, he could have allowed that I and millions of other black people leading lives like mine are real too.

These words alone do much to vouch for McWhorter's reality, authenticity and wholeness. I'd guess that Wilson himself would have seen and felt this although he might have disagreed with McWhorter's belief that his play was sending a "message" and with his narrowing the import of Faulkner's statement about the presence of the past.

Those elements of the past which form parts of what we call our identity—family, religion, ethnic background, class, biological being including gender, strength and health, our place in the communities of which we're a part—almost surely lead to internal as well as external conflicts in the course of our life. Perhaps only those who never feel such conflicts can be called inauthentic and unreal. One talent of the dramatist and prose fiction writer is to stage the conflicts, that is, to so isolate or exaggerate one or more of the conflicting elements that it upsets the status quo of the drama's beginning and begins its drive toward another status, tragic, comic or some combination of them. The bliss of the audience or readers is to get swept up in this two- or thirty-hour transfiguration in such a way that our own reality is enriched with what we've seen, heard or read. The work of very powerful dramatists and novelists will in time alter, indeed, become the culture, that is, the very "reality on the ground."

How wonderful it would be if there were in Iraq today a few dramatists with August Wilson–like gifts whose plays could enchant great numbers of Shia and Sunni with the dramatization of their complex identities in such a way as to get their fingers off gun triggers and their minds into the reflectiveness of Wilson's audiences or, for that matter, McWhorter's commentary.

Post 47
May 16, 2007
Today is Studs Terkel's ninety-fifth birthday, and tributes to him are being played over WFMT, the station on which he interviewed, played

records and reminisced sometimes five times a week between 1942 and 1997. When I first heard Studs, I thought he rattled on too loosely, unmoored by grammar or anything but misty benevolence. His first interview with me, probably around 1960, was surprisingly better. Studs was well-prepared. There were underlines throughout the book we were discussing, and again, if memory serves, he seemed to have a good take on it. Over the years, I'd see him at parties and funerals, on the street, my home and then during interviews. There I was more and more impressed by his preparation, his seriousness, his understanding, his easy charm, his—yes—goodness. In the *Nation,* I reviewed his first book, *Division Street America,* in relation to such other books of oral history as Oscar Lewis's *Children of Sanchez,* contrasting them with works of fiction from the *Canterbury Tales* on. I said Studs was no Chaucer but a kind of Harry Bailly, the pilgrims' amiable host. (Studs asked me who Bailly was.) Two years ago, I sat with him over lunch before the Printers' Row Book Fair where in separate booths we were to read. Although "practically deaf," and a beat or two slower, he was more or less as he'd always been, the easy pace of being Studs assimilating age better than most of us do. This Chicagoan, himself no chicken, couldn't help feeling a sort of love for him.

In the newspapers today, I read the obituary of another American monument, Jerry Falwell. Although I'd only seen and heard him on television, and although I found most of his views either abhorrent, naïve, ignorant or intrusively mean and wild, I was often surprised by his apparent amiability, lack of theatricality and occasional spasms of common sense. The obituary revealed other surprises: he was an American go-getter who, just as his father expanded one small restaurant into a chain to which were added service stations and at least one well-known night club, expanded an almost unattended church into one with a huge congregation, then started his own church and, finally, Liberty, the fundamentalist university of which he was chancellor till his death yesterday. His Moral Majority is said to have elected Ronald Reagan, and speaking at Liberty U. is almost a prerequisite for getting the Republican nomination for president. (The first posthumous speaker will be Newt Gingrich; the last Falwellian speaker was John McCain.)

Which of these two men has had a greater impact on their country? Almost everyone would opt for Falwell, for there is little doubt that as far as present-day political power goes, it was his. I prefer to think that

Studs' books and decades of radio work, his genial intelligence, the fusion of common sense with empathy, his political and esthetic sensitivity and then the editorial gifts which make his books a remarkable biographical history of his time and country, will in years to come be seen as having made a more enduring and profound contribution to national well-being. I'll close with lines from a poet Studs and this blogger admire, Alane Rollings:

> My Dead, having lived, must be kept, somehow, alive . . .
> What they'd been was me. The only way to keep them
> was to hold closely as I could
> all the borrowed elements that recompose me by the hour
> on this substantial planet where I live.
> —"Sweetness Night and Day," from *To Be in this Number*

Post 48
May 19, 2007
Much to do, little time. And desire is greater than strength, willpower, patience.

Much of what one wanted for years is a way out of bounds: flying a plane; becoming a skier; running a state.

Today an editor-friend proposed writing a small book about some thing which would cast a different light on the U.S. (One book in the series is about the hamburger, another about inventing a state, a third about Cage's *4'33"*, a fourth about Gypsy Rose Lee.) Would this be within my powers? Perhaps, but my priority remains prose fiction, and I think of ability as I never used to, as limited, and thus rationed. It used to be that I could tackle such a book and still write stories. The two would often strengthen and stimulate each other.

There's so much one sees, hears, reads and imagines which suggests other things. So there's an essay in the new *Antioch Review* about contemporary Israeli poetry. I've never heard of the four poets described by the excellent essayist, John Taylor, but they sound terrific. It's too late for me to learn Hebrew. (All I know now is the "Sch'ma Yisroel," and I'm not sure that I know that.) I could get their books, some from an Israeli press co-founded by the daughter of friends of mine, Adina Hoffman, but at least I can draw a little attention their way. So here are a few

lines from two of the poets, first, Anton Pincas (b. 1935), translated by
Taylor out of Emmanuel Mose's French:

> In our ancient sea
> Nothing's new.
> Only the wind varies.
> I don't think
> I've missed anything.

The next lines are those of Aharon Shabtai (b. 1939), translated by Peter Cole:

> I take an oath of loyalty to the table
> Coated with white Formica, a cup full of pens, the ashtray.
> I dreamed that the state had passed out of existence
> And with our children we'd settled down in the three volumes of
> the dictionary.
> My house will stand beside the word mix, *on the way to* morals.
> I'll risk my life for the sake of a single rectangle alone—
> The bed that belongs to Tanya and me—two meters by a meter-
> and-a-half . . .

May readers of the blog make whatever can be deduced or extrapolated from these lines. My pleasure is in their energy, humor, challenge,
form of assertion; my sense is that there's much going on in Israel beside soldiering, debating, science, advanced agriculture and wall-build-
ing.

I've thought much recently about ways of living as an old person.
One of my contemporaries, a brilliant economist, keeps up amazingly
with what goes on in his field and in fields—distant from economics—
where he sees problems that can be described and handled with economic tools. I've noticed that for the past few years, much of what he's
published is collaborative. I mean to ask him if collaboration is a way of
handling whatever years have done to or with his still very keen but perhaps altered way of thinking.[10] Blogging is something I began nine
months ago. I've gotten used to doing the short pieces I turn out. I

---

10. His answer was that (1) time is limited and (2) many economists want to work with him.

think of them as etudes. Some have been in the form of playlets, a couple are poems. Usually "studies" are studies for something larger. Mine are—how I wish—Chopinesque etudes, that is, ends in themselves.

I'll end—as this form allows me to end—with the last few lines of the Shabtai poem quoted above.

> I saw the pictures of the prime minister and minister of defense
> in the morning paper, smeared with a reddish lacquer, like a
>   prostitute's nails.
> I drive my thoughts far away from them now—
> to a can of baked beans, to two sausages and Chinese parsley.

> It is time for lunch.

Post 49
May 26, 2007
They're advertising discounted fares to Teheran for $623.00. The airline slogan is "Book Now and Save Big." You find it in the margin of pieces reporting on the months-long interrogation and now imprisonment of the Iranian American scholar Haleh Esfandiari, director of the Middle East Program at the Woodrow Wilson School of International Affairs. Dr. Esfandiari was finishing one of her bi-annual visits to her ninety-three-year-old mother and preparing to return to her job and husband, the Iranian Jewish scholar Professor Shaul Bakhash of George Mason University, when she was robbed of her passport at knifepoint by four thugs. She went to the authorities to secure the necessary travel papers. First, she was heard, then lengthily—over weeks—interrogated, then accused of being a Zionist and American spy and finally—as of this date[11]—locked up in the infamously sinister Evin Prison where, some years ago, Zahra Kazemi, a Canadian Iranian journalist, was beaten to death and where, a year ago, the Canadian Iranian philosopher Ramun Jahanbigloo was confined until he "confessed" that his work played a role in inciting "a velvet revolution" against the benign regime of Pres-

---

11. On August 21, she was released from prison after paying a sum of three million rials (about $300,000). In a public statement, she said that she was well-treated in prison. On September 12, back in the U.S., this enchanting person told Gwen Ifill of the *Lehrer News Hour* of the schedule of exercise, reading and writing a book in her head which got her through 105 days of solitary confinement. Her interrogators and guards apparently rose to her high level of courtesy and decency. Only Satan himself could have resisted her.

ident Ahmadinijad. Two other Westerners are now enduring similar hospitality, Robert Levinson, an FBI agent, and Jamchat Parnaz, who works for U.S.-funded Radio Farda. I suppose that those who wish can make a stronger case that these two are spies and Zionist agents than can be made against Dr. Esfandiari, but in this world, a world in which thousands of people from almost every country function, justice is irrelevant, if not something to be mocked.

Anybody can indict almost anyone for wrongdoing. Make this unbeautiful underside of international relations the public side, cease all diplomatic talk, display flotillas of might in neighboring waters, form, incite, ignite and supply groups who are or will be enemies, and before long, the world's arms makers will be doubling the dividends of their stockholders.

I suppose it helps to have a tradition of wrathful vengeance behind one. (See *The Sopranos*.) Recently, the more excitable portion of the Moslem world was infuriated at Pope Benedict XVI's citation of a Byzantine king's words about a sanguinary tendency in Islamic recruitment. This noble tradition may have been inaugurated by the Prophet himself. After the Jewish tribal leader and poet Ka'b ibn al-Asharf not only opposed his efforts but wrote poems which were thought to be insulting to Moslem women, Muhammad is said to have said, "He [Ka'b] has openly assumed enmity to us and speaks evil of us and he has gone over to the polytheists and has made them gather against us for fighting." He called upon his followers to kill Ka'b. Muhammad ibn Maslama offered his services and those of four others. By pretending to have turned against the Prophet, Muhammad ibn Maslama and the others enticed Ka'b out of his fortress on a moonlit night, and killed him.

Anyone for Teheran? Book Now and Save Big.

Post 50

June 8, 2007

I write now from our Georgian "foot in the earth," where we arrived two days ago. For the last few years, after spending eight hours at O'Hare waiting first for a plane, then for a crew, we've driven here from Chicago. The route passes through six other states, Indiana, Ohio, Kentucky, Tennessee, North and South Carolina. We usually overnight in eastern Tennessee on the edge of the Great Smokies, whose winding roads we drive over the next morning. What never fails to strike us is the sheer wealth of the country, the ubiquity of comfort, hundreds and hundreds of motels whose rooms have cable television, microwave ovens, little fridges, ironing boards, clean sheets and towels. In winter, heat, in summer, air conditioning. The prices range from thirty to a hundred or so dollars which include a breakfast, bagels, juice, coffee, sometimes a waffle—make it yourself—and cereal.

Then the restaurants. A few stops can boast only a McDonald's or a Wendy's, but even these purveyors have a few tasty, well-prepared non-lethal dishes to offer, and their bathrooms are clean. In most stops, there are six or eight restaurants, staffed by amiable, often charming waitresses (only a few have waiters, equally pleasant) and hostesses. Sometimes the food is very good, not up to Charley Trotter's or Lutece, but after ten driving hours, delicious, cheap and of course, plentiful. (If you seek obesity samples, come to any of them.)

Another thing that strikes us is the ease of fast travel, the general competence of drivers which involves knowledge of the rules of the road, some unwritten, and even courtesy. On this trip, we were held up once, on Indiana's I-65 near Indianapolis. A "semi turned over, the wrecker's lifting it," a young, professorial-looking truck driver who'd listened to the traffic report station told me when I rolled down the window to ask if he could see what was going on. The two traffic lanes were immobilized for twenty minutes, loosened a bit for another twenty and then dissolved into freedom. Driving the autobahns—which used to have no speed limits posted—I used to think that the only reason they weren't rivers of blood was the restraint that poured in over the radios in cantatas of Bach and sonatas of Haydn. Though one can occasionally find such music fountains here or, of course, play CDs or tapes, my guess is that what comes over the radios of most of the voyagers is not Bach and Haydn. Whatever, though, it seems to do the civilizing trick.

I won't talk of landscape except to say there are lovely patches of barn-and-silo-studded fields in southern Indiana and Ohio, the hills of Kentucky and Tennessee are often spectacular, the Smokies are beautiful in the morning with mist rising mystically toward the sun. As for the buildings, there is no visible master plan, and one doesn't feel that the builders were inspired by F. L. Wright or Senor Calatrava.

Place names: always interesting. Our puzzling favorite: Stinking Creek, Tennessee.

Anyway, here we are in our little nest, thirty miles east of Savannah, where the Savannah River debouches into the Atlantic Ocean. We've been to the Tybee market (the town's only grocery), we've cleaned the pigeon droppings from the porch, and seen the first tankers heading for the port. The a/c and ice-maker are performing as they should, it's in the 90s but at 9 A.M. and 7 P.M. it's a delight to swim in the pool. The few people we know here seem as glad to have us back as we are to see them. The knowledgeable postal clerk with the mustache says he's glad we're back, the fine, intelligent black woman, founder and chief of Relax First, renews our friendship as we make my first massage appointment.

Changes: a surf shop has replaced the takeout Chinese restaurant, Cap'n Chris' restaurant is now the first floor of what will be a six-flat condominium, the Surf Motel has expanded and grown pink as a baby's bottom, but at least on this first glance, our place is still our place, and things are more or less okay. Tonight I'll read the Goethe novella *Elective Affinities,* and tomorrow morning watch the fierce little Belgian Justine Henin dismantle the smiling Serbian teenager Ana Ivanovic.

Given the fragility of flesh and the vicissitudes of fate and fortune, we American burghers can live wonderfully comfortable lives, given, that is, that we have the normal human ability to avoid for any protracted time immersion in the endless brutality which gifted journalists and photographers report to the gifted editors who package it in assimilable narrative segments.

Post 51

June 11, 2007

Fans of Roger Federer and *The Sopranos* had a mixed weekend.

Federer had some grand moments, his off-and-on speed, high-and-low spin and flat shots to Nadal's backhand threw the indomitable Majorcan for as close to a loop as we've seen, and there were enough surprising, ungettable backhands and forehands to give our beloved Federer sixteen break points and the second set; but the Nadal-wall did not come down, and at crucial points, the twenty-one-year-old hit beautiful passing and drop shots which with the heat brought down the great champion ("mi amigo Roger," said the gracious winner) once again, *battu sur la terre battue de* Roland Garros.[12]

---

12. My friend Richard Strier thinks that Federer wants to lose this slam so that unlike Alexander after he had nothing more to conquer, he wouldn't weep tears of void.

At night, the final, beautifully surprising end to the marvelous long television drama *The Sopranos*. Has the televison audience ever before been so esthetically shocked?

The final episode of *The Sopranos* had everything but familiarity. For those of us lusting for revenge, Phil Leotardi was gunned down in front of his wife and baby grandchildren and, for horror-frisson, their SUV's tire rolled over Grandpa's white head.

For those of us who need ends tied up a la Flaubert, we had Tony's visits to the mindless Uncle Junior, comatose Syl, and that human smorgasbord, Janice. For Soprano-comedy, we had a good dose of the mystical old murderer, Paulie Walnuts. For those looking ahead, we learned that Meadow, influenced by seeing her daddy manhandled by the FBI, would become a civil rights attorney and that A.J., saved from suicide and tempted away from enlisiting in the army by a high-sounding job in Carmine's movie production company, would not go on reciting the gloomy line from Yeats' (pronounced to rhyme with Pete's) "Second Coming."

The episode was filled with characters watching television shows and listening to rap and other songs, the popular shapers of attitudes and narrative expectations. Then David Chase planted characters and shots which in such narratives suggested some of the melodramatic conclusions many of us thought we wanted, so that the last ten minutes were full of tension. (Was that fellow in a cap going to blast Tony's head off?) The final moments saw Meadow having trouble parking, then rushing off to join her parents and A.J. at the restaurant, her face full of the anxiety of being late but for us, the *Sopranos*-trained audience, another suggestion of imminent catastrophe. And then, blackout. It was over. Like the Sopranos themselves, their audience would have to live in the vaguely troubling suspense of more or less ordinary life. David Chase, like a very few novelists at their very best, had devised a conclusion which was not a form of collapse but of questioning, one which forced a reexamination of the whole episode, if not the entire series. A beautiful triumph.

Post 52

July 5, 2007

The Independence Day fireworks were beautiful to watch and hear from our little porch on Tybee Island. Garrison Keillor's *Writer's Almanac* had informed us that it was also Hawthorne's birthday and the one on which

Thoreau had moved into his Walden cabin (made by him as Jefferson had made the lap-desk on which he wrote the thirteen-hundred-odd words of the Declaration). I remembered the famous coincidental deaths this day in 1826 when, hundreds of miles apart, the octogenarians Adams and Jefferson breathed their last on that fiftieth anniversary of the day they'd done so much to make great. I remembered too the trip they'd made to visit English gardens and Stratford-on-Avon, the usually restrained Jefferson going down on his knees to pluck a loose sliver from a chair Shakespeare may have sat on. Those were the days, although I believe that excellent Nebraskan, Warren Buffet, that the average American lives better today than John D. Rockefeller did not all that long ago. Watching Venus Williams outhit Maria Sharapova from Wimbledon as I drank iced coffee and lay back after swimming the day's laps in the condo pool convinced me that the Great Investor was right again. Philip Roth tells me that someone he knows—and trusts—is editing Saul Bellow's letters. We've each received enough of them to know that the collected letters may well be one of the great books of our literature. For a son's forthcoming birthday, I ordered Karajan's Berlin Philharmonic recording of the nine Beethoven symphonies, thinking his two small children would grow up with some of this sublimity in their heads, and then wondered how much my own life owed to Beethoven, how many thousands of hours in these almost eighty years have been sweetened and deepened by what in his fifty-seven years he conjured out of the small reservation of noise we take in as music. Obviously incalculable, but what a debt I owe (if I think in Buffetian terms). As to what I owe Jefferson, that too is incalculable, although it's not unlikely that at least some of his stupendous contribution to the country would have been done by others of that remarkable group we call our "founding fathers" or such amazing "sons" as his young friend Merriwether Lewis, who killed himself a few years after his tremendous exploration. In any event, the beauty of the fireworks exploding into gorgeous fragments in the black sky over the ocean had to do, one felt, with the brevity of human celebration.

Post 53
July 12, 2007
I enjoyed Cass Sunstein's recent speculations on the possible transition from the present conservative (rather than centrist) Roberts-led court to a liberal one of the sort over which Chief Justice Warren presided.

My interest in court matter was ignited sixty-seven years ago when I read Drew Pearson and Robert S. Allen's *The Nine Old Men* and wrote in my Hunter College Model School yearbook that I wanted to be a Supreme Court justice. The chief redeemers of that beknighted court, Brandeis and Cardoza, were Jews, as high as such young Jews as I could go in that era. I still remember some of the names and faces of the backward justices, McReynolds, Van Deventer, Pierce Butler, who so irked my beloved FDR that he suggested appointing one justice for every septuagenarian and older one.

Although my ambition altered from law to literature a year or so later, I've never ceased being absorbed by the justices and their decisions. Yet, although for some years I used to go to Washington, DC, twice a year to visit a daughter and her family, I never saw anything but the exterior of the classical court building and until a few years ago, never spoke with a justice.

The justice was David Souter and the occasion was the memorial service for Gerald Gunther, the great constitutional scholar whose biography of Judge Learned Hand had, Souter said, guided his judicial thinking. This was the substance of his eulogy; mine was more personal. I had known Gunther at Stuyvesant High School as Gunther Gutenstein and had not heard of, let alone from him, till 1973, when he wrote me from Cambridge, MA, that he'd just read a novel of mine set there and found a handful of mistakes which he was good enough to correct in case there was a later edition. After this, he "came clean," and said he wrote in this corrective way because he remembered that I'd been chairman of the Arista Committee which, back in 1944, had interviewed him for membership. I'd asked him to differentiate the work of Henry, William and Harry James.

He wrote that he knew only the famous trumpeter married then to the WWII "pin-up" Betty Grable and that even now, decades later, he was embarrassed by his ignorance.

My friend Philip Kurland informed me who Gunther was, and I then began noticing quotes from him in the *Times, Time* and the *New Republic,* but we didn't become reacquainted and then close friends till I went to the Center for Advanced Studies in the Behavioral Sciences in Stanford in 1999.

Justice Souter and I talked briefly after the last eulogy was delivered and then a bit more after dinner at the beautiful Gunther house that evening. What I most vividly remember was his reply to my wondering if he saw any augmentation of his side (Breyer, Stevens and Ginsberg—another eulogist of Gunther, her mentor) coming along. He said he did and then amazed me and everyone to whom I recounted what he said, by saying "Clarence Thomas."

The answer made me think of the court in a different way. I now envisaged a small group of intimate colleagues who exchanged and shared much more than legal opinions. Thomas and Souter had clearly had talks of a different sort than most of us imagined. That Thomas could be charming I knew after hearing him speak at a library here in Savannah which as a boy had helped him leap over the terrible obstacles African American boys and girls faced as they dreamed beyond the provincial aridity of the lives of those around them.

However, to extrapolate charm into legal opinion was something Souter, not I or such legal friends as Gerhard Casper or Richard Posner, could do. After all, one saw the uncrossable gulf in the close friendship of Justices Ginsberg and Scalia, whose families spent every New Year's Eve together but who in crucial opinions almost always voted on opposite sides.

So I enjoyed Cass Sunstein's well-rooted imagination of another liberal court but retain Hamlet's caution to Horatio that there are more things in Supreme Court matters than there are in even Justice Souter's optimism.

July 24, 2007
Yesterday, I emailed the following Letter to the Editor:

> Re. the removal of five benign polyps from President Bush's colon, would it be infra dig to recall Evelyn Waugh's comment on the excision of a benign tumor from Randolph Churchill: "Odd that they removed Randolph's only benign part"?

The *Times* has a more benign collective nature than this correspondent who, for a witticism, even someone else's, knifes his more tolerant opinion of our chief exec. G.W. is no more malign than the next fellow, only more harmful; his deficiencies are of another order, some of which can be explained by Lord Acton's most famous observation. After all these years as prexy, G.W.B. still displays the awkwardness of little girls dressed up in Mommy's shoes and skirts. All presidents exhibit some of this awkwardness, but all I know anything about (I've read biographies of Filmore, Tyler, Garfield, Bush's ancestor Pierce and the underrated Chester Arthur, as well as most of their betters) outgrew it in a year or so.

I'm reminded of the proprieties of institutions and offices by an email from the writer John Coetzee, suggesting that I suspend judgment about his forthcoming (in January 2008) novel because the layout of the *New York Review of Books* did an excerpt of it a "disservice." In book form, two or three different streams of text will run parallel across the page whereas in the *NYRB*'s four-column layout, the two streams were cut off—or dammed. (I wonder if the fugal set-up will have more of the quality of Mallarme's "Un Coup de Des n'abolira jamais le hazard," than of Faulkner's alternation of chapters from two narratives, *The Wild Palm*s and "Old Man." We'll see next January. I suspect we'll be on to another Coetzeean invention, one closer to that section of Roth's *Sabbath's Theater* in which the main narrative is "undercut" by one in footnotes.

There is ten thousand times more noise generated by the three- or four-week vacation the Iraqi parliament will soon be taking unless the noise from our vacationing senators, representatives and—unfortunately—unvacationing TV and editorial commentators shames them into comparing themselves unfavorably with the coalition troops trudging through 130-degree heat with backbreaking backpacks. Perhaps G.W.B. ought to sacrifice his vacant days in Crawford and/or Kennebunkport as another mark of his sacrifice, sympathy and understanding.

A final and historical note on the surprising sympathies of men in power: after Hitler's murder of Roehm and a couple of hundred others in the "Night of the Long Knives," an admiring Josef Stalin, ten years the Austrian's senior, said to Mikoyan, "Some fellow that Hitler! Splendid! That's a very skilful operation."

Post 55
August 4, 2007

> We all come down and drown in the Mississippi River.
> —Hold Steady (Craig Finn), "Stuck between Stations"

The song is about the poet John Berryman walking with the Devil down Washington Avenue before throwing himself over the bridge connecting the east and west campuses of the U. of Minnesota where he taught. Berryman missed the water but succeeded in the suicide which is said to have been on his agenda since as a boy he heard the shot which his father fired into his own head.

This scheduled self-destruction on one Minneapolis bridge was very different from the unscheduled, unplanned, unwanted deaths of the drivers and passengers whose cars followed the downward plunge of "fatigued" steel into the Mississippi thirty-five years later. There was, though, as there almost always is, a treasury of human poetry springing from the words and actions of those who survived and those who suffered from those who didn't.

One almost wordless poet was a twenty-year-old gym coordinator, Jeremy Hernandez, who'd taken his job because he couldn't afford the tuition in the auto mechanics course he'd started. In tank top, slender, slightly mustached, mild and weary, Jeremy stood beside the small, lovely Natalie Morales of NBC as she coaxed a few words from him about what he'd done, which was to "follow his feet," leap over seats, kicking aside water coolers in the yellow school bus, kicking open the back door and then passing child after child out to those who brought them to safety. "They were like my brothers and sisters," he said in explanation. "I loved them. They would have done the same for me." As what Natalie and her NBC contacts, Matt Lauer and Meredith Viera, felt would be a sort of crowning acknowledgment of his "heroism," they bade Jeremy look at the monitor where was displayed his picture "on the front page of the *New York Times*." What to them would have been the fulfillment of a life's ambition was not part of Jeremy's world. Perhaps he'd heard of the newspaper, he surely had never read it or perhaps even seen it in his neighborhood. His neighborhood was filled with the Hispanic, African American and Whatever boys and girls, one of whom, age five, was already a wiser commentator and more fluent orator than the not unsympathetic Morales and company.

Two days later, appeared on the same network a truck driver whose truck just managed to keep from hitting the school bus before crashing thirty-five feet below. Its burly, bald, fiftyish driver turned out to be another poet who slowly and perfectly described waving at the children in the bus and sounding his horn for them, then plunging into a nothing where he first smelled the diesel from his fuel tank. "I knew it was slow to burn," but burn it would, and as he went on describing what he did, he was cut off by the NBC male anchor bowing to the anti-poetic, anti-human network schedule. (This elicited sympathetic praise of the driver by the most human and charming of today's anchors, Amy Robach, before she yielded to the network's moronic scissors.)

These were but two of the vignettes which like waves fixed on canvas by Hiroshige or Monet were taken out of the flux of life by the terrible event and turned into embodiments of mourning and redemption by the memorializing shears of television and the more generously detailed and artistic words of newspaper and magazine reporters.

John Berryman, whom I knew and cared for and whose amazing, idiosyncratic poems and brilliant biographical treatments of Stephen Crane and Shakespeare I admire and reread, would, I think, have been stirred, perhaps to verse, by this terrible accident so close to the non-accident which ended his life.

Post 56
August 14, 2007

> All the vulgar issues of life were a matter of indifference to this lofty soul,
> to whom nothing had yet afforded a profound emotion.
> —Stendhal, "The Rose and the Green" (trans Richard Howard)

Only weeks after the first complete human genome, that of the great bio-chemist James Watson, was posted on the Internet, we are getting reports of theories of transformation influenced by wondrous confidence in genetic determinism. It took far more time for the understanding of perspective to alter the nature of painting than for this new influence to determine the direction of economic and political analysis. A recent example is reported in the August 10 issue of the *NY Times:*

> Gregory Clark, an economic historian at the University of California, Davis, believes that the Industrial Revolution—the surge in economic growth that occurred first in England around 1800—occurred because of a change in the nature of the human population. The change was one in which people gradually developed the strange new behaviors required to make a modern economy work. The middle-class values of nonviolence, literacy, long working hours and a willingness to save emerged only recently in human history, Dr. Clark argues.

The change, Dr. Clark believes, was due to the survival of society's wealthier, successful people whose genetic constitution had coded these values.

Watson, himself, though a believer in genetic determinism, says more modestly of his own success, "It must be something. I walked fast." Also, his "devotion to intellectual things was helped by the fact that I was a puny boy." He wishes the genetic blueprint of his schizophrenic son had been available because he and his wife "had never handled him right . . . you don't really want to say someone is not likely to have a future."

We constantly make motivic examinations of people, past and present, and give or withhold support for those running for office on somewhat flimsy evidence. I myself have thought more about the nature of President Bush than about most of the characters I invented for stories I wrote. In stories, I use whatever elements of character are needed to deepen the narrative, no others. As for President Bush's character, even though my habit is to subvert my initial response to Speech X or Policy Y, there is so much Bush-evidence that I make frequent emendations in my characterization of and feelings toward him. So in the September 2007 issue of the *Atlantic* there is a telling piece by Matthew Scully, one of Bush's three senior speechwriters from 1999 until 2004. The main thrust of the piece is the exposure of the self-promoting speechwriter Mike Gerson who, despite the collaborating of such gullible (or falsifying) reporters as Bob Woodward, did not write most of the famous Bush lines and phrases ("axis of evil") for which he's given credit. En route to the Gerson-demolition, Scully, who seems to this perhaps gullible reader a reliable, decent and intelligent person, speaks of Bush's basic modesty and ability. Working closely with the man before and during his presidency, Scully writes that "I know one is now supposed to sigh with regret at how mistaken we all were about Bush in those [pre–Iraq War] days . . . and yet I think I recognize greatness when it steps before me, and the sight of George W. Bush in those days left an impression that has never worn off." This certainly softened the almost contemptuous feeling about the president which I'd been holding for quite a while.

My evaluation is not based on inspection of his genetic blueprint.

It is a byplay of the power of the purse that every few years another country, large or small, will gush with tennis talent. Once or twice the gush is in a family's backyard, say, that of the Bulgarian Maleeva sisters or the more famous one of Richard and Oracene Williams and their now super-duper star offspring, Venus and Serena.

Tennis is so clear about triumph and defeat, fine and poor play, good and bad luck that the non-tennis world looks careless, clumsy, brutal and lethal, if not insane, but in this post I want to vent spleen on the debris of error falling out of the larger world, the world which human technical ingenuity has constructed to bring ease and security to such burghers as myself. The errors here annoy, enrage and preoccupy us to the exclusion of facing, if not solving, those greater, weightier problems of which we know largely through newspaper and television. Half of these arise in the damaged souls of our fellow human beings, the other half through "nature," that "god" who in the aftermath of volcanos, tsunamis, forest fires and hurricanes is thanked by trembling survivors as they stare at the ash pile that was their home, their neighborhood, their town.

In the last week, I have spent hours on the phone dealing with entities which exist to ease my life, the phone company, a home security service, a brokerage and the corporations which install and service our cable television, our air conditioning and our clothes drier. All these have in a harmony of disharmony, a contagion of error, a tsunami of stupidity, failed us, either through billing or executive errors. Some of these are related to our return to a household after a three-month absence, although I thought that I'd carefully alerted one and all to the change.

My phone manner has degenerated from patience, politeness and gratitude to rage and threat. My internal lipid count has risen, my soul has shown itself to be weaker, stupider and more vicious than even I suspected. I am indeed just the sort of selfish, self-aggrandizing person revolutionaries would love to exterminate. Indeed, in an occasional moment not darkened by frustration and rage, I see myself as the sort of person who, elevated to some position of power, could translate such annoyances into policies over which another part of me rages as I read the paper or watch the news.

Two days ago, we'd run into another sort of worldly clot: after an overnight in Spring Green, Wisconsin (where, incidentally, its pride, Frank Lloyd Wright's Taliesin, was difficult to find), we drove back on the fine toll road, I-90, only to be ensnared in a massive gridlock caused by the installation of a toll booth, near O'Hare airport. Decades ago, Cortazar, the Argentinian writer, depicted hell as an automobile gridlock. You bet.

Home, I read my friend Alan Krueger's new book, *What Makes a Terrorist*, which demonstrates that the terrorist is a middle-class, reasonably well-educated person such as I. It also discusses the twisted statistics in a State Department assessment of terrorist activity which Krueger had earlier discovered. (This discovery led to a Colin Powell retraction but not to the formation of a statistical entity in the department.) Then I read a few stories by my old friend Jean Justice. These deal with the often subtle misunderstandings and misappraisals which darken the life of her protagonists. "It is," I think, "all of a piece."

When Roger Federer slams a forehand winner or Justine Henin aces her opponent, the consequences are clear, defined, limited and absolute. Now and then, the "better player" is outplayed and loses, but usually, the tennis world is one in which excellence is rewarded and errors are immediately punished.

If one is very patient, careful, hard-working and lucky, such results appear in some of one's own domestic and business life. If one is lucky enough to live in a country run largely on such rational principles as checks and balances, there is probably a preponderance of good national fortune.

Of course, every life ends in a kind of tragedy, every country eventually withers away, every triumph loses its glory, but if one builds this sense of ultimate failure into one's expectations, it should ease the pains and largely derivative horrors which compose even the most fortunate burgher lives. Or so I ease myself as I wait to watch the woman's final on my new flat-screen, high-definition television set.

Post 58
September 25, 2007

I.

Once again, Iran's President Ahmadinijad's reputation was rescued by the ineptitude, rudeness and stupidity of a well-known reporter and then by those opponents of his who reenact the Yeats depiction of a world of discourse in which "the worst are full of passionate intensity." On the *60 Minutes* interview with Scott Pelley, Ahmadinijad showed himself—as in time past he'd done with such other famous and inept interviewers as Mike Wallace and Brian Williams—good-humored, well-informed and patient under rude, persistent, clumsy questioning. So, instead of accepting and building on Ahmadinijad's response to his question about Iran's working toward nuclear weapons, namely, that the day of such weapons' utility had long passed, Pelley accused him of not answering his question. Which of course evoked a rational, still good-humored response that he, Ahmadinijad, was not a Guantanamo Bay prisoner being interrogated by the CIA but the elected president of the country in which they sat.

Yesterday, we had the usual, media-selected opposition to Columbia University's invitation to Ahmadinijad to participate in a Q and A with faculty and students. (The anchor robots seemed nervous when unfrenzied students and faculty spelled out the case for open forums, free speech and debates.) Small disappointments: level-headed Hillary Clinton, after, one guesses, a staff cost-and-benefit assessment of responses, said had she been president of Columbia, she would not have issued such an invitation, a version of George Bush's response, except that his was preceded by a more sensible, "It's okay with me, though I don't think I'd have invited him." At least, neither called Ahmadinijad a "crazy madman," the redundant depiction that went unchallenged by "debaters" on CNBC or a "mean-spirited, petty dictator," which was Columbia President Bollinger's hospitable introduction which Ahmadinijad quickly and quietly disposed of in a two-sentence remark about Iranian notions of hospitality.

In Iran's national concourse for university places, Ahmadinijad came out no. 132 out of 400,000. He has an M.A. in civil engineering, a Ph.D. in transport and planning, was on the short list of 65 (out of 550) outstanding world mayors when he was mayor of Teheran, and ran a skillful campaign to become president of his country. Far from being a dictator, he was rebuked by the ayatollahs for, among other things, suggesting that women be allowed to attend public sporting events (he has two daughters as well as a son), is openly challenged by newspapers and students, and is not in control of the army or other major sources of Iranian power. As for his notorious proclamations about Israel, the

Holocaust and—as of yesterday—homosexual freedom, he did as well as a believer could, saying that although he is not anti-Semitic and that Jews in Iran are actually favored as far as parliamentary representation goes, he did not look kindly on the "Zionist state" because it was an occupying power and one unfair to its ethnic minorities. As for the Holocaust, he granted that it may have happened but that like everything else, it should be further researched. (Nobody asked him if he thought the existence of Iran as a legitimate state or the cheese composition of the moon warranted further research.) As for the limitations on homosexuals, he said there were none in Iran. (This drew the loudest laugh, perhaps even from that portion of the audience—estimated at 30 percent—that was behind him all the way.) As for women, he considered them superior beings and they were so treated in his country. He cited their presence in the universities, business and government: there were two women deputy premiers. It was clear that this unshaven, "casually dressed," necktieless homunculus relished the intellectual sport of university "debate" especially on a worldwide stage, and that he'd mastered the skills of public challenge: circumlocution, good humor, "you-too"-ism and "Now-let-me-ask-you-a-question."

A professor for six years, a public figure for many more, Mahmoud Ahmadinijad is, like it or not, well on his way to becoming another of the oil-elevated populists who take up that portion of the world stage not dominated by the heads of oil-consuming democracies and out-and-out terrorists.

I suggest that we welcome the best of Ahmadinijad: his Moslem tolerance, if not love, for all people, his proclaimed opposition to war and nuclear weapons, his desire to enter into world debate and world trade. Accept his necktieless ease, unshaven face and his mix of arrogance and pride, answer logically his more outrageous statements, and turn down our own rhetorical burners as a way of persuading him to lower his.

II. Iconography

(a) There's a splendid photograph on the back of the latest issues of the Harvard and University of Chicago magazines. It is, I believe, an ad for NetJets, and shows the company's owner, Warren Buffet, sitting in one of the plane's comfortable lounges beside his young friend Bill Gates. They are in shirt sleeves, Buffet in suspenders. Gates is smiling broadly and looks relaxed and happy; Buffet, less openly expressive, also looks at ease. In front of them on a table are two glasses of what may be Coca-Cola (another Buffet company), two hands of a card game I can't identify except that it's not the bridge Buffet adores and which they've played together, a section of a newspaper resting on a handsome leather notebook near Gates (another section emerges from his briefcase), a dish of candies, another of some sort of salad, another with halves of a muffin. On a side table in the rear is a vase of fresh flowers. Portrait of Two Amiable, Congenial, Benevolent Billionaires as constructed by well-remunerated PR specialists.

(b) At last week's congressional hearings, iconographers could count nine rows of ribbons on the left side of General David Petraeus's uniform, each standing for some accomplishment or area of service. They rose toward the four silver stars of his rank and other symbolic insignia which I could not make out on television as he read his clearly written statement and answered questions from the members of the Armed Services Committees, the first chaired by a Grant Wood–looking sexagenarian, Ike Skelton (perhaps a cousin of the late comedian Red, whom he resembles). As usual in nationally publicized hearings, the questioning of the general and of his diplomatic counterpart Ryan Crocker, was an occasion for members of the committees to exhibit their own expertise, well-traveled knowledge, high-minded stances and fitness for even higher office. The general, lucidly, patiently and as openly as his place in—to use a phrase he used often—"the chain of command" allowed, defended his mission, claimed it was en route to being fulfilled and then, once or twice, opened further to say that he did not know how it fit into the larger picture of American security (this in response to a question from John Warner to whom longevity has supplied the kind of wisdom respected by colleagues and commentators). No one had apparently read Petraeus's 337-page Ph.D. (Princeton) dissertation dealing with the failures of Vietnam and other American wars fought by too-few troops with too little public support, despite its obvious contradiction of his present mission. Indeed, no one seemed up to the lucid patience of this disciplined soldier who'd emerged from his modest Cornwall-on-Hudson upbringing (his father, Sixtus, an immigrant Dutch sea captain), his graduation from nearby West Point, whose superintendent's daughter he married after graduation. The portrait here seemed to be a version of Patience on a Monument, the "Monument" being the eternal sameness of actionless schmoos.

Pirate Jenny to Pilgrim Jenna

> Beelzebub, Apollyon, and Legion . . . contrived here to set up a fair; a fair
> wherein should be sold all sorts of vanity . . . at this fair are all such
> merchandise sold as houses, lands, trades, places, honors, preferments, titles,
> countries, kingdoms, lusts, pleasures; and delights of all sorts, as harlots,
> wives, husbands, children, masters, servants, lives, blood, bodies, souls,
> silver, gold, pearls, precious stones, and what not. And moreover, at this fair
> there is at all times to be seen jugglings, cheats, games, plays, fools, apes,
> knaves, and rogues, and that of every kind. Here are to be seen, too, and
> that for nothing, thefts, murders, adulteries, false-swearers. . . .
> —John Bunyan, *Pilgrim's Progress* (1678)

Fifteen or so years ago, I subscribed to *Vanity Fair*—Tina Brown was
editing it then—and enjoyed it for two or three months till I felt the
repetitiveness of its stories: almost all, whoever the subject—they were
almost all profiles—movie star, magnate, couturier, athlete, politician,
rose spectacularly, balanced on the razor edge of triumph, then fell
more or less catastrophically, the chief component of falling a form of
vanity or hubris.

Yesterday, my wife brought home the October issue of the magazine, hundreds of sleek pages of young beauties advertising clothes,
perfumes, resorts, yachts, planes. Within this paradise of merchandise
were articles about the beautiful and famous, all sprinkled with some
hitherto secret sadness, but essentially aglow in triumph. There was also
an annotated list of the one hundred rulers and shakers of fashion, industry, trade, building, news-making and digitalized (virtual) pleasure-
giving. The net worth of this editorially crowned one hundred must
equal the GNP of all but a dozen or so nations. (The richest of all, a
Mexican named Carlos Slim Helu, was unknown to me;[13] I felt as I do
not knowing calculus or Greek.)

---

13. A friend of mine reported the following: "I had dinner last fall with Carlos Slim, supposedly
the richest man on this planet. It was at his office, with a half dozen of his stooges. All he did was
show me his art—which is outstanding—and talk. He certainly wasn't interested in listening to me
or anyone else." My colleague Walter Kaegi told me that "Slim" derived from "Selim" and that the
billionaire was of Lebanese origin.

There are also at least—I haven't finished reading the issue—two articles on President Bush, one on his comedic gift, his failure to use it and to use his wife and daughters as a way of stemming his declining popularity.

I don't know whether the president, Rove or Rove's successor read the piece or whether they/he had decided independently to trot out the suggested artillery, but last night, just after I watched the Chicago Cubs win their division title, my wife and I watched Diane Sawyer interview and go on the road with Jenna Bush, the president's twenty-five-year-old blond daughter. The road went through the shack-lined slums, AIDS-darkened alleys and bare schoolrooms of Jamaica and Haiti, where Jenna has been teaching. (Her Secret Service protectors were blended in as inconspicuously as possible, but my terrible thought was that a more alert al Qaeda brigade could have secured a huge prize here.)

Jenna is a dear young woman, poised, sensible, good-hearted, well-spoken, an enthusiast and sympathizer. When Diane, with the aged reporter's intrusive coarseness, ever in search of some emotional or behavioral twist, informed a sixteen(?)-year-old AIDS-suffering girl who talked with quiet despair about losing her good job, her neighbor's respect, her hope, indeed her life, that the Miss Jenna to whom she talked was the daughter of the American president, crooked white teeth bucked out of the dark face. A shy, amazed smile preceded a timid plea for help, for a visa. All Jenna could do was hug her, perhaps a redemptive moment in the girl's life.

The *NY Times* this morning indicated that the Sawyer interview was the opening salvo of a publicity tour for a book, *Ana's Story,* which Jenna's written about another tragic, AIDS-blighted girl. Jenna is donating her share of the profits to UNICEF.

Such generosity augments the grace, sweetness and quiet intelligence of this daughter about whom till now most knew little but sophomoric hijinks and a sense that she was Antoinetting around while the world burned, a kind of Pirate Jenny. The Sawyer interview altered this view and may do for Jenna's father what nothing short of his announcing the end of the Iraq War would. Next to Sawyer's itchy professionalism, Jenna was fresh, modest, unspoiled, a model of good upbringing, a large credit to her parents. In her way, she was a modern pilgrim passing beyond the temptations of *Vanity Fair* on the road to what stands in me-

dia terms for the Celestial City, the abstention from the jewels of privilege, the reaching down and helping pull up a few of the blighted billions born and raised far from the "preferments . . . kingdoms . . . precious stones and what not" of *Vanity Fair.*

Post 60
October 2, 2007

Doubting Thomas

> Una citta nella cutta, cinta da mura e soggeta ad altre regole. [A city within a
> city, surrounded by walls and subject to different rules.]
> —Italo Calvino, *La giornata d'uno scrutatore*

Why not leave well-enough alone? Sixteen years since his confirmation
as Thurgood Marshall's replacement on the Supreme Court, a leading
member of the Court's conservative block, a favorite of American conservatives (presiding at Rush Limbaugh's wedding to his third wife,
speaker at important conservative dinners), a genial, amiable colleague,
living comfortably in rural Virginia, young enough at fifty-nine to—*deo
volente*—serve longer than any other Supreme Court Justice, why stir terrible old fires? Is it because within the serenity of our outer city is another city subject to different pressures, operating under different rules?

The subject of critical biographies and articles, many much fiercer
than the one delivered almost twenty years ago by old Judge Leon Hig-
ginbotham (warning the new justice not to forget those of his race who
could profit as he had from affirmative action and special quotas),
Clarence Thomas apparently decided that giving counter-interviews
was not enough. And so he wrote a memoir telling what really drove
him and what really happened in the first forty-three years of his life: *My
Grandfather's Son,* the finely titled account of the father-deserted
Clarence who with his brother was sent by his mother to live with her
father after their small house burned to the ground. There young
Clarence encountered the discipline which led to self-respect and also
knowledge of the ugly discriminations which, if you just bitched and
moaned and whined, would undo that self-respect and leave you helpless on the road, another social burden.

At sixteen, after hearing a fellow seminarian saying he hoped that
the just-shot Martin Luther King, "that son of a bitch, would die,"

Clarence left the seminary and his Catholic faith. "You have disappointed and betrayed me," said his grandfather and kicked him out of the house. The memoir, a tribute to that grandfather, is also, in its odd way, a vaunting rebuke to the rebuker.

One rebuke leads to another. Common sense, if not wisdom, should have told Thomas not to raise again the almost-ghost of Anita Hill, whose sober senatorial testimony stained his life with a dye (lie-dye or truth) that no legal or personal triumph washed away. So he creates a new counter to the old charge in the form of a nasty portrait of an edgy, mediocre worker, a quick striker at whomever she sensed invaded her self-importance.

All these sixteen years, Professor Anita Hill had not publicly revisited the famous hours of vituperation, vulgarity and mendacity (see David Brock's confession of false reporting and characterization in his confessional memoir) on which the Thomas senatorial hearing concluded. Thomas's confirmation and years of court service stood, however marshy the ground on which they stood. But now, apparently unwilling or unable to bear the old indictment of sexist manipulating, the "lies" and perhaps even the racist oratory ("hi-tech lynching") he brilliantly delivered to cover them, Justice Thomas publishes this memoir. (Another substitute for the lie detector test he knew he could not take?) So Professor Hill came out of the academic shadows, and wrote a fine counter in today's *New York Times* saying that Thomas should not reinvent her in the course of recounting his life.

Unable not to return to the scene of our crime, unable to forget and thus unable to believe that others forget, knowing somehow that murder will out though it hath no tongue and must speak with miraculous organ, Clarence Thomas, back again in the Roman Catholic Church of his youth and seminary training, delivered this inverted form of a Catholic confession, a personal memoir whose truths conceal the inner city of other truths.

Post 61
October 16, 2007

Socrates on Globalization

The most recent IMF report discusses such results of globalization as the increased wealth in all participating countries and all social quintiles, along with a widening of the gap between top and lowest quintiles due largely to the technology transfers which have made skilled, education-dependent work ever more valuable even as profit-seekers shift as many low chores as possible to unskilled, low-paid workers.

The theme of the champions of human capital since Adam Smith rings a bell with all teachers: education is the key to personal advancement. Unlike the goods which we take home in containers to examine and treasure at our leisure, education is—as Montaigne pointed out in "Of Physiognomy"—swallowed on the spot and, short of torture, cannot be ripped from us. In that same essay, though, Montaigne takes a poke at education. Here he is:

> We are all of us richer than we think we are; but we are taught to borrow and to beg, and brought up more to make use of what is another's than of our own. Man can in nothing fix himself to his actual necessity: of pleasure, wealth, and power, he grasps at more than he can hold; his greediness is incapable of moderation. And I find that in curiosity of knowing he is the same; he cuts himself out more work than he can do, and more than he needs to do: extending the utility of knowledge, to the full of its matter.
>
> Tis a good, if duly considered, which has in it, as the other goods of men have, a great deal of vanity and weakness, proper and natural to itself, and that costs very dear. Its acquisition is far more hazardous than that of all other meat or drink; for, as to other things, what we have bought we carry home in some vessel, and there have full leisure to examine our purchase, how much we shall eat or drink of it, and when: but sciences we can, at the very first, stow into no other vessel than the soul; we swallow them in buying, and return from the market, either already infected or amended: there are some that only burden and overcharge the stomach, instead of nourishing; and, moreover, some, that under color of curing, poison us.
>
> I have been pleased, in places where I have been, to see men in devotion vow ignorance as well as chastity, poverty, and penitence: 'tis also a gelding of our unruly appetites, to blunt this cupidity that spurs us on to the study of books, and to deprive the soul of this voluptuous complacency that tickles us with the opinion of knowledge: and 'tis plenarily to accomplish the vow of poverty, to add unto it that of the mind. We need little doctrine to live at our ease; and Socrates teaches us, that this is in us, and the way how to

find it, and the manner how to use it . . . What if knowledge, trying to arm us with new defenses against natural inconveniences, has more imprinted in our fancies their weight and greatness, than her reasons and subtleties to secure us from them.

Of course, Montaigne is offering us the very thing he condemns, wise counsel in print, but one supposes that, however modest he may be, he allies himself with Socrates as the purveyor of necessary wisdom.

The IMF report deals largely with the sort of learning neither Socrates nor Montaigne considers: the technical intelligence which invents, operates and interprets the evermore abstract "machinery" of modern production and distribution. We have had at least since Mary Shelley's exhibition of Dr. Frankenstein's creation warnings about the dangers of such technical genius. Oppenheimer's citation of the Bhaghavad Gita as he watched the atomic explosion in the New Mexican desert is perhaps the best-known of such warnings.

Montaigne summons the Socratic notion that we have in us whatever wisdom we need (restated movingly in Bellow's *Mr. Sammler's Planet:* "We know, we know, we know, we know"), but this doesn't apply to what makes us able to buy the Lexus, the thirty-thousand-square-foot mansion, the Netjet or, for that matter, the cell phone, the virtual reality games, the iPod and the dinner at the three-star restaurant. Yet, yet, yet, we do know, don't we, that what ultimately counts is already in us and that with a nudge or two from a Montaigne, a Socrates or a Bellow, we can tune into it.

Post 62

October 21, 2007

Frank Rich's column today begins and ends with a suicide. The first is that of Charles D. Riecher, the air force's second-highest procurement officer, who killed himself two weeks after a *Washington Post* expose; the last that of Colonel Ted Westhusing, who was training Iraqi military and whose suicide note read, "I cannot support a msn [mission] that leads to corruption, human rights abuse and liars . . . I am sullied." Rich's column documents the corruption—jobs and money in return for lucrative business contracts with Boeing, Blackwater and those turning the enormous, shoddy, ill-built U.S. embassy in Baghdad into a monument of corruption and waste.

For relief from Rich's latest horror story about the soft carelessness of the money-eating, pious, murderous, perhaps-criminal administration, I read one of the short, brilliant stories in Denis Johnson's little book *Jesus' Son*. It's called "Dirty Weddings," and begins with the narrator taking his girlfriend Michelle to an NYC abortion clinic where he acts up and is thrown out, first among picketers who throw holy water on him and then into an El train where he observes in the windows flashing by kids watching TV, women putting on makeup, men spooning soup into their faces, the morning's debris of breakfast, quarrels, numbness, passion. A sixteen-year-old girl, lost in a cocaine paradise, leads him to a slum hotel where he buys some for himself. He tells us that Michelle left him for a man who failed to read her suicide note lying beside him on the pillow; he realizes how much he loved her and concludes, "I know they argue about whether or not it's right, whether or not the baby is alive at this point or that point in its growth inside the womb. This wasn't about that. It wasn't what the lawyers did. It wasn't what the doctors did, it wasn't what the woman did. It was what the mother and father did together."

I suppose what I'm feeling here is the moral preached in 90 percent of sermons and taught in 90 percent of schools and churches, that the things which drive us up the wall are ultimately in our own minds, choices and actions, and that like Colonel Westhusing it is we ourselves who sully and are sullied, we ourselves who mother and father the creations we then choose to abort.

Post 63
November 2, 2007
"I'm really scared," the *NY Times* reports Oren Ashkenazi of TVC Television and Cinema Wardrobe Cleaners saying about the imminent Hollywood writers' strike. TVC "processes" up to two thousand "garments" each night for television programs such as *24* and is not "set up for retail customers." Ditto for Green Set, a thirteen-acre nursery which rents plants to set decorators, for Hollywood tour guides, for Letterman, Leno, Daly and Colbert whose unscripted tongues will flop in their mouths like those of parched dogs, for restaurant cashiers and waiters, hotel managers and laundresses, script buyers, grips, electricians, actors, wardrobe mistresses, even for animators whose work along with that of "reality" programs advanced what drove the embattled writers of televi-

sion drama to this first strike in nineteen years. Patric M. Verrone, the leader of the Writers Guild of America (West), was himself an animator. He cleaned the guild of those in management's pocket and rejected the producers' offer of a contract which did not adequately boost the writers' share of DVD sales and that of any other technology which draws its original powers from the minds of writers. With this "Give me residuals or give me death," our new Patric(k) is ready to plunge Southern California further down the abyss torn out of its sun-drenched hide by the collapse of the housing market and the incineration of thousands of its expensive acres, some of this begun with almost equal innocence by ten-year-old boys "playing with matches."

To us writers unbound by fellowship in guilds, perhaps exulting a bit snootily in our independence (especially if, like Wagner's Walther von Stolzing—a name as suggestive as Oren Ashkenazi's—we've won a prize), it might be in order to remember the words the greatest of the master-singers, Hans Sachs, addressed to the exulting Walther:

> Don't scorn the Masters. Honor their art. Not to your ancestors, your coat-of-arms, your spear or sword but to the fact that you're a poet acknowledged by these Masters is the source of your happiness. Our Masters cared for the art in their own way, cherished it as they thought best and kept it genuine. If it didn't stay as aristocratic as of old, when courts and princes blessed it, in the stress of evil years, it remained German [cinematic] and true, and if it flourished nowhere but where all is stress and strain, you see how honorable it stayed. What more do you want from the Masters? Watch out! Evil tricks threaten us. If the German people [American film comedy and drama] should one day decay under false, foreign rule, soon no prince will understand his people and foreign mist with foreign vanity will take root in German land and none will know what German is and was.

Of course, even this laborious version of Hans Sach's warning sounds marvelous within Wagner's gorgeous music. May some equivalent of that float over the Hollywood negotiating tables so that a few hundred million Americans can continue to make a stab at understanding at least melodramatic and farcical versions of ourselves and so that Oren Ashkenazi can continue to process his two thousand garments every night.

A commentator on my last blog suggested that it was time to shut this blog down. I took to the suggestion, thinking that I was being too self-indulgent, letting these blogs go in every which direction, expressions of a fickle and perhaps unstable mentality. But this then is what they are, unpaid snippets of a long life that includes sixty years of writing in a semi-professional (unpaid articles and stories for literary magazines) and then professional way.

I was thinking about this as I drove north for my granddaughter's second birthday and heard the news of Norman Mailer's death in the hospital where, twenty-nine years earlier, my mother died. It made me think of her astonished fury when she saw the angry little hole his cigarette made on her precious coffee table. He and I had been talking, perhaps drinking a little, and, in Norman's case, obliviously and carelessly. It was in the semi-relaxed, semi-intense mode which is once recorded in the piece which he named "Hip, Hell and the Navigator," and included in the book *Advertisements for Myself,* reprinted in at least one anthology and talked about every now and then as his favorite interview. Apparently Lionel Trilling has either hailed or mocked it as a piece of extraordinary theology, which back in the late fifties would have gratified Norman enormously. He was not at the top of the wave. The two novels which followed *The Naked and the Dead, The Deer Park* and *Barbary Shore,* had been poorly reviewed, rightly so, except that half *The Deer Park* was, I thought, strong and interesting. That came up in the interview. I thought that his writing a preface to the dramatic version of the novel which said that its setting was actually Hell was a pretty inexpensive way of recharging the exhausted story. I can't remember if that initiated the switch from the discussion of Hip and its meaning for a writer to theology, but it was Norman's sudden, epiphanic insight that God, like Norman himself, was involved in a great struggle, and that much of what puzzled, dismayed and tormented his creatures could be traced to this which was to so please Norman later when he readied the interview for publication, first in the *Western Review* and then in the book which was to once again turn him into what mattered so much to him, the great literary challenger of the given, the obvious, the status quo ante Norman.

His competitiveness was well-known. Since I was a friend of Saul

Bellow, he usually asked me what Bellow was about. I'd told him about *Henderson the Rain King,* which I'd just read in manuscript. "Guess that makes him Number One," he said, reflectively, sadly. I remember that this was said from the wheel of his car. Out each of the rear windows stuck the head of a black pointer, striking, if contradictory turn signals. Such an odd, innocent picture; and so odd and innocent a driver.

Yes, this greatly talented man, who could tell you where the grocer bought his suits and what radio programs he listened to, who knew why the Cape Canaveral launchings brought out every tinkerer within five hundred miles, who knew why Jack Kennedy's hauling his injured shipmate to safety as he did (teeth gripped on the man's belt) revealed his ferocity, this brilliant reporter of the world's stuff, had a depth of innocence which he'd grown to dislike almost as much as he disliked and disowned the handsome Jewish boy swaddled in his herringbone suit on the back cover of *The Naked and the Dead.* "I never looked like that," he told me. In his eyes, he never did. As he disowned that boy, so he poured Nietszchean and other highfalutin' glop over the brilliant worldly reports of prize fights and movie stars, political conventions and the space program, burying his reportorial gift under Zarathustrian rubble.

A few times between his trips to where we summered in Twin Lakes, Connecticut, I drove down to the house where he and his beautiful wife, Adele Morales, lived in the dull countryside of southern Connecticut. The town's other literary light was Van Wyck Brooks; I don't think they'd met. There one would be coaxed into an old cedar orgone box to smoke marijuana or into an improvised ring where crouching, gesturing Norman would spar with you, his face menacingly innocent, his punches making little breezes by your ear.

When he stabbed Adele in the breast and was put into Bellevue, I wrote him that I'd testify to his sanity or essential benevolence and got back a touching penciled letter of gratitude and semi-contrition.

The few times I've seen him in the last twenty years, he was in official positions (president of PEN) or at the annual luncheon of the American Academy of Arts and Letters. His gray hair was waved, his blue eyes were genial under agitated eyebrows, he was beautifully dressed and looked more like a banker than many at Davos. I'd become more and more the quiet burgher, Norman more and more the contrarian, often brilliant commentator and manufacturer of books which I think much of him knew were not the marvelous novels he wished to write. When the excellent book on Gary Gilmore received the National Book Award for Fiction, I wrote him (and the *Times*) that it was so carefully and deliberately a documentary work that it should have received the award for non-fiction. He wrote a good letter of partial agreement, but Jim Atlas, then working for the *Times,* felt the letters were somehow "self-serving," and they weren't published. The *New York Review of Books* did publish a comic exchange between us about what Norman had said or didn't say to an elevator operator after he'd finished talking at a Modern Languages Association meeting in Chicago. The dispute, genial as it was, saddened me as I drove north now on the Outer Drive, for it indicated the distance which had come between this decent, fascinating man and me which of course now would never be spanned.

Post 65

November 22, 2007

Amadou Cisse, a quiet, intelligent twenty-nine-year-old Senegalese man, recently finished the requirements for his doctorate in chemistry and was to receive his diploma in a few days at Rockefeller Chapel at the University of Chicago. "You'll have to call me 'Doctor' now," he told his younger brother Alioune, for whose wedding last summer he made his last trip back home. Professor Steven Sibener said he was proud of him and had the emptied bottle of champagne in Amadou's honor up on the shelf with those of his other successful doctoral students. On Monday, November 20, about 1:30 A.M., Cisse walked home from what might have been a congratulatory party. Not far from his home on one of the darker streets just beyond the university neighborhood, another young man got out of a car and shot him fatally in the chest. Neither his wallet nor his books were taken. The killer sprang back into his two-colored car and drove off.

As a toddler, Amadou lost his father fighting in a war with Gambia. His mother, a nurse, raised him, Alioune, and sister Ndeye in a quiet section of Dakar. At sixteen, Amadou won a World Federation scholarship to study in the Sangre de Cristo mountains in New Mexico. This was followed by a scholarship to Bates College in Maine and then another to the doctoral program at Chicago. He was one of the outstanding Senegalese students of his generation.

While family gathered in hot Dakar and a Senegalese expat community plus some of the bereft students Amadou had generously tutored gathered in chill Chicago, Alioune spoke to a *Chicago Tribune* reporter about Amadou. "He sent me a check every month so that I could pursue my own studies at the U. of Toulouse without continuing to work at a gas station. The checks were never late." He said that his brother wanted to reform Senegal, wanted to run for office, even the presidency. He was, he added, "very intelligent."

The day's *NY Times* reports that the streets of Dakar are swarming with street hawkers whom the country's old president wants to ban from doing what they've been doing from time immemorial. I don't remember seeing them on my one day in Dakar in mid-February 1981. En route from Casablanca to Freetown, we stopped overnight in the Senegalese capital, taken a cab downtown to the Place d'Independence, then walked around dark streets, ducking into a *boulangerie* here, a café there, then taking a bus back to our hotel. It was a forty-minute ride, the bus was crowded, we were the only "Europeans" aboard, a distinction that earned us rapid looks of amiable curiosity. My slight nervousness dissolved in a minute, I remember feeling secure, part of a human fellowship which was expressed in alerting us to our stop and pointing us through the darkness to our hotel.

According to Alioune, Amadou felt the same sort of fellowship in Chicago. He thought it a beautiful, wonderful city. As for his thoughts in the last seconds of his life, we can only speculate. Did he see a face that in some ways was like his own except for the hatred, fear and fury pouring from it? Had he been asked for money and refused to give it, or was this a territorial confrontation, Amadou on a street claimed by the shooter and his gang peers, a version of what Amadou's father had suffered a quarter of a century ago on the soil of Gambia? Or was it a version of the envy, frustration and mad hunger for celebrity which, forty-four years ago today in Dallas, saw the extinction of another young man of great achievement and promise?

Whatever, the diabolism of the human narrative had surfaced again, and one of the world's most valuable beings rich in learning, generosity, goodness and ambition was snuffed out for nothing by a few cents worth of lead expelled from a thirty-dollar handgun.[14]

Post 66
December 28, 2007

Yesterday morning, en route to the hospital to have a blood sample taken for analysis, I heard on the radio that Benazir Bhutto had been shot and blown up along with about twenty of her followers and the suicide bomber, "a thin young man on a motorbike."

Pervez Musharraf griped a couple of weeks ago that Western support for Mrs. Bhutto had to do with her beautiful English and the fact that "she is very good-looking." Mrs. Bhutto's articulate intelligence, beauty and fine, strong manner surely increased the admiration and even devotion my wife and I had for her as she handled fluently and frankly the questions of the excellent *Lehrer News Hour* interviewer Margaret Warner; Warner's second interview with her ended with the two intelligent fifty-year-old women clearly admiring and liking each other.

I don't know what kind of life Margaret Warner has led, but it is almost surely much less dramatic than Bhutto's. Whose life wouldn't be? The first woman leader of a Moslem country (in 1988 when she was thirty-five), Mrs. Bhutto was accused of and dismissed for corruption; she ran and won a second time in 1993, was again accused and dismissed. Apparently, opposition to her came not only from Moslem traditionalists but from the Punjab elite and land-owning "feudals" she accused of being the "destabilizers" of Pakistan.

---

14. Compare the "short happy life" of Amadou Cisse with those of the boys described in Andrea Elliott's remarkable piece "Where Boys Grow to Be Jihadis," in the November 25, 2007, Sunday *NY Times Magazine*. The proto-jihadis remind me more of the Beverly Hills idlers in Brett Easton Ellis' *Less Than Zero* than of, say, St Francis of Assisi, another well-to-do young convert to abnegation and devotion, if not martyrdom. From drug-peddling hooligans to reborn devotees, the proto-jihadis were schooled by imams, peers and inflamed interpretations of world politics. Amadou's actual murderers were Chicago teenagers led by one Eric Walker, age sixteen, the age when Amadou received his scholarship from the World Federation. Eric told the police he needed money so borrowed an old Pontiac from a neighbor, collected a gang and went out for a spree, targeting U. of Chicago students. Their first victim got away; from the second, they collected one dollar and credit cards; from the third, a wallet; from the fourth, a pen. The fifth, Cisse, had no money and was shot dead. Walker, like Amadou, lost his father when a toddler, but unlike him, he collected not scholarships but a record: drug possession and possession of a stolen motor vehicle. He will be tried as an adult. As of November 29, the actual trigger puller of the murder weapon has not been named.

Mrs. Bhutto was no stranger to bloody violence and prison life; her father was executed by the state he served as prime minister; two of her brothers were killed under suspicious circumstances. Azif Zardari, the man Mrs. Bhutto married twenty years ago, the father of her three children, has been accused of corruption, exonerated by Pakistan's auditor general, accused again and jailed for years. The accusations involve receiving commissions from such firms as France's Dassault Aviation for getting Pakistani contracts. There are also accusations of gold smuggling. The Swiss and Polish governments have supposedly sent documents to Pakistani prosecutors which include the incrimination of Mrs. Bhutto. Her recent return to Pakistan, first as a possible collaborator with Musharraf, then as his chief opponent in the January 8 election, involved exoneration from such charges. I myself don't know if the indictments are part of Pakistan's political volatility or of Zardari and Mrs. Bhutto's criminal greed.

How often did Mrs. Bhutto looked back longingly at the learning years of her life? After early schooling in Pakistan, she came to Harvard in 1969 and graduated four years later cum laude and Phi Beta Kappa. She then went to Lady Margaret Hall, Oxford, for four years of philosophy, politics and economics. There she was elected the first woman president of the Oxford Union. Perhaps such *Lehrjahre* sharpened the ambition to succeed and redeem her father and to become one of the great women of Islam. Whether she proved to be a good, mediocre or terrible public servant (there are informed opinions behind each claim), whether she did enough for women and women's rights—an early plank in her platform, whether she weakened the power of the country's elites, I don't know. It was apparently enough to buoy her popularity as head of the Pakistan People's Party, the country's largest. She did not, apparently, see herself as a martyr. She told the interviewer Ann Curry that she wanted to live, that like her father who told her the day before his death that he would never see his grandchildren, she wanted to see hers, but before that, she felt that it was her duty to save her country. For that, she had the courage to face the dangers she knew well.

Courage led her to the Rawalpindi rally and then to the AK-47 bullets fired by the "thin man on a motorcycle" when she raised her head from the limousine carrying her away from it yesterday. She died with her political boots on, in the full spin of impassioned politics.

Two days earlier, my wife and I watched a smaller saga of violence, scooped by CNN from one of its boiling cauldrons, Baghdad. Three masked men spotted a sturdy, jolly five-year-old boy, Yousouf, playing outside his home. They poured gasoline over him and ignited it. The rest of the program involved the almost miraculous salvation of the boy, his father risking his life to reach the CNN offices in Baghdad, and making a broadcast of Yousouf's fate (not excluding close looks at his horribly burnt face). The broadcast raised enough money to bring the family to California where a wonderful cosmetic surgeon, Percy Grossman, began the many operations which will make Yousouf look more or less like other boys his age.

What my mind cannot digest is the minds of the three masked men as they did what they did to this little boy and as they are today. I can usually imagine myself doing very bad and even good things which I've not come close to actually doing. My professional work has involved putting myself into different situations and imagining them as seen by different sorts of people. However, the actions of these three men I cannot imagine. Horrors go on every single minute on this planet. We all know the names of today's central stations of cruelty, Sri Lanka, Darfur, Iraq, we read daily of horrors erupting there and almost everywhere else on earth. I can imagine most of them. I can imagine the mind of the "thin man on the motorbike" who killed Benazir Bhutto, but the minds of Yousouf's incinerators pass beyond me. Is Yousouf but a footnote in their fierce mental history? Do they even remember the seconds it took to douse him with gasoline, to light the match and fire it up? I have no idea.

Post 67

January 11, 2008

Nicholas Schmidle's excellent article "Next-Gen Taliban," in the January 6 Sunday Magazine Section of the *NY Times,*[15] revealed what one should have known or guessed, that the Pakistan jihadi movement is far from homogenous but is instead a flux of more or less radical groups, the younger ones believing that the suicide bomber is the answer to the B-52 bomber. After reading Schmidle's piece, the most anti-Musharraf Westerner will more than likely feel some sympathy with his effort to control this flux while at least mimicking adherence to a democratic

---

15. Two days after the article was published, Pakistan expelled Schmidle.

Pakistan. The average literate Westerner during the Vietnam War became at least superficially acquainted with the geography, demography and history of what had before been a blank or perhaps a colorful fuzz in his mental world; so now Islam, its varied practitioners, devotees and lethally fanatic adherents, are part of our preoccupation and study. Even if the destruction of the World Trade Center six and a quarter years ago is no longer part of our daily fears and nightly terrors, most of us feel that our own lives are to greater or lesser degree affected by the doings and beliefs of Rehman, the Ghazi brothers, Fazlullah and the others named in Schmidle's piece, perhaps not as significantly as what's happening in India and China or even London and Paris, but nonetheless to such a degree that we are obliged to learn something about them.

Yesterday afternoon, I listened to the charming director Peter Sellars rant about his—to me—detestable notion that the operas, plays and oratorios he stages are made vivid and important by their relevance to the problems with which front pages and presidential candidates daily bombard us. That evening, after the television news, I dove back into the world of *Framley Park,* Anthony Trollope's 150-year-old novel about the gentry, clergy, ladies and politics of that time, not for one moment thinking of George Bush, the Taliban, Tony Blair, Iraq or the current presidential campaigners. I was far away from them in a world where I cared about Mark Robarts' financial stupidity and Lady Lufton's attempted recruitment of the almost madly upright, impoverished pastor, Reverend Mr. Crawley. These "characters" were nearer to me than Rehman, Musharraf or the now dead Ghazi brothers, and I cared about what happened to them as much as I cared about what happened to Barack Obama, Hillary Clinton, Fred Thompson and Mitt Romney (fascinating in their way). I understood how Trollope's work helps form our interpretation of such "political" events as Hillary Clinton's almost-tears and the almost-disappearance of the five military-aged civilian sons of the war partisan Romney, but I refused to do what Sellars apparently wanted his audiences to do, feel the contemporary relevance of Trollope's novel as he believed the audiences of his productions of Euripedes' *Herakles* and *The Marriage of Figaro* did. Since Sellars compares athletes to artists, I wonder if he wanted us to think of Iraq and George Bush when a USC back crashed into an Illini linesman or of the Ghazi brothers in the Red Mosque when Mike Tyson chewed off Evander Holyfield's ear.

What relief that a few brilliant craftsman (including Sellars) create marvelous edifices in which millions through centuries can shelter themselves from the bombardments of the new generation of Taliban and the tedious speeches of those wanting to direct the world from the Oval Office.

Post 68

January 21, 2008

The last forty-eight hours of the Australian Open have seen some terrific matches, champions eliminated, champions pushed to the brink of elimination, marvelous players battling for almost five hours, winning and losing by inches here or there. These great athletes, trained for years to deal with the exhausting ups and down of tennis matches (there are always "faults" and lost points, almost always lost games and lost sets), deal with victory and defeat with the gallant, professional decorum of Arthurian knights.

Meanwhile, the country is overrun by other professionals who are battling day after day, night after night, their physical exertions every bit as intense and even more protracted than those of the tennis professionals. They are older, their physical gifts seem ordinary, and yet their ability to talk for hours and hours, to smile and smile and smile, to answer questions of every sort, to fly hundreds of miles every day, to guard with fanatic care every word that comes out of their mouths and every gesture they make, and to do this for week after week, month after month, convinces you that they have extra supplies of whatever humans need to endure things like five-set tennis matches under hot suns.

Though these political athletes confront each other directly only in rare and supervised "debates," they are clearly in the battle of their lives for rewards of power and historical celebrity that have tempted the human species as long as it has been human.

Which class of human beings gives us more pleasure? For me, the answer is easy. Even though most of the political athletes are knowledgeable, agreeable people of more than average intellectual power, they become for me some of the most boring human beings I've ever encountered, whereas the tennis athletes engage in matches which often see me almost as absorbed and sometimes as tense as they are. Both sorts of athletes are performing a small variety of actions, repeating them over and over with but the smallest variation, yet such is the nature of their respective professions, that the brevity and small space of the tennis athletes build toward climax as works of art do, whereas the scale of the presidential campaign, despite the individual contests which punctuate it, disperses and adulterates one's interest. The context of low-grade, repetitive punditry which envelops the political doings blunts and even destroys most of the intellectual interest in what happens. Unless one is an impassioned partisan, one's interest not only flags but turns one away from what one knows are significant contests.

Clinton, Edwards, Thompson, Giuliani, McCain, Obama, Romney, Huckabee, Biden, Dodd and Paul are distinct individuals whom one recognizes and whose backgrounds and views one knows. Why is it that after months of differentiating them, they blend into two barely distinctive potions of tedium who serve to lower the importance of the worldly difficulties whose solutions they offer?

And how one sickens of the pronoun "I" and the recital of the steadiness, prescience, legislative and executive accomplishment which even the most modest "I" cannot stop trumpeting? A tennis fan compares interviews with tennis players and imagines what he'd think of them if they spoke of themselves as the politicians do. It might be said, "They're not running for office," but they too want to be liked and admired. Can't the politicians learn from them about modesty, praise for one's opponents, temperate assessments of the problems ahead, humorous, self-deprecating accounts of old battles?

Even so devoted a tennis fan as I can tire of the game (I did back in 1992 when I "covered" Wimbledon for the *Chicago Tribune*), but this fatigue isn't permanent, and though I often turn off a match which is too one-sided, I'm far from renouncing the game and believe that I will watch matches with pleasure on my deathbed.

Whereas the campaign and the campaigners who are engaged in what will surely affect my income, my fears, my feelings about my country and the world tend to estrange me from them as, in the grooves of their ambition, they seem to estrange themselves from those noble elements which launched their political lives.

Post 69
January 27, 2008
I know what's happened to my feelings about Bill Clinton, so I assume that the same change has taken place in others.

I've been a fan of Clinton's since his first presidential campaign, I voted for him twice and felt for him deeply when the congressional lynch mob Clarence Thomas took unto himself ganged up to throw him out of office. In one of Philip Roth's novels there are pages about the sanctimony and hypocrisy of those days; a former student of ours (Roth's and mine), a young writer named Isabel Cole, wrote me from Berlin, "Why are Americans surprised that they voted a man into office?" The louder the sanctimonious racket, the angrier I got about the smirking virtue-sellers who raised it. I found the "Depends on what 'is' means" testimony an exhibition of strength and courage unique in presidential annals and delighted in the great public's forgiveness and "None of our business" response to the congressional and journalistic hypocrites. I enjoyed the subsequent years of Clinton's popularity, relished the quiet intelligence as he, say, gave a brilliant *tour d'horizon* of world affairs or refreshed debate by giving down-to-earth translations of difficult economic or political problems.

Now in the winter of 2008, Clinton's speeches for his wife and against Barack Obama have infuriated me. They have the simplistic, insinuatingly suggestive stupidity he used to counter. They are devious in the way his accusers accused him of being. They are mean-spirited in an "I-don't-give-a-damn-about-anything-else" mode, "anything else" standing for the Democratic Party and whoever becomes its candidate. He black-baits as if an older, meaner Arkansas voice were let loose in him; he distorts Obama's remarks about Republicans and Reagan as if he were the liar the impeachment-mad Republicans claimed he was.

What the psychological explanation is, I don't know. Some have suggested that he's making up to Hillary for his liaisons with Monica Lewinsky et al. Some say he's trying to sink Hillary's candidacy because he can't bear the public displays of marital solidarity he goes through on every platform on which they both stand, or because, for many years, he's disliked her forcefulness, detailed knowledge and Clintonesque grasp of matters small and large.

I don't know and don't care about his motives. All I know is that the charming, decent, empathetic, learned, hard-working, sincere human being I once thought so wonderful, is now covered with the marble dust of the statue he himself has been daily demolishing.

A fine piece about Iraq by George Packer in the Winter 2008 issue of
World Affairs concludes:

> The war began as folly; it became a tragedy when the hopes and
> lives of Iraqis and Americans began to be expended by the thou-
> sands.
>
> "I can never blame the Americans alone," an Iraqi refugee
> named Firas told me in early 2007. "It's the Iraqis who destroyed
> their country, with the help of the Americans, under the American
> eye." To gain this wisdom, Firas had to lose almost everything.
> What would it take for Americans to understand what Firas al-
> ready does? A recognition that Iraq was everyone's loss, whichever
> side you were on.

Beginnings are difficult to make out (When did the American Civil
War actually begin?), conclusions are even more complex (From the
Gettysburg Address through *Gone With the Wind,* discuss the significance and effects of the American Civil War), but human life consists in
some degree of the decisions about what has happened to and around
oneself. To someone like myself, who finds himself surprisingly but un-
mistakably on the brink of his eightieth birthday, the pressure of such
assessment is a tragic-comic fact.

The after effects of WWI, the Depression and FDR, WWII, Hiroshima, Korea, prosperity, the discovery of Europe and one's academic and family life, Vietnam and Watergate, world travels and one's
book-writing, the coming of age, grandparenthood, Iraq, the 2008 presidency and now the endgame is a barebones summary of a life. Day by
day, though, one lives, somewhat less mobile, less ambitious, if not resigned, at least more at peace about one's limited if fairly straightforward existence, although aware of the weakness, foolishness and inade-
quacy which soils too much of it. Old age is, as I think L. P. Hartley
wrote fifty-odd years ago, another country. Most of one's relatives,
friends and colleagues have died. One knows that one won't see much
of what happens to one's grandchildren or younger friends. The world,
one believes, will be essentially the same, and perhaps some of what one
has done will affect a few people in ten, fifty or even a hundred years.
(This isn't a preoccupation or an ambition.)

In the last few days, one has heard from a graduate school acquaintance, not heard from in decades. He has read something one wrote forty years ago and reports on it and on his own troubled retirement. In the mail yesterday, the manuscript of a beautiful short story by a close friend who has for five months been suffering the first writer's block of his life, about an actor who can no longer act, who has an affair with the lesbian daughter of old friends, converting her for a while into a heterosexual woman. He resumes his successful acting life, but after the young woman resumes her lesbian life, he lapses into the suicidal state he hasn't managed to complete and completes it. Over the weekend, a good friend reports on the latest condition of her fine daughter, who is the victim of Obsessive Compulsive Disorder, and on the decision of her ex-husband, the girl's father, to move from Chicago to Harvard, where his new companion is a brilliant reporter of and fighter against genocide. Yesterday, on the coldest day of Chicago's worst winter in twenty years, I went to see the dermatologist about the auto-immune condition which has troubled me for three years. It is, I think, my fifth column. Annoying as it is and weak as the medication taken for it has made me, I consider myself lucky to have in eighty years escaped lethal diseases and deaths or awful injuries to my children and grandchildren, and to be more or less independent financially and—with the help of a wonderful wife—physically and emotionally.

I write this post as a sort of birthday announcement to the few sympathetic and the fewer, I believe, unsympathetic readers of the Open University blog which has in this last part of a fifty-five-year literary career given me another outlet. Unlike Packer's version of the Iraq War as everyone's loss, my narrow view is able to think of my eighty mostly uncelebrated years as a gain for me and in a very small way for most of those who've been part of them.

Post 71

February 28, 2008

Of the trillion words written and spoken by William Buckley, I was the recipient of but one, "Delicious," which accompanied a check for two hundred dollars, payment for the only piece I published in the *National Review* (where from 1960 some of my books had been generously reviewed by the likes of then twenty-three-year-old Joan Didion and the brilliant classicist, critic and caricaturist Guy Davenport). My view of

Buckley himself had been tempered by humane snippets garnered from our common friend, Hugh Kenner. I never took to Buckley's preachments or his self-relishing wit. The eruptive flash of his tooth-bright smile was to me like chalk on a blackboard. As far as conservative thinking went, I was, after all, on the same campus as Milton Friedman, Leo Strauss (the influences on Willmore Kendall, Buckley's Yale guru) and Richard Weaver (whose famous course in Expository Writing I took over with his amiable help), had read Russell Kirk, James Burnham and other popular conservatives and periodically questioned graduate students about Edmond Burke, Dr. Johnson and other great conservative writers. Nonetheless, Buckley's death removes another familiar piece of my world and is mourned as the Margaret in Hopkins' famous poem mourns the "goldenrod unleaving": "It is Margaret you mourn for."

I'd just finished reading Emile Zola's marvelous novel *Pot-Bouille* (1882), translated a century ago under the odd title *Restless House*. (The French means something like "Stewpot.") The book charts the two years of young Octave Mouret's stay in a "most respectable" Parisian apartment house. With systematic power and extraordinary mimicry, Zola strips, floor by floor, family by family, every ounce of respectability from every tenant. Avarice, snobbery, shabby vanity, brutality, cruelty, unbridled, pleasureless lust, impotence, unfeelingness, mendacity and what-have-you are scarcely veiled by social and religious genuflections and proclamations. The hypocritical tenants bully, connive, cheat, lie and struggle to death's door in intramural ferocity. The novel ends in one of the famous scenes of world literature, the self-delivery of her baby by the semi-imbecilic maid of the Josserand family, Adele, who, after managing to cut the umbilical cord and resting for an hour in the bloody birth mess, struggles down to the trash cans where she deposits the baby. Surrounded by the tenants' high-minded denunciation of a recent plague of infanticide, Adele fears imprisonment. The book ends with this murder and with a final shower of self-boosting assertion, of domestic, civic, political and religious virtue.

The book is dated by one of the tenants' denunciation of Renan ("He should be burned at the stake") and his just published *Life of Jesus* (1863). This is two years after Octave moved into the veneer-thin splendor of the apartment house and just after he has married the beautiful, unfeeling widow who runs the small department store which she and Octave will transform into the Printemps-like grandeur of *Au Bonheur des Dames,* title and setting of a later volume in the twenty-volume Rougon-Macquart series, Zola's depiction of the rise and fall of genetically determined members of the two families and their society.

Sixteen years after *Pot-Bouille,* Zola would publish (in Clemenceau's newspaper) *J'accuse,* his famous denunciation of the French government's indictment and imprisonment of the Jewish officer Alfred Dreyfus. The subsequent uproar forced Zola to flee to England and perhaps, in 1902, back in France, led to what might have been the murderous, at any rate lethal blocking of the furnace which asphyxiated him.

Compared to Zola's depiction-creation of the social, political, economic, moral and spiritual horror of nineteenth-century France, Buckley's account of the America of 1950 to the hour of his death this week is that of a squeaky wheel compared to the B-minor Mass.

Post 72
March 5, 2008

Why Hillary Drops Her Final "G"s

Why isn't it noticed, or, if noticed, not commented upon? At least in her Ohio and Texas talks, Hillary Clinton drops the final "g" from the "-ing" words (participles, gerunds), an annoyance, especially to those who've heard her talking to other people and groups where not one "g" is dropped and she sounds like the young woman who gave a famous Wellesley College commencement address, was one of America's one hundred most successful lawyers, was first lady of Arkansas and the United States and has been a successful U.S. senator from New York State for eight years.

Of course, it's clear that Hillary wants to sound more like the audience of "ordinary" people she's pumpin' for votes. Most of us act and talk differently with the grocer than our colleagues, but it's unusual for politicians to be so conspicuously different as Hillary is before audiences. Changing your political position is considered a no-no for politicians; Hillary been fairly successful explaining such changes. The g-dropping, though, points to something else in this amazingly successful woman's life. It recalls the fuss made out of her changes of hairdo in her first lady years, her marital juggling in the Hillary-humiliation time of Monica Lewinsky. (By the way, how is it that no comedian has suggested that the now famous 3:00 A.M. phone call to the White House came from Monica?) Many women who know that they don don other selves in front of their husband's colleagues, hunting and poker buddies understand and sympathize with Hillary's adaptations and alterations.

Those who have seen Hillary on *Saturday Night Live* or heard her mocking version of Obama's speeches see that she has histrionic gifts. ("Give her an 'A' for presentation," was Obama's response to the mockery.) More women than men will understand and sympathize with what lies behind Hillary's accommodations and acting, behind the dropped "g"s and the changed hairdos. Many—most?—men will be annoyed by them, and by the shift from straight talk to strident proclamation ("I'm a fighter"; "I've been tested"; I know, I've seen, I've been, I've done, I-I-I-I-I-I).

La donna e mobile was the seducer duke's lyric justification for his own mobility; *cosi fan tutte* is the not-so-long-outmoded Mozart–Da Ponte view of women Many—most?—women, with and without university degrees, have personally endured it.

When did it start for Hillary Diana Rodham? Was it when she began undercutting her father's Republican shibboleths? Did her ninety-two-page B.A. thesis on Saul Alinsky embody the early changes, masked there by a "nuanced" academic style?

Five years she kept the courting Bill Clinton on her string, deciding to marry him (after, not necessarily because) she'd failed the Washington, DC, bar exam and passed the Arkansas one.

That this woman, distinguished as remarkably able since her twentieth year—and by no one more than the husband who in Little Rock and Washington appointed her to important roles and who now campaigns for her—feels that she has to jump through the hoops of dropping "g"s arouses more pity than disgust.

Post 73
March 30, 2008

The three weeks since the last blog have been more significant for the blogger than his readers. He slipped into the counter-world of illness, curled into chills and fever, sleeping and dozing, not eating, scarcely moving. After a week of this, twenty pounds lighter, weak as wet string, the powers of recovery began taking over via the wonderful wife, the family members (those too young to understand Grandpa's condition having the most therapeutic power), the generous (Medicare-covered) outreach of modern medicine—a personal strength trainer, a 280-pound neckless oblong of command—"Hokay. Next hexercize"—a dear, ancient nurse who drew from a cracked cowhide satchel the apparatus of vital signs and a computer to register them, the email counsel of first-rate doctors and the drugs, selected edibles and routines they advised.

A friend called, shocked at turning seventy-five—"How did I get here?"—and we talked about the death of a publisher, Aaron Asher, one of the last true men-of-letters publishers, who published us and Saul Bellow and Lyndon Johnson's memoirs. Aaron had stories of the late president driving him on the ranch, slowing only for Secret Service men to refill his glass of bourbon, of Lady Bird serving him first at dinner, their discovery that day of the My Lai massacre and checking their files (Aaron: "Did they have an entry for Massacres?"). We talked of his new (unreleased) book and about the late work of authors, the diminished energy for length, the ways of reconfecting familiar material, then our reading—he was relishing Thomas Mann's great stories, his favorites "Mario and the Magician" and "Disorder and Early Sorrow," throwing in with habitual generosity, "You and he are among the few who write with tenderness about the family," and much more, the warm talk of old friends, tonic consolation, nostalgic enrichment.

Then too, there were the music, newspapers, magazines, books, television series (the amazing *The Wire*) and Netflix (the wonderful installments of Michael Apted's peerless series which films a dozen English people every seven years), indeed much that has composed so large a part of especially recent life.

As for the great world, how much has it changed in these three weeks? Clearly Iraq is reboiling with tribal and criminal ferocity perhaps triggered by the American Surge. Cafés and bookstores which were open, markets to which one could send one's children for bread and fruit, are again stages of murder. The other festering spots of the world fester as ever.

On the intensely lit American stage, the political candidates perform along the lines of their complex characters, Hillary Clinton, gripping furiously to what her years of battles and triumphs seem to entitle her, fabricates, dodges, advocates, defends, charms, antagonizes, attacks; Barack Obama generally becomes more complex and straighter as he keeps uncovering what keeps his amazing presidential drive going; John McCain gives occasional glimpses of what sustained his reputation as an independent thinker and doer, while around all three of them, the dramatis personae form, part of the national Oberammergau, Kerrys, Richardsons, Liebermans, Caseys, Ferrarros, Carvilles, sense, nonsense and hyperbole pouring from them sufficiently to keep the commentary world in motion.

It is good to be back.

Post 74
April 14, 2008

Real heroes seldom look like their predecessors or textbook models. Ben Shalom Bernanke reminds me of Lewis Carroll's Dormouse. Small, bald, pepper-and-salt bearded, his voice repressed toward monotone, this ex-student of the Talmud, son of a Dillon, SC, pharmacist and a schoolteacher, taught himself calculus, got the highest SAT scores in his state, worked as a waiter to help put himself through his Harvard summa cum laude B.A. and, according to a friend of mine who knows him, endured and clearly overcame serious personal phobic crises. Out of this human swirl emerged a Roland, a Galahad, an El Cid who under enormous pressure led to the making of a decision that may well have saved the world economy plunging into a black hole. Through light and dark hours, estimating the consequences of not acting or acting poorly, gathering with other dedicated guardians of the economy, he helped work out the decision to keep Bear Stearns from the collapse whose blasted filaments would almost surely have brought on economic catastrophe. To hear him on April 2 and 3 responding to the well-informed, often belligerent, often self-serving "inquiries" of congressmen, one saw the epitome of thoughtful, forceful, knowledgeable reason. Here we had the true civil servant at his best, a model, as far as I'm concerned, of the person who under pressure makes crucial decisions.

As I listen with familiar but renewed joy to a fine pianist (Cecile Licad) play Chopin's G-minor Ballade (Opus 23), some of the human strength which has been drained these last weeks from my old body flowed in, and I felt the luck of being left with the genial inventions and creations of human genius. In his way, little Ben Bernanke was helping create the conditions out of which such creations and inventions come.

I'd been having trouble finding something truly engaging to read, but three days ago, I dropped the new book that hadn't drawn me in and took up two old favorites, the prose of George Orwell and the stories of W. S. Maugham. I read Orwell on Mark Twain as a "licensed jester," his portion of Voltairean disgust and outrage muted by his enchantment with success and by the prudential decorum of his wife, his brilliance surviving largely in his portraits of an age otherwise irrecoverable. A harsher judgment than my own but as always in Orwell, one felt that a fine, independent intelligence has made one that had to be considered. Then Maugham: two stories of the far east, "A Vessal of Wrath" and "Flotsam and Jetsam." The exactitude and surprise of observations, the unexpected, piquant detail and the powerful underplayed feeling for the happy, Dutch hedonist who runs the Malaysian colony or against the hate-charged, failing rubber plantation whose hating couple welcome the malaria-struck white man who's carried into their home took me thousands of miles and hours away from the markets Bernanke and company had saved, and I could hardly wait to see what would happen to the puritanical evangelist who brings the dissolute Ginger Ted to the malaria-struck island terrified that he will rape her or what had driven the couple in the other house to remain together despite the hatred which colored every inch of the air around them.

But lesser Maugham stories tired me, and I took up *Anna Karenina* and rose into narrative sublimity, just reading here and there about Dolly and her children, Levin working with the peasants, Anna's amazing stream of consciousness as she heads for the railroad station and her suicide. I wish I knew Russian so that I could relish, say, what D. S. Mirsky says about Tolstoy's style (its combination of idiomatic Russian nobleman speech and complex French syntax) but there is enough here for a thousand enchanted readings.

Finally, a film, the amazing *There Will Be Blood,* with a central portrait unmatched by anything I've seen in film including *Citizen Kane,* Daniel Day-Lewis' Daniel Plainview. I haven't read the book on which Paul Anderson's script is based, Upton Sinclair's *Oil,* but I suspect it is an attack on capitalism and religion. The film could be reduced to such "meaning," but that would be like reducing Ben Bernanke into a standard bureaucrat and Tolstoy into another merely excellent writer.

Post 75
April 24, 2008

Nothing like a few days in hospital to refresh—at least revise—one's usual view of the world. The hospital world of repair, renewal, rescue, of injury, illness, the breaking and broken, the sinking and the sunk, is unto itself, connected here and there but essentially cut off from the world of buses, bakeries, borrowing and earning. Its thousand technicians, doctors, interns, nurses, cleaners and transportationers inhabit the bright, immaculate corridors and labs, concentrating on their complex occupations almost in the center of which—the "almost" can become a problem—is oneself. In the tiny den of one's self-manipulable hospital bed—television, lights and sometimes nurses at one's finger—one is visited day and night by technicians who take and retake one's "vital signs," by interns, residents and doctors who tap one's chest, feel one's glands, listen to one's lungs and heart, ask and re-ask questions about one's susceptibilities and habits ("Are you diabetic?" "Do you take any street drugs?") and discuss one's condition and its possible causes and remedies.

No private rooms available, I was curtained away from two successive roommates, men decades younger than I but so assailed by difficulty that I felt like a prince of health. They were diabetics, blind, they beshat themselves and were in diapers, but each was far more alert than the doctors who raised their voices addressing them. They were ironic, funny, skeptical, contemptuous of the attempt to treat them as children or morons.

The first of my two nights, I couldn't sleep. There was every sort of noise, loud-speakered summonses to nurses, television chatter, the intrusions of the pursuers of vital signs. The second night, my doctor prescribed a sleep-inducing drug and I awoke hours later amazed that nighttime had been annihilated. Finally, but two days in, the joy of having the doctors of my two teams (one was the hematologists debating the cause of my anemia) concur in discharging me. I was "transported" in a wheelchair by one of the good-spirited transportationers to the beawninged entrance where my wife waited with the car. And then the oddly unfamiliar but oh-so-welcome world of streets, houses, trees, CTA buses and cars where I've spent most of the last half century.

It was the Monday before the Pennsylvania primary where my brilliant neighbor, Barack Obama, was trashed and trounced by the almost

188

madly driven wife of the great political performer who, but weeks before, had my allegiance, admiration and affection. In my own bed, fed the food I loved, I broke off the endlessly repetitive commentary of MSNBC and watched my beloved Cubs play the kind of baseball which sees them in their division's first place. I then read a few more pages of *War and Peace,* which I was reading in the hospital, more astonished than ever by its fascinating human strands beautifully, magically interwoven. (Daniel Mendelssohn, otherwise writing well about Herodotus in the *New Yorker,* foolishly compares his wildly, uncontrollably restless pages on the rise and fall of Persia to Tolstoy's powerfully, subtly assembled masterpiece.)

Home.

The luck of being home with anything material I could want. Now and then, though, one's heart half-broke watching and hearing stories of thousands being foreclosed and thrown out of theirs or, worse, of hundreds of millions over the planet with nothing to eat, their gorgeous huge-eyed babies wordlessly begging that they might live a few more less tormented days. The insights of Malthus and Darwin are inscribed on the tragic human faces and swollen bodies. Senators Clinton, McCain and Obama, one of whom would soon have the sort of power which might extend, alter and even brighten at least some of these existences, subtly and not so subtly trashed each other and demeaned their otherwise superior selves. "What," the thought came to me, "if Tolstoy were president? How much would that alter the world?" Depends if it's the wise, omniscient, tolerant Tolstoy of the great novels or the preachy whack job of the sex-and—septuagenarian decades. Anyway, the wise Tolstoy couldn't get elected, or, if elected, couldn't rule.

Still, the Cubs and Tolstoy's book eased my easily easable spirit, and I slept without benefit of medication.

Post 76

May 2, 2008

I haven't learned my Iraq lesson yet. I want the U.S. to pluck Robert Mugabe out of his criminal fastness in Zimbabwe and drop him, parachuteless, from forty thousand feet during which he'll have enough seconds to reflect upon the horrors he has inflicted on the country of which he was once a benefactor.

"Do unto others . . ."

If Ian Smith had allowed the jailed Mugabe to attend the funeral of his three-year-old son, who knows how many people, decades later, might have been spared Mugabe-inflicted viciousness. In jail for ten years, schoolteacher Mugabe earned three degrees from the U. of London Extension Division. Soon after he came to power, Zimbabwe's educational system was Africa's best. Child mortality dropped, national prosperity seemed possible. Land owned by six thousand white citizens was expropriated and distributed to blacks, too many of them Mugabe stooges. Do unto others . . . When Cecil Rhodes, who'd given his name to the land which became Zimbabwe, expropriated the land which those settlers eventually owned, was questioned about its propriety, his graceful response was, "I prefer land to niggers."

When drought hit the country, the long-stored hatred in Mugabe burst into what wrecked his country: life expectancy the worst in Africa, inflation at 1000 percent, political opponents jailed and tortured, starvation and chaos in the streets.

Corruptio optimi pessimi. Lilies that fester smell far worse than weeds.

The bespectacled octogenarian with the gleaming wicked head is trying to squirm out of last month's electoral defeat. Soldiers and police are bribed to obey him, the seething populace is waiting for African and world leaders to ratify their choice and expel the monster, but they are molasses slow to act; the United Nations secretariat mutters; the American administration condemns, but as of today, Mugabe reigns.

Post 77

June 7, 2008

Thirty-six hours ago, on our annual trek to our summer residence on Tybee Island, Georgia, my wife and I stopped at a Comfort Inn in Dandridge, Tennessee (the only town named after our founder-president's wife, Martha Dandridge Washington), a few miles west of the Great Smoky mountains. For dinner, we ate very well and very cheaply (for both of us, under thirty dollars including a 30 percent tip) at a Perkins restaurant. Around us were tables full of contented, obese patrons, many of whom left with cartons of leftovers.

A few days before, I'd seen on the *CBS Evening News* a vignette from another small Tennessee town, Dover, on the other side of the state, near Nashville.

This featured the distribution of boxes of free food to hundreds of ordinary-looking, mostly white people of all ages, the boxes handed over by volunteers who looked much like the recipients. Interviewed by a reporter, the latter said that they were both humbled and grateful, but there was also a sense that something was wrong. They were all workers, hard workers; some held two jobs. They'd been overwhelmed by the price of food, gasoline and newly revised mortgage payments. This food distribution was a matter of life and death.

There were two worms in this charitable apple: (1) many applicants were habitually turned away every distribution day and (2) this was the last of the distributions: Tennessee had run out of the funds which purchased the food.

I'd put away my turkey, stuffing, cranberry sauce, hash-brown potato casserole, salad, fresh strawberry pie and coffee, part of my mind on those decent-looking and -talking Tennessee men, women and children hoisting the boxes of free food. I thought, "Is this the Irrawady Delta of Myanmar, the Zimbabwe of the monster Mugabe, the postquake Chinese villages, New Orleans in the days after Katrina? No, this is fat old USA," and though, as we ate, the unemployment rate leaped ahead to 5.5 percent, the price of oil soared another eleven dollars a barrel and the stock market plunged 394 points (the stale participles constitute the tragic basso rilievo of these days), most of my colleagues and friends were doing, as usual, pretty well. Yes, I'd been paying close to four dollars a gallon for our Toyota's fuel, but days earlier I'd received from my few shares of Exxon and Conoco what amounted to half of my first year's salary as an instructor at Connecticut College for Women back in 1954–55 (thirty-five hundred dollars, on which I'd somehow supported four people).

But something is rotten in the state of Tennessee, something seriously wrong in the good old USA.

Now here at Tybee, on the table next to my bed is a fat paperback edition of Adam Smith's *Inquiry into the Nature and Causes of the Wealth of Nations* with a fine introduction by my friend Alan Krueger, the prize-winning Princeton economist. Krueger quotes Smith: "It is but equity . . . that they who feed, clothe and lodge the whole body of the people, should have such a share of their own labour as to be themselves tolerably well-fed, clothed and lodged." And the great champion of the free market's power supplied a sort of solution to the defunded misery of the Dover distribution: "It is not very unreasonable that the rich should contribute to the public expense not only in proportion to their revenue but something more than in that proportion."

My 30 percent tip in Perkins did not suffice. My support of stockholder proposals which the directors (against whom I habitually voted) suggest be voted down did not suffice.

Is the solution above my pay grade, not part of my JD ("job description," as Maria Sharapova explained after her exit from the French Open to crowd boos when reporters asked why she was disliked)? Not really. My puzzlement and anger at the Dover hunger line lead to this blog post and to questions about solutions to its readers, including my economist friends and perhaps my neighbor and one-time colleague Senator Obama: *What can, what should be done about this American misery?*

Post 78
June 19, 2008
The most level-headed, wise and modestly self-assured of George W. Bush's appointees, Robert Gates, has proposed a Rooseveltian enrichment of the already de-Rumsfelded Pentagon, the funding of social scientists and other professional researchers to work on such defense problems as China and Iraq:

> . . . Gates has compared the initiative—named Minerva, after the Roman goddess of wisdom (and warriors)—to the government's effort to pump up its intellectual capital during the cold war after the Soviet Union launched Sputnik in 1957.
>
> Although the Pentagon regularly finances science and engineering research, systematic support for the social sciences and humanities has been rare. Minerva is the first systematic effort in this area since the Vietnam War, said Thomas G. Mahnken, deputy assistant secretary of defense for policy planning, whose office will be overseeing the project.
> —*NY Times,* June 18, 2008

There is mention of humanities scholars, not poets and novelists, a loss. (In *Three Days of the Condor,* the Robert Redford character works for a small CIA outfit that reads such bizarre material in order to pick up out-of-the-box suggestions for unspecified machinations.)

I just finished John Updike's novel *Terrorist,* one of his many recent books which most critics slammed. But Updike may be the wisest of all

American observers, and I trust that Minervans will read—though it won't be necessary to fund—him. The novel is full of acute observations, usually made by characters who haven't passed the politically correct exam. Here, Hermione Fogel, the spinster assistant of a Tom Ridge–like secretary of home security, comments on the new breed of security screeners:

> In a land of multiplying security gates, the gatekeepers multiply also. To the well-paid professionals who traveled the airways and frequented the newly fortified government buildings, it appears that a dusky underclass has been given tyrannical power. Comfortable lives that even a decade ago moved fluently through circuits of privilege and assumed access now encounter sticking points at what seem every step, while maddeningly deliberate guards ponder driving licenses and boarding passes. Where once a confident manner, a correct suit and tie and a business card measuring two by three and a half inches had opened doors, the switch is no longer tripped, the door remains closed. How can the fluid, hydraulically responsive workings of capitalism, let alone the commerce of intellectual exchange and the social life of extended families, function through such obdurate thicknesses of precaution? The enemy has achieved his goal: business and recreation in the West are gummed up: exorbitantly so.

Whether or not this observation will serve Secretary Gates and his Minervan cohorts I don't know, but its free-floating intelligence is the sort of thing which at least limbers up intellectual muscles.

I'm now seventy-five pages into Denis Johnson's NBA-winning novel *Tree of Smoke,* and though one-seventh of the text isn't enough for judgments, it looks as if one of its American war themes seems to be the fluidity of alliance and enmity. (Japan, an enemy in 1945, is an ally today, Russia, an ally in 1945, was an enemy through the Cold War and is now—what?) Not a great insight but in Johnsonian detail, powerful. It might be obliquely covered in a joke from another novel read last week, James Salter's *Light Years:*

> . . . there were two drunks on an elevator . . . A woman got on—she was completely nude. They just stood there and didn't say anything. After she got off, one turned to the other. "You know," he said, "'s funny, my wife has an outfit exactly like that."

The Pentagon Minervans shouldn't ignore jokes, irony, sarcasm, cynicism or wit of any sort. The human enterprise, even in its destructive and diabolic forms, turns just as often on these axes as on the doom-heavy ones Messrs. Bush, Cheney, Petraeus and McCain apparently prefer.

Post 79

July 17, 2008

Ten days ago, I watched "Venus Wimbledon," as her family calls her, defeat her younger sister Serena for her fifth Wimbledon championship. One's pleasure in this, the best of the sisters' matches I've seen, was marred only by the self-gratulatory garrulity of Mary Carillo, whom, year after year, NBC couples with the adolescent stooge Ted Robinson and the informed, surprisingly modest John McEnroe, who, unlike the others, actually stops talking when the players are going about their business.

The day after the sister match, there was a marvelous and moving men's final in which Roger Federer, playing at or near the top of his game, suffered what he said was the worst loss of his life, a five-setter, to Rafael Nadal. The last game was played in semi-darkness, which Federer mentioned as a factor in his loss. Still, the beauty and power of tennis was here—"the best match I've ever seen," said the superlative-lover McEnroe—and put to shame much of the political rot of the planet.

On Bastille Day, the UN condemned the monster who rules Sudan for genocide, a brief eclipse of the monstrosities of Robert Mugabe, the octogenarian who gripped again the reins of the country he's ruled and ruined.

Oddly, there's a stroke of silver in this monster's portrait. A brilliant bit of journalism by the *Washington Post*'s Craig Timberg revealed that the day after Zimbabwe's March 29th election, Mugabe told his circle of cronies that he'd lost and would resign. "No, you won't," was the response of General Constantine Chiwenga, the chief of staff who went on to order the old thug that there would be another election which he would win. Chwenga's fellow usurpers unleashed the one hundred thousand thugs of their Thugarchy. These killed, raped and drove out of the country the opposition. And, sure enough, on June 27th, the old monster was reelected.

All of us who complain about the Zimbabwean misery—including many of those at the recent African conference in Egypt—can't cohere into a fist to smash him. This week, Thomas Friedman wrote of the outrageous cowardice of Vladimir Putin and Thabo Mbeki, whose ambassadors vetoed a Mugabe-punishing resolution at the UN.

Of such irresponsible cowards, Celsus, the powerful and witty critic of Christianity whose work we know because Origen quotes him extensively in *Contra Celsus (m)*, wrote:

> . . . if they will take wives, and bring up children, and taste of the fruits of the earth, and partake of all the blessings of life, and bear its appointed sorrows (for nature herself hath allotted sorrows to all men; for sorrows must exist, and earth is the only place for them), then must they discharge the duties of life until they are released from its bond . . .

Would that the fortitude and civility of Rafa, Roger and the *soeurs* Williams could be installed in those of us with the power and responsibility to counter the monstrosity which disfigures humanity in the actions of Mugabe and his cronies, and Omar al-Bashir and his.

Post 80

July 23, 2008

Now we know why Barack Obama spent so much time in the gym those last days in Chicago before taking off for Afghanistan. He was practicing jump shots, preparing for the sensational twenty-five-footer he sank in the Kabul gym in front of cheering U.S. troops.

All practitioners prepare. Professionals are defined as much by preparation as performance. Great professionals focus on key moments, often "unexpected" occasions and opportunities. The great practitioner takes a longer view than the people around him. The fine, diligent *New Yorker* piece by Ryan Lizza about Obama making his slow, challenged way to political office in and through Chicago shows him learning the ropes and continually abandoning them for other ropes, other learning, other modes of advancement. The same goes for his negotiating with University of Chicago law deans and professors who wanted to recruit this brilliant, attentive young man, one going so far as to tell him after a political defeat that he had no future in politics but might well have a great career in the academy and then perhaps as a public intellectual, a la Judge Richard Posner. Obama accepted an office, a stipend and some lecturing on constitutional law but nurtured his political career, his long view, as he wanted.

Because of the recent Wimbledon tournament, I think of Richard Williams, seeing the money and glory earned by women tennis players, buying a book on the sport in order to learn it and then working thousands of hours with two of his daughters to make them international champions.

These are great triumphs of practice and professionalism. The knowledge of oneself, the people around, contemporary conditions and future possibilities is so great for both these men, one is tempted to use the word "genius" for them.

The basketball shot that Obama made in that gym was photographed and sent around the world. I expect that it will become what is too frequently called "iconic," and will be found in history books or their digital equivalents for a long time.

This week I reread a marvelous book, fifty years old this year. It is the Prince of Lampedusa's only novel, *Il Gattopardo, The Leopard*. It is about the last days of such Sicilian aristocrats as the nineteenth-century prince Don Fabrizio de Salina as Garibaldi's eight hundred red shirts invade the island and tumble the feeble Royalist troops of Fabrizio's helpless acquaintance King Ferdinand. Fabrizio's knowledge of his friends and family, particularly his beloved, impoverished nephew Tancredi, is matched by a remarkable and remarkably articulated sense of his land, Sicily, and its people, particularly such shrewd, bourgeois graspers as Don Calogero Sedara, whose wealth and the mind-boggling beauty of whose daughter will give Tancredi if not a princely life like his uncle's, one as close to it as the new era permits. Shortly after the triumph of the Victor Emmanuele regime which will unite Italy into a single state, a representative of the regime, a wise old Piedmontese aristocrat, Chevalley, is sent to invite Don Fabrizio to become a senator and thus help determine Sicily's future. Don Fabrizio courteously declines the offer and then shares what he knows and feels about Sicily, knowledge and feeling which help explain his refusal.

In Sicily it doesn't matter if things are done well or badly; the sin, which we Sicilians never forgive, is simply that of "doing" at all

. . . Sleep, my dear Chevalley, sleep, that is what Sicilians want, and they will always hate anyone who tries to wake them, even in order to bring them the most wonderful gifts . . . All Sicilian expression, even the most violent, is really wish-fulfillment: our sensuality is a hankering for oblivion, our shooting and knifing a hankering for death; our laziness, our spiced and drugged sherbets, a hankering for voluptuous immobility . . . novelties attract us only when they are dead, incapable of arousing vital currents; that is what gives rise to the . . . constant formation of myths . . . which are really nothing but sinister attempts to plunge us back into a past that attracts us only because it's dead. . . . Sicilians never want to improve for the simple reason that they think themselves perfect; their vanity is stronger than their misery . . . [what] we ourselves call pride in reality is blindness.

Richard Williams and the even more eloquent Barack Obama may never express their knowledge of what surrounds or nurtures them as richly or poetically as Lampedusa's *Gattopardo,* but I think each understands the obstacles before them with some of the same profundity and originality. This is some of what underlay both this year's Wimbledon women's final and the wonderful three-point shot which Barack Obama made before the troops, the American voting public and history this week in Kabul.

August 3, 2008
I'm not going to pussyfoot here: John McCain is, day by day, disgracing himself, converting a reputation as an independent, honest man of wit and wisdom who, during the Vietnam War, as a prisoner in the Hanoi Hilton, behaved under torture and torment with the kind of courage and tenacity very few could come anywhere near matching. Yes, he gave a statement his captors wanted but made it clear to Americans that his being didn't stand behind his words. He resisted offers of release knowing that shame would follow him all his life and stain his unblemished military family's escutcheon.

In the Senate, he sank to what he called his lowest point when he was "fooled" into becoming one of the senatorial stooges of a savings and loan tycoon/crook, and bore the notorious label as one of the Keating Five. For this singular departure from his political standard, he apologized.

In 2000, running against George Bush, he endured the filthy innuendos of the Bush campaign. At a debate, seated beside Bush who was assuring him he had nothing to do with the filth, he said, "Don't give me that shit. And take your hand off me." A photograph (recently reprinted in *TIME*) shows him glaring at Bush with pure hatred. His later embraces of the successful opponent were awkward only partially because the arms broken in prison were incapable of more physical conviction.

Now McCain is using ads and giving speeches which are almost as debased as those of that 2000 Bush campaign. Questioned, he defends them. Such usually fine commentators as David Brooks claim that the senator must campaign in this rut of attack because the campaign McCain's admirers expected and hoped for wasn't drawing sufficient attention. This is as low and foolish as Brooks has gone in his brilliant journalistic career. Why shouldn't McCain break through the Obama magic or "mania" by going on doggedly and decently, ignoring the so-called pragmatists in his campaign and ignoring polls, simply exhibit the straightforward, witty and sometimes heroic self who became an exemplary public servant? I am not the only one who might then alter my Obama allegiance and vote for him. In any case, he would be defeated as an honorable person instead of as a weakened old man who sold out to his lowest and stupidest self.

August 11, 2008
The Beijing Olympics began at 8:00 P.M. on the eighth day of the eighth month of 2008. Sacred numbers. (A baby in Seattle, born then, was said to weigh eight pounds.) I watched the stupendous razzle-dazzle at my brother-in-law's house on Savannah's Isle of Hope. No razzle-dazzle here, just the Skidaway River shining through the great twisted oaks and Spanish moss, alongside which strolled solitary walkers, joggers, mothers wheeling baby carriages and well-fed drivers of golf carts, a moving frieze against the beautiful, after-storm sky.

On the Beijing spectacle of spectacles, thousands of synchronized dancers, acrobats and gymnasts gyrated on enormous digitalized scrolls. They whirled around a translucent blue ball, then gave way to gorgeous fireworks and a flying athlete who, aloft, ignited the scroll-shaped cauldron with the torch that had been carried—and booed—around the earth. The Olympics were open. A parade of athletes, grouped by nationality and dressed by famous designers, circled the great field; the last contingent was the Chinese. It was headed by the seven-foot basketball player, Yao Ming, who walked beside and later carried tiny Lin Hao, the nine-year-old Sichuan schoolboy who'd dug himself out of the earthquake-made rubble where twenty of his thirty classmates had died and then gone back into it to dig out two of them. Asked why, he said it was his responsibility, he'd been a hall monitor. More than all the fireworks and athletes put together, little Lin Hao had innocently brought China back into the world community.

My wife, a student of Chinese and China, said that one of the crucial tenets of Chinese culture is "Responsibility for Others." The jewel in the crown.

Back home, a call came telling us that our friend Ted Solotaroff died this afternoon of 08/08/08. The caller, his stepdaughter, said he'd been peaceful, talking to his wife and another stepdaughter when a thunder storm broke out. The noise must have startled something which broke what little was left of him.

Ted was part of a young University of Chicago literary group of the fifties, the third dead these last sixteen months. I called to tell the other survivor, Philip Roth, and we spoke about Ted, who'd written, half a century ago, the first serious criticism of Roth's work.

Like Roth, Solotaroff did not finish graduate work at the university. Like Roth, he went on to New York. He had a job on the literary section of the *New York Herald Tribune*. Then he became an editor of *Commentary* and at Harper Collins. He edited *New American Writing,* which first published many outstanding writers, and wrote fine reviews and essays for such publications as *TLS* and the *New Republic.* In his last years, he published his best work, two books of memoir. He was at work on the third when he died. In short, the exemplary career of a responsible citizen of the republic of letters or—to give the title of his collection of essays—the "literary community."

On Saturday, August 9, another jewel in the crown of international decency died in Houston. Mahmoud Darwish was the leading poet of Palestine, and his life will be celebrated by three days of national mourning. He spoke and wrote about the attempt to expel his Palestinian brothers from history, but also wrote, "I will continue to humanise even the enemy . . . The first teacher who taught me Hebrew was a Jew. The first love affair in my life was with a Jewish girl. The first judge who sent me to prison was a Jewish woman. So from the beginning, I didn't see Jews as devils or angels but as human beings." Several of his poems are to Jewish lovers. "These poems take the side of love not war."

Lin Hao, Ted Solotaroff, Mahmoud Darwish. These jewels in the human crown shine more and more brightly as brutality, greed and meanness erupt in Ossetia, Darfur, Zimbabwe and a hundred other pits of ugliness on the human map.

August 22, 2008

In 1873, Charles Francis Adams (son of John Quincy and father of Henry) wrote of his disgust that William Seward's nomination for the presidency in 1860 was defeated by a "person selected partly on account of the absence of positive qualities so far as known to the public, and absolutely without the advantage of any experience in national affairs beyond the little that can be learned by an occupation for two years of a seat in the House of Representatives."

I doubt that the McCain campaign will be citing this description of Abraham Lincoln.

August 28, 2008

Bidenbrooks

Uncle Charlie, Mama Biden, Beau Biden, Malia Obama and, yes, "my friend, John McCain." The dramatis personae grows and, with it, that of the protagonists, Barack and Joe, Michelle and Jill. And look who's part of it? Bill, Hill and Chel, whom we've "known" for years. Plus John Lewis of Georgia, Bill Ayres of Hyde Park and, like Hamlet's ghost, Martin (once Michael) King of Georgia and Lyndon Johnson who, age twenty-one, taught Mexican American kids in Cotullo, Texas, and prepared himself to give the great address on civil rights which caused Martin Luther King, in a distant motel room, to weep.

We "don't know" Obama?

Hell, we know him and his running mate better than we know some of our uncles, maybe, in a way, ourselves. We know them almost as well as we know the characters in a good novel, Mann's *Buddenbrooks,* say, so maybe we should call this piece Bidenbrooks.

Buddenbrooks, though, was subtitled "The Decline of a Family," and all the biographies we take in though newspapers and television are about The Rise of a Family, or, at least, The Rise of the Protagonist.

The convention talks and "videos" (some made—gratis—by Stephen Spielberg and starring—gratis again—Tom Hanks) have the great American, if not international, arc, Triumph after Disaster. The other arc, Triumph to Disaster, is the story of the opponents, the Republicans from 2000 to 2008, John McCain from his heroic days as captive of the Vietnamese in 1965 to John McCain, captive of the Republican Right Wing in 2008.

The convention stories roused tears and smiles. When Beau Biden, Delaware's attorney general, weeks shy of National Guard duty in Iraq, described the catastrophic death of his mother and sister, the hospitalization of his brother Hunter and himself, the nightly Amtrak trips of his father, Joe, to their hospital beds and the paternal constancy that shaped his life, Michelle Obama was not the only one in the Denver auditorium who was blotting tears.

When John Kerry, himself the victim, four years earlier, of an ugly fiction, evoked Barack's Uncle Charlie who enlisted in the army the day after Pearl Harbor and then waved Uncle Charlie to his feet, or when Joe Biden waved another white-haired elder, his mother, to hers, the audience in the auditorium and over the television world felt the depth and rootage of the goodness and bravery that could, once again, lead the country to glory.

Thomas, Antonie and little Hanno Buddenbrooks fell into one disaster after another, and the great Buddenbrooks family of Luebeck, Germany, tumbled into the abyss of economic oblivion (and artistic immortality), but Joe Biden and Barack Obama were on the ladder of political eminence which, in the Oval Office and the Executive Office Building, would rescue their country from such an abyss and achieve the ever-contingent immortality of history.

September 3, 2008
The political parties employ expert iconographers who, in their way, rival the great Erwin Panofsky in expertise. Panofsky explained the symbolic intent of the order of diners in paintings of the Last Supper; the political iconographers arrange the order of sitters and speakers on the dais, the pictures in back of the president as he speaks from the Oval Office, or, as in the following case, that of candidate greeters at an airfield.

A few minutes ago (it's 1:30 P.M. Wednesday, the day Sarah Palin will speak to the Republican Convention in St. Paul, Minnesota), I watched John McCain walk down the ladder from his gleaming campaign plane and go down the line of a dozen people waiting to welcome him. First, there was a hug and kiss for Cindy McCain, his blond, rich, stalwart second wife, then an embrace for a short dark young woman whom I assumed was their adopted daughter, Bridget, then a few young men and women whom, I again assumed, were his sons, daughters and in-laws. Then there was an embrace for Sarah Palin, attired in what seemed to this untrained eye a poorly tailored light suit. She was succeeded by her blue-suited husband, Todd, and a young couple who'd been holding hands: Bristol Palin, looking pretty and not—to me—five months pregnant. She clearly introduced McCain to her young swain, eighteen-year-old Levi Johnston (whose blog about not wanting "kids" had been withdrawn from cyberspace after a few hours of notoriety there). McCain spent a minute, a large bounty of what's called "face time," talking with young Levi. My guess is that he either said, "I hear you're quite a hockey player" or "What you're going through is somewhat like my first experience of combat. It's tough, but it'll make you strong. Lots of luck."

He hugged two of the other Palin girls (the Down's syndrome baby wasn't around) and then stood in the middle of what turned into a family portrait before exchanging some words—of encouragement, one guessed—to Sarah before going his separate way.

So, the iconographers wanted us to read, we have a Republican family, new but solid in the face of whatever criticism has been shot out of "left liberal bloggers" about the failure of this self-applauding, forty-four-year-old partner with a still great figure, the good family mother who apparently didn't convince her eldest daughter to wait till the wedding night before fornicating or to see that her lover used condoms (though that might be a part of her belief that condoms should not be distributed in high school). McCain's feminine hook to catch the Hillary vote was off with the iconographers and professional speechwriters to get ready for her speech to the convention. The three- or four-minute airport scene exhibits the human variety (dark Bridget next to blond Cindy, eighteen-year-old Levi next to pretty Bristol) and passionate overflow (the levees breached only here and there) of these lovers and ex-lovers now cohering into what might possibly run the United States

and thus alter, bend and break the lives of several billion far less powerful human beings.

September 8, 2008

I've been reading *Passions,* twenty delightful stories of Isaac Bashevis
Singer. Most of the stories center about the unexpected intrusion of
odd, often unattractive women into the lives of men, old, young, married, celibate, intelligent and experienced, stupid and naïve. These
women live down the hall or show up as distant, if never-known, relatives. They are almost always annoying and yet they exert powerful
charms. Sometimes the male who succumbs to them thinks of them as
dybbuks.

I think of them now because the men overmastered by these
women remind me of the Republicans and certain others who have suc-
cumbed to the attractions of Sarah Palin.

Of course most sudden celebrity in a news-and-novelty-parched
society like ours has something bizarre about it. Those who help create
the celebrity know that it is best packaged in interesting, unusual "narratives." Even a new athletic hero such as Michael Phelps was fitted out
in such a way that his enormous appetite (for food) and need for sleep
became the comic handles by which even those uninterested in
Olympic swimming records took hold of him.

Palin had an especially rich narrative. Indeed, in view of the important role she was assigned by her "creator," Senator McCain, the narrative which introduced her was quickly followed by a counter-narrative,
and then by other narratives, favorable and unfavorable. This will continue as she keeps making public appearances and as long as information about her is elicited from her old friends and enemies in Wasilla,
Juneau, her colleges, her husband's friends, her daughters' schoolmates.

My suggestion here that the celerity and power of her immersion in
the political story are like the bizarre, scarcely explicable domination of
Singer's heroines is to introduce the Jungian sense that an archetype is at
work and that we should be aware of that as we rationally appraise this
woman's capability. The suggestion extends to John McCain's "instinctive" or "intuitive" choice of her. What does his choice say about the
sort of decision-making he will be making day by day if he's elected
president?

September 27, 2008

First thoughts about the first McCain-Obama debate:

McCain did better than I thought he'd do, which doesn't mean that he was as good as the postmen here on Tybee Island would have been. All that "I've seen," "I've been," "I know" was nearly as vulgar as his refrain: "Senator Obama doesn't understand."

The disintegrating self is uglier to watch than to suffer. The McCain so eloquently seen, heard, felt and described by David Brooks is not the McCain who is falling apart in so many ways: the choice of Palin, the behavior last week: "I'll stop the campaign" and delay the debate; even his attempt at drama last night ("Kennedy is in the hospital" when Kennedy left the hospital today). He was never a genius (near the bottom of his academy class) and—perhaps the result of being almost as fatherless as Obama and, like Reagan, the son of an alcoholic—emotionally insecure, a gambler (no accident that he crashed five planes) and now, under the pressure of campaigning, exhibiting the erosions of his seventy-two years, and you have McCain today. In view of all this, I expected and, yes, hoped for more incoherence (though there was God's plenty anyway), if not collapse.

Obama as well had too much "I" stuff, but he was gracious ("John—is right," a graciousness the McCain campaign converted into an ad that makes Obama McCain's endorser), confident, knowledgeable enough, firm in the face of McCain's accusations and intelligent, but there was too little nuance in him (after all, most Ossetians hate Georgian dominance and want the status Russia gave them) and too little of his rich humor. Unlike McCain's chilly discourtesy, Obama seemed like the decent man he is, but not the inventive and surprising man he also is. He didn't convey sufficient appreciation of the miseries and failures he mentioned, he was too often on automatic pilot. Disappointing, but in the culture of winner-loser, he was clearly the winner.

October 4, 2008

The political word today is that the Republicans will return to personal attacks on Obama and Biden to draw attention away from McCain's erratic performance during the days before the passage of the Great Rescue/Bailout/U.S.-as-Sweden bill. We are supposedly to hear again about the Reverend Wright, the unreverend Tony Lezko and William Ayers, the unrepentent Weatherman.

Of these three Chicagoans, I know only the last. I've been to three or four small dinner parties with Ayers and his wife, Bernardine Dohrn, once hailed as the Weathermen's Dolores Ibarruri ("La Pasionaria"), a fiery, beautiful Muse and orator. (Incidentally, I never heard the word "Weatherwoman.")

Dohrn is still attractive, Ayers has an adolescent fizzle in his sexagenarian bones. Dohrn is more subdued, uninterested in fame. She told me that her husband wanted to pursue movie interest in them, but that she didn't. "They only care about the sex and violence." Once, Ayers was about to tell the four other people at dinner how they'd gotten Eldridge Cleaver from a California prison to a Moroccan haven but Dohrn skillfully buttoned his lip.

I did not know them back in the late sixties and early seventies. The excitement at the University of Chicago centered about the refusal to grant tenure to Marlene Dixon, angry students occupied the Administration Building, formed improvisatory theater groups, passed out material about such professors as Daniel Boorstin and held rallies. I attended one of these and believe I learned more about revolution there than I'd learned from Carlyle or Barnaby Rudge. The radicals were led by the Weatherman Howie Machtinger. He conducted the meeting masterfully, a young Lenin or, to take an example I'd witnessed in the French parliament, the Communist leader Jacques Duclos. My own contribution to the U. of Chicago uprising was a series of satiric poems published in the student newspaper—site of the warring opinions—which earned a denunciation in which Machtinger called me a mother-fucker.[16]

At dinner, thirty-eight years later, Ayers and Dohrn did not seem to hold the poems against me, and I didn't hold their fiery and criminally violent behavior against them. As in Chekhov's wonderful story "Old Age," time had planed down the sharp edges and brought one-time antagonists into each others' arms.

As far as I know, Ayers and Dohrn are loyal to the selves which led both of them to jail (though not for long), but they were busy doing other things, useful things, Ayers as educator, Dohrn as a legal counselor. They'd raised the child of a Weatherman who'd been jailed, they were taking care of Bernadine's ill mother, they were doing many things

---

16. Of the three such indictments of which I know, this was the only one that appeared in print. The second one came from an unsuccessful trinket-peddler in Rabat who qualified the epithet with the intensifier "Jewish."

educated community activists were doing. Apparently one of these things brought at least Ayers into contact with another, much younger community activist, Barack Obama.

If Democrats want to deal in an ugly way with McCain, they can talk about the jail sentence served by Cindy McCain's uncle and the suspended sentence her father "served" in connection with illegal activities in their beer distribution business. They can revive the stories of his wildness, his adulterous relationship with Cindy when his first wife (mother of some of his children) was disfigured in an auto accident, his inappropriate senatorial activity on behalf of the crook Charles Keating and perhaps his not very glorious pre-prison record in the naval air force.

Let's hope that this doesn't happen, and let's hope we've heard the last of William Ayers, Tony Rezko and Jeremiah Wright.[17]

October 2008

The Debate's Real Loss

It's fifty minutes after the vice presidential debate between Sarah Palin and Joe Biden. The losers were David Brooks, Mark Shields and other commentators supposedly hired by television executives for intelligence, sensitivity and ability to articulate clear-eyed responses and titillate viewers with their amusing and thoughtful reactions to political events. That these two regulars on PBS's *News Hour* failed to see that Sarah Palin's brassy, blind narcissism, chirpy ignorance, evasiveness, broken syntax, self-vaunting folksiness and robotic falsity disqualified her for important public office should mark their end as commentators. That they did not commend the essentially thoughtful, well- and widely informed performance of Joe Biden should cancel their contracts. The contrast between his intelligence and her stupidity, yes, stupidity, was too clear to be missed by all but blazing partisans.

Yes, this writer is partisan, but makes some attempt to accurately appraise what he sees and hears. That is more important than most causes. Otherwise, value systems will disintegrate and the boundaries

---

17. I write this as I watch my beloved Chicago Cubs enact their annual ritual of humiliation. Perhaps their name should be changed from Chicago Cubs to Chicago Goats (as in "scapegoats").

between right and wrong, vice and virtue, truth and falsity will be destroyed. Brooks and Shields abandoned the standard to which they've given more than lip service.

I've been proud that Brooks had been a student of mine at the University of Chicago. That pride has turned to ashes. As for Shields, it has been a minor pleasure to hear political insights he'd gathered over years of reportorial work.

No more. [I still listen to and admire them.] Working such special streets of punditry as "Who came up to expectations?" "Would Biden gaffe his way into headlines?" or "Would Palin again reveal the ignorance she showed on the Katie Couric interview?" this Gallagher and Sheehan of savvy politics failed to distinguish what was basic, namely which of these two candidates could head the American government. May they rot in Commentator Hell.

October 24, 2008

A long-gone friend of mine asked a hard-scrabbling Tennessee farmer why his favorite movies were the Astaire-Rogers fables of elegant people cavorting in phony-fancy London hotels and Venetian canals before bursting into wonderful songs and dances. "I been poor all my life," said the farmer. "When I go to the movies, I like to see rich people cuttin' up."

This answer is a part of my lack of angry reaction to the $150,000 spent by the Republican campaign on Sarah Palin's clothes. My Lord, there's an Everest of criticism to heap on the ignorant, perky pol whom weary, foolish McCain scooped up from the sex-inflected encomia piled up by the conservative journalists who were dined and charmed by her on their Juneau vacation cruises. (The most besotted and praise-drunk was that jocular disciple of Leo Strauss William Kristol, son of Irving K. and the so un-Palinesque Gertrude Himmelfarb.) Why go into them now when most of the country seems to have seen her almost-horrifying, almost-farcical inadequacy? (I'm beginning to feel sorry for her, beginning to spot sad gleams of virtue in her.)

So let her be dolled up, combed, styled and Neiman-Marcused. After all, she's more part of entertainment than politics. Her ability is in no small part theatrical. Give her a few weeks training and she might get a regular job on *Saturday Night Live,* perhaps parodying Tina Fey parodying herself being offered a time share by Martin Scorsese.

Reagan said that his professional actor's experience was the most useful ingredient of his presidential work. I think Palin's political experience gives her much of what she can use for TV comedy.

February 3, 2009

On John Updike

The transition from observation to written description was swifter and smoother in Updike than in that of any human being of whom I know.

The other extraordinary Updike distinction was the constancy and pressure of his attention. Wherever he went—and he went everywhere—the mind was observing, categorizing, relishing and putting into words what it saw-felt-heard-smelled-tasted-imagined.

Has there ever been anyone who wrote more interestingly, if, at times, excessively, about more things: the American way of packaging, the hysteria of ideology, the charms of Doris Day, the look, smell and feel of genitalia, a mother's failure as a writer, children's anger, the break-up of marriage, Emerson's essays, the Cold War, '89 Toyotas, Ted Williams, zippers, the Master's golf tournament, the cello, hundreds and hundreds of scenes, people, trends, events, objects?

A great writer?

Not in some ways. That is, of Updike's fifty-odd books, there are perhaps only three or four which hold a reader from line one to the finish in such a way that he is shaken to the point of tears. Offhand, the only one I can think of is *Rabbit at Rest,* and that requires that you've read the three previous Rabbit books and that you inure yourself to the author's need to describe in detail whatever the narrative touches no matter that this slows, and sometimes subverts, the narrative flow.

The short story was an easier gear for this amazing literary intelligence. In perhaps fifty stories, Updike's narrative gift did not run out of emotional fuel. Many of them can be read over and over with the delight one gets only from literary mastery.

Seldom has sheer intelligence been coupled with great narrative or dramatic gift. Shakespeare is the acme of such fusion; Tolstoy, Proust and Joyce are the closest novelists have gotten to it. Updike's novels may not have it, but his remarkable literary criticism does. It is as masterful as it is in part because Updike can summarize and even energize other people's narratives in such a way that they don't merely illustrate the critical points he's making about their work but add a narrative dimension to the criticism, a sort of dessert special.

I don't believe that any country has ever had a writer who brought depths of understanding, often beautiful and uproarious understanding, to so much. What a national, what an international resource this man was.

His to me unexpected, even shocking death leaves an unfillable void. To counter the despair such a void brings, one counters with "How lucky we've been to have had Updike writing for more than fifty years."

III

❦

Hosting

Glimpse, Encounter, Acquaintance, Friendship

⤞⧆⤝

5:00 P.M. ON A SPRING DAY in 1963, one hundred yards south on the Florian's side of the Piazza San Marco, I walked past a gallery on Via 22 Settembre which that year was selling apple paintings by the most commercially successful lousy painter in Venice. The show window was full of gleaming red apples, and as I gave them the usual look of amused disgust, I saw mirrored in it the face of a middle-aged, balding man with a facial tic who was walking in the opposite direction. Our eyes met in esthetic fellowship reinforced with smiles of superiority.

If I hadn't recognized Andre Malraux, I would still have enjoyed that second of fellowship, but that this blink-of-an-eye fellowship was with the author of *The Voices of Silence* added that special suntan of distinguished celebrity which creates or at least augments what's memorable.

If not Malraux, but a lovely woman had been my esthetic fellow, that too would have imbued the second with gold, but of a sort not treated here where the subject is the sovereign touch of literary fame. I want to write about the way my life has been enriched by such glimpses and by more extended relationships with people of accomplishment in my own line of work. The half-second "with Malraux"—whom I'd not seen before and wouldn't again—is here called a "glimpse," and will be differentiated from what will be called "encounter," "acquaintance" and "friendship."[1]

---

1. I want to exclude from this essay what are some of my richest associations with writers, including the very richest, that with my wife, Alane Rollings, whose poetry (the last of her five published volumes is *To Be in This Number,* Northwestern U. Press, 2005) is too deeply involved with my feelings to write about in the limits of this essay. Then there are the special relationships with those of my students who've become wonderful writers, the late Austin Wright, Douglas Unger, Robert Coover, Peter LaSalle, James Schiffer, Peter Cooley, Campbell McGrath and, happily, quite a few others. Pride in and often friendship for them constitutes a category in itself.

Why has the Malraux glimpse stayed in my head with such clarity for more than forty years? Most such moments remain out of consciousness and pass unrecorded; others surface without summoning— "involuntary memory" is Proust's term for this—to play various roles in our reflective, literary, erotic, sensual and intellectual life. A Malraux-like glimpse may be more significant than, say, an acquaintance, even a friendship, which, once terminated, may die barely remembered. It rescues from life's flux what has a yet-to-be-defined definition that makes a part of one's life special, beautiful, meaningful.[2] Colette's probably right about the use of images—"By means of an image we are often able to hold on to our lost belongings"—but my sense of the glimpse-image is more that of a modest epiphany, a second slightly charged with surprise and pleasure.

2

I want to describe four encounters which occurred at different times of my life with four different writers. The first occurred in 1942. I was fourteen and had been reading with great joy novels of Sinclair Lewis, *Main Street, Arrowsmith, Babbitt,* and *It Can't Happen Here.* I was walking home through Central Park after an appointment with Dr. Murray Bass, the first of the wonderful doctors I've had in my long life. Fifty yards away, I spotted the tall, skinny, slouching Lewis himself. With the stalker's savage joy, I headed for him. Spotting me spot him, Lewis moved away. I followed. He moved faster, then higher, up one of the small rock cliffs whose every crack, crevice, bulge and contour was part of my childhood geography. I followed him. "Mr. Lewis?" Fedora off, blue eyes weary with submission, he acknowledged the identification. I was gripped, though not repelled, by his notorious face, its pits and

---

2. In January 2004, I saw the Taj Mahal, something I'd avoided doing as a cliché of tourism in my first Indian visit in the summer of 1973. After making my way through several guarded barriers and paying several largish fees, I passed through a narrow door and saw the famous building. That first glimpse was to my surprise surprising, a vision of symmetry floating its intense whiteness into the blue sky, an epiphany-like glimpse which lasted about five seconds and makes me wonder what its relationship is to the Malraux glimpse. Is there an esthetic or, for that matter, an economic theory which explains such power? February 23, 2007: An op-ed piece in the *Times* says that fans unsatisfied by star glimpses are getting star tattoos. The antiquity of the power of distinction is recorded in a stock example from a seventh-century Sanskrit text, *The Ornaments of Poetry,* by Bhamaha: "Eminent men, like roadside trees, provide shelter / shade and fruit."

trenches the sign of some awful engagement with disease or decay. No matter, I had my man. I told him that I was reading and loving his novels. He was polite and, though unsmiling, not unkind. He asked me which books I'd read. I rattled off the titles. There was some other chatter, the only thing remembered now the fact that he was living at the El Dorado six or seven blocks north of our 84th Street Central Park West apartment. We must have shaken hands goodbye, and I went home to dazzle my parents and sister with the fish I'd hooked.[3]

The second encounter took place in 1952 when I was living in Frankfurt/Main, working for the Department of the Army teaching illiterate soldiers math and reading. I read in the *Frankfurter Allgemeine Zeitung* that Thomas Mann was going to be visiting Bad Gastein about the time that my wife and I were going to Salzburg for a festival performance of Berg's *Wozzeck*. A few years earlier, my aunt Mildred had married the brother-in-law of Helen Lowe-Porter, Mann's English-language translator. I wrote to ask her to get Mann's address from her new sister-in-law, who did not supply it, but suggested that I get it from Professor Theodore Adorno, who was also living in Frankfurt. I called Adorno, got the address of Mann's son Michael in the Salzkammergut and wrote the great man to ask if he could possibly see me in Bad Gastein. I received a short handwritten note in German saying that yes, on such and such a day, he could see me and, for my "*Orientierung,*" supplied the name and address of his Gastein pension. I showed this inky screed to the German secretaries, who were as excited by it as believers would be by a splinter of the cross.

The day after hearing Berg's marvelous opera, I took the train to Bad Gastein and walked to the pension where Mann and his wife were staying. They were out walking. I sat and waited till I heard, "Mr. Stern." There was this trim gray couple, the man in tweed cap, knickers, sweater and jacket, the short-haired wife in tweed skirt. We walked a few hundred yards to a restaurant overlooking the beautiful mountains. "Are you a writer?" Mann asked. Although I considered myself a writer, I'd published nothing except in college literary magazines and was now working as a teacher. "No," I said. (Perhaps this accounted for the only note of the visit Mann recorded in his diaries, which I read forty years

---

3. I did not invite him home, as, two years earlier, I'd invited the old pianist Artur Schnabel, with whom I was walking on Central Park West, to use our piano. Schnabel thanked me but said that he had one of his own.

later. "Mittagessen mit Mr. Stern aus New York." The editor's footnote read that he hadn't been able to identify "Mr. Stern.")

Over lunch, I told Mann that I was reading *Doctor Faustus*. "That's too difficult," he said. "I was extending the language as much as possible there." He recommended the much simpler short novel about a woman who mistakes a cancerous flow for the return of her menstrual period, *The Black Swan*. We talked about Berg, Bartok, Salzburg, Frankfurt—he remembered the beautiful Roemer houses which in the Frankfurt of 1952 were in ruins around the bomb-blasted cathedral—then mentioned with a touch of bitter amusement a letter he'd just received accusing him of being an American author. "German is my country," he'd replied to the letter writer. He talked about German as a great lyric language and praised a poet of whom I'd then not heard, Georg Trakl. (Back in Frankfurt, I bought a volume and began translating the poems.) He was open and amiable, though somehow distant. He also said a few things which I'd read in his book, *Die Enstehung des Doktor Faustus.*[4] With his wife, he was intimate and slightly infantile. She was mistress of ceremonies, domestic boss and familiar love. She ordered the lunch, drove the car, cut his hair and told him the daily score. The only German sentence of his I remember was his obedient "Ich hab' mein Pullover aufgezogen" (I took my sweater off). At the end of the two hours, back at the pension, there was a Jamesian moment. Throughout lunch, Mann had not removed his sunglasses. When I said "Goodbye," he took them off and revealed blazing blue eyes.

Mann was the first of the writers I considered "great" whom I was to meet, and the encounter I took with unearned confidence as the stamp of my ability to exist on the same planet if not level with greatness, and if not in books, at least in life.

The third encounter took place in Rome in 1963. There was a literary conference on the Via Nazionale. I arrived early and immediately identified the other early arrival, Jean Paul Sartre. I went to him, mentioned our common friend, Paolo Milano, the literary critic. We sat down at a café, had coffee and talked about all sorts of things, the most memorable of which had to do with Sartre's notion that writers in colonized countries constituted the true avant-garde since they wrestled

---

4. One I remember had to do with his speaking English to his wife for the first time when he woke from an operation at Billings Hospital in Chicago. "I needed a new language for pain."

with the experience of the colonized in the language of the colonizer. I asked him about his relationship to the artists about whom he wrote, Tintoretto, Flaubert, Genet and others. "I begin close to or distant from them and in the course of writing, move in the opposite direction." As for Genet, "He systematically contradicts everything I wrote about him." I found Sartre exceptionally sympathetic, attentive, unpretentious, kind. Without fuss, he bought all the drinks and supplied the cigarettes for the group of writers who joined us. His face was more pleasant than I'd expected. One eye leaned almost on his nose, but otherwise the face was engagingly pleasant. The Irish poet Patrick Kavanagh staggered to the table on the arm of his companion, Desmond O'Grady. He said to me, "Ask Mr. Sartre why he turned down the Nobel Prize. Forty [or however many] thousand pounds." Sartre said that he was an unusual size and couldn't find a tailor to make tails for him. Kavanagh rebuked him for the sacrifice. Sartre was unfailingly courteous. It was clear that he'd long ago learned how to rebuff rudeness and worse intrusions. It was a surprise to me that part of his intelligence was this gift for diplomacy. Whether it was the source of what I regarded as his generosity and tolerance or whether it simply revealed them, it supplied an aspect of the man of which I'd not read. The encounter was significant not only for that but for giving me a sense of his fine low voice, the clarity, simplicity and ease of his French.

The fourth encounter, chosen from others because it's the only one with a Japanese author, was with Shuntaro Tanikawa, the Japanese poet with whom my wife and the two fine graduate students assigned to be our guides in Tokyo had tea in a Tokyo hotel in 1997. I'd been lecturing to a group of fifty or sixty Japanese graduate students who were getting a special University of Chicago degree via courses from Chicago professors coming to Japan, then taking a full load of courses during two summer quarters on the Chicago campus. The program attracted many interesting adult students; one who attended my talks was a society woman who'd gone to the same school as the Japanese empress. She was a neighbor of Shuntaro, Japan's most distinguished poet. She said she'd speak to him about a meeting, gave him the only novel of mine translated into Japanese and told me a few days later that he'd be delighted to meet me. Our two splendid guides—to whom we'd become quite close and from whom we learned more about Japanese domestic and personal matters than we could have found out in months of less intimate acquaintance—were thrilled by the chance of meeting him, perhaps some compensation for the many hours easing us into the right subway cars and accompanying us around the city. The five of us had tea on the second floor of a good hotel whose name I will not bother disinterring from my journals. I'd thought we'd need the young women for translation, but Shuntaro spoke excellent English, had spent time in America, was influenced by American life and poets, had faithful American translators and was miles deeper into our country than we were into his. Here is some of his poem "My Favorite Things," the title taken from an Oscar Hammerstein lyric quoted in the poem:

> No matter how much
> I like a thing
> Actually owning it
> Somewhat bores me . . .
> Poor Oscar.
> Your forced Rhymes
> Sound just awful

Part Two is dedicated to John Coltrane, who sounds just fine.

Shuntaro had the sort of courtesy someone like me thinks it takes as long to create as the lush green of an English lawn. It was afloat in an amiability which transported you. It made a wonderful ninety minutes. Shuntaro gave us his books, including the one from which the Hammerstein-Coltrane poem was taken, "At Midnight in the Kitchen I Just Wanted to Talk to You," translated with the ease the title bespeaks by William I. Elliott[5] and Kazuo Kawamura.

When we said goodbye, I towered, a bit shamefully, over the small, bald fellow, but did feel a flow of affection passing between us. From Chicago, I wrote him and received a good letter in return, but that has been the end of the encounter.

3

Acquaintances are for me extended relationships which almost always involve friendship, if not intimacy, but which are not components of

---

5. November 8, 2007: Philip Roth writes me that Elliott was a good friend of his at the U. of Chicago graduate school. "He went off to live in Japan and marry a Japanese woman."

one's life as friendships are. Usually acquaintances are sought out, arrangements to meet are made fairly long in advance or involve a level of formality which friendships usually don't require. They can be very important in one's life and for one's work, and they are often precious in themselves, but they aren't a natural part of life as friendships are. Their brevity actually augments their preciousness and memorability. My friendships with writers are compounded of far more incidents, conversations, gestures and scenes than I can remember or classify. In addition, most friendships have clear stages of intimacy which sometimes include estrangements, whereas after the move from introduction to amiability and even ease, acquaintances are less variable, once the basic relationship is established. There may be high and low points, some even dramatic, but the difference is that between the special dinner plates brought out for occasions and the good familiar plates off which one eats every day. Some acquaintances endure over years, some are restricted to a time and place, some are clearly warmer than others, but they are alike in the ways I've said and can thus be described under this special rubric although acquaintances can be, were and are real friends.

In books,[6] I've described acquaintance with Samuel Beckett, Ralph Ellison, Ezra Pound, Flannery O'Connor, Robert Lowell, Norman Mailer, Lillian Hellman, Howard Nemerov, Uwe Johnson, Bernard Malamud and a dozen other writers. I will take the liberty here of simply alerting the interested reader to them and will add only that if, as Leonardo—or was it Cellini?—said, a piece of sculpture has fourteen different aspects, human beings have many many more. Each acquaintance is built on one's relationship to different aspects of oneself and one's acquaintance. Some involve an old master certifying something about an aspiring tyro; some are the literary rivalries of contemporaries which may develop into friendships or fall into jealousy or antipathy; some are a sum of many casual occasions which can become increasingly amusing and even heartwarming; some move from strong bonding to oblivion as one or the other moves away or correspondence becomes more burden than pleasure. So seeing Eudora Welty on her five or six trips over thirty-odd years to Chicago made for familiarity short of friendship or great warmth. As for Stephen Spender, I kept running

---

6. *One Person and Another; On Writers and Writing; The Books in Fred Hampton's Apartment; The Invention of the Real; The Position of the Body; What Us What Was.*

into him, sometimes in embarrassing ways, such as when, having arranged a lunch with my old teacher Robert Lowell, I brought along Mel Lasky and he brought along Spender, this a month after these two former editors of *Encounter* had had a bitter public dispute about the CIA's funding of their magazine. Writers encountered daily at one of the few conferences I've attended could turn into good *amis de la semaine* (like the Norwegian novelist Kjarten Floegstad, met first in Valencia in 1987 and seen twice in later years in Chicago) or just familiar luncheon companions (Octavio Paz at the same conference). Ezra Pound, seen weekly over a year, was never a friend, but a piece of incarnate history whose mostly cryptic utterances and, once, moving self-revelation which could have been made to an abstract posterity as much as it was to me I've written about several times, once in the novel *Stitch,* where Pound was turned into a sculptor who'd carved the equivalent of the *Cantos* on an island in the lagoon. Sam Beckett's warmth made him something between an almost-friend and a friend, but I only saw him for ninety minutes at a time, and the times were separated by a year. He did once call Bellow in California to ask him to thank me for sending him a biography of Nancy Cunard, about whom we'd talked.

At another time, perhaps I'll figure out the algorithm of acquaintance, but here, somewhat weary of speculation, I'll move on to friendship.

4

The most difficult relationships (I'm tempted to keep what I'd first typed, "relationshops") to write about in the terms proposed here—the influence of other writers, more or less independent of their books, on one's work—is friendship, particularly one of not years but decades, such as those I had with Saul Bellow, Donald Justice, Philip Roth, Tom Rogers, Edgar Bowers, Norman Maclean and a few other writers. One can talk about the development and maintenance of standards, so that one wants to move and amuse these friends whose own standards are high and who help you maintain them by criticizing your early drafts and arguing over books, your own and theirs, but such conversations and critiques are parts of lives which involve many personal matters and feelings. It is special talking about one's personal life with people of special sensitivity, sympathy, comic energy and long acquaintance with you and your problems. With some friends you do it more than others; with some you yield to their peculiar views of your life more or less because their take, different from your own, interests you. Some friends give excellent, some poor advice. Both Bellow and Roth, two of my closest literary friends, have at different times given me what I considered and still consider bad advice about what to do in important situations (divorcing and reconciling), and I don't know if that's because their view of me and my situation was askew or if their own imagination or hunger for more dramatic resolutions than those which fit my temperament and situation motivated them. With Justice, whom I knew from the age of sixteen until he died almost sixty years later, there was very little intimate talk. We were close, but very seldom did we talk about, say, the erotic parts of each other's lives. Once when there was a rift in one of our families, one of us helped repair it by urging that a particular step be taken; and when Don had a heart attack, I was one of the first he called from his hospital bed. For almost sixty years, along with delight in each other's company, there was the sense that we would help and stand by each other, though as our literary and even political opinions diverged more and more—Justice's were more conservative—we wrote and saw each other less frequently. I remain close to his wife, Jean, herself a very fine short story writer.

To deal with friendship in another way, I'm going to end this essay by scooping up a section of the journals I've kept for almost sixty years to show how one of these old friends worked into the life I chose to record on a few days in 1967.

September 18, 1967

> NICKY [my then six-year-old son]: I fell off a boat once.
> MRS. AGIN [mother of his friend Richard]: How terrible, Nicky. What happened?
> NICKY: I don't know. I wasn't asleep long enough to find out.
> *Singing to himself in front of TV:* What's a nice girl like you doin' in a place like this?
>
> *Playing the Monkey Pick-up game while the TV news showed Sandburg's funeral and the somewhat too rich voice of the poet was heard saying: ". . . and men live like birds in the woods." Nicky (not looking up from*

his string of monkeys): Birds! They do not. *(And looking up a few seconds later, disgusted):* What does he mean? Like birds?

Andrew [son, then ten] watching "I Spy," which took place on Delos and other beautiful Greek islands, after I'd deplored the script and wished for more beautiful views: This is "I Spy," not "Greece."

September 19, 1967
Saul came in most depressed. Chicago is hateful, no life in the streets, nowhere to go, he's fiercely lonely. Daniel [his then four-year-old son] had abused him and kept on till he'd had to slap him. Then, working over Berghof's punk version of Seize the Day, *he saw how much that and other books of his centered about men who had no real commitment to high life, only scorn of low life. (We'd been talking of Svetlana [Stalin's daughter] and the interview with Lady Bird J in the* NY Times.) *Then he revived talking about the miseries of his relatives: his brother-in-law Charlie Kauff-man, ex-plumber who pulled teeth in Appalachia and who only wants to die ("I didn't make it this time," he said after his last attack), about his sister blind to the perversity of one son, the kleptomaniac, and her other son's suicide; on to the crazy orthodox household of Sam, his rabbinical, ex-baseball player son T. and his wife's absorption in the fossil world of orthodoxy, then on to Morris's boy, now a CPA and sure to be involved in some scheme who called him only when Kup [gossip columnist of the* Chicago Sun-Times*] printed a choice item as if to gloat about "sappy old Uncle Saul." In large part, his pessimism, like mine, is related to the fact that he hasn't worked since Maggie's case last Friday. Finally, a comic description of the painting of genitalia which Susan hung in the living room.*

October 24
Yesterday Saul read about 10–15 pages of Cantabile's meeting with George in the old Russian bath [from the novel Humboldt's Gift*] as good pure narrative as has ever been written. At the Eagle, Saul lambasted Mann (he's teaching* Death in Venice*), fine, but "with that extra layer of fat that makes a fat girl." The "fat is opinion." Saul says he was influenced early by Schopenhauer's "Essay on Style" which says, "They can challenge opinion, never imagination."*

Although I've chosen a section of the journals which includes our professional work instead of, say, one in which we went down to Maxwell Street to buy a suit or went to a hockey game with friends or sons, one can see that the relationship did not have the selective intensity of ones which are built on and even for transience. This relationship was just a familiar, if exceptionally revelatory, part of our daily life. I've learned, not only with sadness, that such relationships don't end with the friend's death but become a rich, perhaps transformational, component of the memories which are so large a part of age.

Scattered Memories of the U. of Chicago
English Department. 1955 et seq.

I

1955.

Every afternoon at 4:00, the English Department met in 409B, a closet-sized ex-storage space on the fourth floor of Wieboldt. All department members were welcome, only a handful came every day; another handful came once in a while. At the center of the regulars was Walter Blair, the wry, rotund, Canadian-born department chair who specialized in American humor, Mark Twain and the tall tale. Walter had coffee boiling and cookies spread on a cracked plate. Stamped by the fearful, ascetic economies of the Depression, Walter and the rest of us four o'clockers somehow felt that the constricted, shabby setting suited our skeptical, Depression-plus-FDR-nourished psyches.

Another regular was Arthur Friedman, a blue-eyed, white-haired, nervously merry and obscene eighteenth-century scholar up from the day's work on his edition of Oliver Goldsmith. Editing texts was one of the scholarly tasks held in high esteem by the department. Even such scholar-critics as the assistant professors Stuart Tave and Gwin Kolb edited texts, Gwin slaving away at *Rasselas,* the tale Samuel Johnson dashed off in a week to defray his mother's funeral expenses, Stuart later editing Robert Bage's odd, Voltairesque novel of 1796, *Hermsprong.* Downstairs, Donald Bond was finishing up his lifework edition of Addison and Steele's great newspapers, *The Spectator* and *The Tatler.*[1] Don-

---

1. Later there'd be Bill Ringler's wonderful editions of Sidney's *Arcadia* and David Bevington's marvelous ones of Shakespeare and other dramatists.

ald, the only Republican in the department, was too refined for our coffee klatches, but Stuart and Gwin, who shared an office in Wb 409A with the one-eyed Texas linguist, James Sledd, were usually there. Gwin and Stuart had both been in the navy, Gwin an ordinary seaman, then an ensign, out of Jackson, Mississippi's Millsaps College, Stuart an officer from the Bronx, who'd driven around Hiroshima not too many weeks after it had been atom-bombed into ash and flesh rubble.

The department was full of ex-soldiers. Another was the medieval scholar Ted Silverstein, baptized "Roughy" by Friedman, perhaps because his heroic mustache and high-decibel geniality reminded the Goldsmith scholar of Teddy Roosevelt and his Rough Riders. Silverstein's squadron had requisitioned the Eiffel Tower for air force intelligence in 1944; a military lilt lingered in his geniality. My office mate, Ernest Sirluck–scrupulous editor of a volume in the Yale Milton— seemed to carry an invisible swagger stick. Son of a provincial Jewish shopkeeper in Manitoba, Sirluck had slid into the locutions and manners of a British officer; he intimidated such nonetheless admiring students as the future poet-editor George Starbuck and the European-trained intellectual George Steiner.[2] Sirluck sometimes showed up at the coffee klatch, but not when Silverstein or Sledd were there. Sledd's sometimes savage humor sprang from a bellicosity sharpened by the humiliation of being an almost able-bodied man who'd not served in the armed forces of our last world war. The "almost" was due to the glass eye acquired after a childhood accident. His ability to pop it into his palm during heated colloquies was part of his black comic repertoire.

The department's token woman,[3] Catherine Ham, had been an officer in the WAVE, the women's branch of the U.S. Navy. In Chicago, her soft, southern authority was exercised as the department's executive assistant, although she also taught a survey course in the humanities. Catherine saw to it that our little coffee closet was more or less habitable.

I loved the coffee hour. Lowest of the low, an instructor, I was the first writer the department had hired as a regular member since Thornton Wilder had served six years in the 1930s. (Wilder didn't teach what

---

2. Young Steiner was enchanted by the brains and roughness of Chicago but spotted genius in only one person with whom he'd once played poker, the young cartoonist Hugh Hefner, then sketching his plans for a magazine called *Stag,* eventually launched on Marilyn Monroe's airbrushed beauty as *Playboy.*

3. What had happened to Chicago's women scholars between the tenure of Edith Rickard and the hiring of Janel Mueller in the 1960s?

later came to be called "creative writing" courses but after class did read the poems and stories of such favorite students as Elder Olsen and Edward Levi.) If I didn't fit Chicago's bill, there'd be little lost: my initial salary was $4850 ($1350 more than I'd earned the year before at Connecticut College for Women in New London). For some years, around Christmas time, I'd be called into the office of the humanities dean, the gruff-voiced, egg-bald Americanist Napier Wilt (another ex-soldier who'd been "gassed" in WWI), who would cheerfully inform me that I was doing all right and deserved the annual raise he was proposing to the administration, $200. Such was the persuasive power of Wilt's genial but dignified patronage that I left his office feeling as if I'd won a trifecta.

To me, there seemed to be no rank pulled in Wilt's division or in the department. It was as democratic (in every sense) as it could be. The coffee hours were full of jokes (Walter's stories and manner were modeled after Will Rogers'), politics—the "semi-idiot" Ike was president, his vice president one of the great original American villains, Richard Nixon. (We should have been more sympathetic to this permanent outsider who as president growled that Eisenhower had not once in eight years invited him inside his house.) A common topic was books, which often meant new books of prose fiction. Almost all members of the department read them, and this meant keeping up with what the best book sections (most newspapers had richer, longer book sections back then[4]) featured as serious fiction.[5] This was another measure of our departmental commonality and cohesion.

We had a living image of unhappy English Departments. Every summer quarter in the late fifties, the bibliographical scholar Fredson Bowers came up to Chicago from the famously unhappy U. of Virginia English Department to teach a couple of courses. I noticed in the first days that Bowers' shoulders were crooked, the right one lower than the

---

4. From the beginning, I reviewed books for Chicago newspapers. It was an augmentation of my small salary but also satisfied my notion of a writer's civic obligation. An extension of that was my asking then Vice President Nixon what books had played a role in his formation. His surprising answer may be found in "The Pursuit of Washington," in *The Books in Fred Hampton's Apartment*.

5. This extended to my early work. When *Golk,* my first novel, was published in 1960, it was read and commented on by almost every member of the department, and when I appeared on television and radio programs, my words were assessed by friendly critics. In later years, I had very few departmental readers, although there were a few faithful readers in other departments.

left. In a week or so, his shoulders straightened out. Then, days before his return to Charlottesville, down went the right shoulder.[6]

Wives were very much a part of departmental life. They were or were given characters, Walter's artistic, pessimistic Carol, Donald's ebullient Judith, the doyenne of the excellent poetry collection then ensconced on the fourth floor of Harper, Norman Maclean's dry, laconic "true westerner" Jessie, Gwin's charming Ruth, Stuart's high-spirited Danish, Edel, and so on. For decades, divorce was nearly unknown. Friedman and Olsen had been divorced, and then in the early seventies, I was divorced and felt like a pariah. Although several wives worked, their identities were often tied to the department, where many spread their husbands' views of each other. One of a thousand fruits of the modern women's movement was the death of "the faculty wife." (I suppose the sepulcher is *Who's Afraid of Virginia Woolf?*)

2

Perhaps a word or two is in order about the remarkable group of graduate students here in the fifties. I've mentioned two, Starbuck and Steiner, who went on to distinguished careers as poet and public intellectual, although Steiner has always been an academic as well. There were such other writers as the poet David Ray, who was also an editor (of *Prairie Schooner*), the fine critic and avant-garde novelist Austin Wright, the literary critic, editor and, more recently, memoir writer Ted Solotaroff and, best known by far, Philip Roth, who came back for Ph.D. work (he had a Chicago M.A.) in 1956 and began writing and publishing even as he sweated miserably over Old English. He left for NYC and the beginning of his marvelous narrative career in 1957. I'll mention here what has become a well-known episode or two of American literary history.[7] In 1957, Dean Wilt granted my request for two thousand dollars to bring active writers to my writing class for a week's

---

6. A few years later, our department tried to recruit him. His wife, the Boston story writer Nancy Hale, gave a winter reading in Mandel Hall. In the middle of a story, she stopped, shivered, went over to her chair, picked up and put on her long mink coat and returned to finish the story. This somehow made it clear to us that she and Bowers would not be coming to Chicago.
7. There are references to this in Molly McQuade's *An Unsentimental Education*.

stay. The first years the money brought four writers—Bellow, Lowell, Nemerov and Peter Taylor—fewer in subsequent ones.[8] Saul Bellow, then teaching in Minnesota, was the first invited writer. Roth, my friend and fellow instructor, wondered if his story "Defender of the Faith" could be the class story discussed by Bellow. It was, Bellow relished it, and the three of us got together after the class, the initial meeting of their long, complex relationship. Next year, the third member of what Bellow would call "the Hart, Schaffner and Marx" of American literature, Bernard Malamud, visited the class and in our University Avenue apartment met Bellow, who happened to be visiting in Chicago.[9] In his fine memoir *First Loves,* Solotaroff describes what meeting Malamud meant for him.

A half-decent account of the varying careers of our many remarkable students would require volumes.

3

The faculty of the seventies, eighties and nineties had reading obligations, which were heavier and heavier with difficult literary theory. For relaxation, many of my younger colleagues were more at home with *Miami Vice* than *Herzog* and drew class illustrations from it and its television peers. Our colleague John Cawelti had pioneered popular culture studies, but although he'd applied close analysis to westerns and the Three Stooges, he himself knew where they stood in the hierarchy of mentality. Such departmental friends of mine as Arthur Heiserman and John Wallace sometimes believed that our newer colleagues didn't. "They dive into the sewers of pop culture not for analysis or sanitation, but to swim," was our unfair Ibsenian criticism.[10] We thought that the consequence of this immersion was the abasement of their culture and

---

8. Later Ellison, Mailer, Lillian Hellman, Flannery O'Connor, Anthony Hecht, Uwe Johnson, John Berryman, Kingsley Amis, J. F. Powers, J. P. Donleavy and many others came.

9. As long as I'm into these encounters of the famous Jewish writers, I was at the party in NYC where Bellow first met Isaac Bashevis Singer, whose "Gimpel the Fool" he had so wonderfully translated; the story was Singer's English-language breakthrough. The apartment was that of the publisher Aaron Asher, a Chicago graduate.

10. I used my position on the Committee on General Studies in Humanities to hire our first specialist in film theory, Gerry Mast (to whom, years earlier, I'd given his lowest undergraduate grade), the first of many brilliant departmental appointments in the field.

the systematic torture of their critical prose. Still, both Heiserman and Wallace joined the board of Shelley Sacks' new periodical, *Critical Inquiry,* which became the home base of the new criticism.[11] Neither of them, though, ever penned a sentence in the labyrinthine mode of Yale-muddled Derridiana. Our generation had modeled style and analytic technique on the essays of Eliot and such "new critics" as John Crowe Ransom and Robert Penn Warren.[12] This slowed, if not destroyed our appreciation of the newer work. I remember trying to get through Gayatri Spivak's introduction to Derrida's *Grammatology.* "Fog escorting mist," was my reaction. Lean, lovely Gayatri in her ash-stained saris spent a couple of quarters here and was reported to extract nightly counsel on all matters from Yale's guru-en-chef, Paul de Man. De Man too spent Chicago time, giving one of the two worst literature lectures (on Proust and a funerary sonnet of Wordsworth) I have ever heard.[13] (The other: Stanley Fish's arrogantly careless slaughter of "Il Penseroso."[14])

The division between new and old eventually turned the curriculum upside down. I remember a meeting in which I asked that special exemption be made: a required course in Shakespeare. The rigorous seventeenth-century scholar Janel Mueller (a champion and engaged consoler of young women students and faculty) led the opposition to this "privileging." It was clear, though, even to the most curmudgeonly of the old timers that new energy had poured into the thinking of English Departments and that much of it came from the dynamic young women who enlivened it. In 1954, I'd been an early reader of Simone de Beauvoir's *The Second Sex,* had indeed discombobulated my classes at Connecticut College that year by making assignments out of it. (My copy of the book was returned with the markings of intense, multiple readings, but the young women of New London could or would not digest the revolutionary contradiction of their upbringing.) Despite Beau-

---

11. After Shelley had smoked himself to death, *CI* was taken over by Tom Mitchell, who made it one of the most influential periodicals in the history of culture.

12. I did publish a few non-critical pieces in *CI,* one of which led to a public brawl—a verbal one—with Joyce C. Oates. I mostly published in such literary periodicals as the *Kenyon, Sewanee, Hudson* and *Partisan* reviews, occasionally in *Harpers* and the *Atlantic Monthly.*

13. I remember being slightly surprised and pleased at an *en face* breakfast with De Man that he ate normally and talked clearly.

14. This earned him the name of Professor Piranha in the short story "Lesson for the Day" (see *Almonds to Zhoof: Collected Stories of Richard Stern*).

voir and such other books as *The Madwoman in the Attic,* I was unprepared for the new ways of looking at and teaching literature, the concentration on what was absent, the clues to social and political inequity discernible in the most familiar novels and poems. That a change of mentality comes with a change of style and manner should not have been as surprising or as dismaying as it was. Luckily, our new people (Ruddick and Kruger, Knight and Hadley, Ash, Postlewaite, Rigal, Berlant and Stewart[15]) were generous, even prodigal, with guidance. It meant not only alterations in our reading and teaching, it meant "new types of [social] architecture, a change of heart." The adjustment was, I think, easier for some of us older men than for such fine women scholars as Elizabeth Helsinger[16] and Janel Mueller, whose training had begun well before graduate school, well before school itself. They had the difficult job of fusing elements of the newer scholarship with their own traditional training, and for a while, some of us thought that their work showed the wrenching of this complex negotiation. As for the critical swamping of the curriculum, it continued for some years but was eventually drained as the department listened to the complaints of its literature-starved students.

The 1950s coffee hour gang had not prided itself on what I'd thought before I came to Chicago was its departmental glory, the critical methods of R. S. Crane and Richard McKeon as embodied in what was then a famous text, *Critics and Criticism,* two of whose contributors, Elder Olsen and Norman Maclean, were active members of the department (although seldom at the coffee klatch). To some degree, even the most classical—"i.e., old-fashioned"—members of the department paid attention to textual analysis in the manner of the Chicago—or "New"—critics, but it was the exacting scholarship of editors and the historical scholarship of such faculty as R. C. ("Cecil") Bald and George Williamson which constituted the departmental ground bass. The courtly Bald (who'd been a bravely outspoken professor in South Africa) worked on Donne's biography, Williamson on the transforma-

---

15. Jackie Stewart's specialty, black films, points to another subject this piece doesn't take up, black studies, whose first professor here was George Kent and whose luminary for ten-plus years has been Ken Warren. Somewhere else I'll describe the scene in which Amiri Baraka and his henchmen entered a room in Wieboldt like mafiosi, claiming first that they had nothing to learn from such as Saul Bellow—who sat within feet of them—and then demanded that the U. of Chicago cough up money to atone for decades of ill treatment.

16. Who became my favorite department chair (a title shared with Jay Schleusener).

tion of seventeenth-century English prose style and on T. S. Eliot (his "Guide" was the first published book on the Anglo-American poet-critic). The ironic skeptic Williamson was also the first-rate editor of *Modern Philology* following the long tenure of Ronald Crane (who had famously reviewed every important work of eighteenth-century scholarship in its annual bibliographical issue).

Crane had retired but was still a presence.[17] A stocky man, white-haired and -mustached, he had the dignity of intellectual self-confidence. He was delighted when his finest and surely best-known student, Wayne Booth, came back in 1962 to teach in the department.[18] Booth's *Rhetoric of Fiction* had already become one of the must-read books for graduate literature students around the world. Its conversational style, immense easy learning and fascinating narrative distinctions seemed a mirror of its author, although Wayne was even more open to every sort of theory and fact, and despite an almost naïve irony, was genuinely, even insistently open about his own self-doubts. It was Wayne's tolerance and intellectual hunger which bridged the gaps in the department and set its critical tone for the next years. In addition, he and his wife, Phyllis, along with their fellow chamber musicians David and Peggy Bevington and the chairs James (with Barbara) Miller and Beth (with Howie) Helsinger, revived the hospitable graciousness which hadn't existed in the early seventies, the years of political-cultural ferocity.

Cecil Bald was acting chairman when I arrived in August 1955. The first day I showed up in his office, he walked me over to the Quadrangle Club and did everything but fill out my application and pay my membership fee (which for an instructor was something like $25, a sum even I could afford). Norman Maclean was president of the club, and helped furnish our apartment with its cast-off chairs and sofas. Over fifty years, I've eaten thousands of lunches there, usually as a regular of the Round Table, almost all of whose early regulars—Jock Weintraub, Donald Lach, Arthur Mann and Bentley Duncan of the History Department, John Wilson, once president of the university, Dr. Bob Lewy,

---

17. I had the pleasure of frequently eating with him in the Quad Club. A *Kenyon Review* piece of mine on *Doctor Zhivago* had wrongly convinced him that I was to be a critic after his own heart and mind.

18. The standards were present to his dying day. Booth was at his hospital bed when a physician came to Crane with reassuring words about his condition. "What's your evidence for that?" Booth reported Crane snapping to the cheery doctor.

and Howard Moltz of psychology, such regular visitors as Hans Kung and an occasional stray woman professor who shocked us into mental paralysis—have died. There are barely enough regulars today to blot out the ghosts who rise over the sandwiches and soups.

The club was a component of the interdisciplinary, inter-departmental cohesions which distinguish the University of Chicago. From the late sixties on, though, young assistant professors shunned it because to them it represented the old, male, largely white hegemony which they regarded as a chief source of the world's inequities. Such views were erupting in Prague and Paris, in Berkeley, Columbia, Ithaca, Kent State and on a hundred other campuses. Most Chicago professors lived within walking distance of the campus. The propinquity enabled them to rally quickly to address students and each other. European émigrés like Bruno Bettelheim brought woeful tales of the German thirties. Crisis-impassioned economists such as Milton Friedman and political scientists such as Hannah Arendt proposed solutions to the underlying sources of the eruption. (Friedman wanted the faculty to get out of TIAA-CREF; George Shultz, then dean of the Business School, felt that the police should have been used to dislodge the students from the Administration Building.) On the other hand, my colleague Jerry McGann dressed a la Byron in black velvet and lace and regarded his classes as cells in which revolutionary ideas were born and propagated. One promising English Department assistant professor resigned to become a postman; another retreated to an arts college in Maine. The Hamlet-like brooding but firm basic principles of the university president, Edward Levi, eventually brought the troubled university into port, scarred but, if anything, strengthened.[19]

4

I was told that in the years before my arrival, there'd been tension in the department between the Crane group and one headed by Williamson, Bald, Blair and Wilt. Not in my time. There was amiability and more than surface respect for each other. Sometimes disagreements about

---

19. Levi would soon do the same for the country. As Gerald Ford's attorney general, he cleaned out the befouled stables of Nixon's Justice Department.

which students should be awarded which fellowships flared up during the annual fellowship award nights—which lasted till well after midnight—but that was the only departure from genial courtesy I noticed. These award sessions were attended by everyone in the department, full professor to instructor. Indeed, when outside appointments were discussed, many senior members elicited the opinions of us juniors. All this made for an easy, ego-boosting ambience. My guess is that the notorious "Tenure Syndrome"—which showed up in the children of department members up for tenure—didn't exist back then.

Other elements of departmental cohesion were parties, bi-annual ones given by the Blairs in their apartment, and occasional ones given by all other members, senior and junior. The esprit of manly drinking a la Hemingway led to crises for such members as Maclean, a devoted Hemingwayite[20] who could and did drink a lot, and Olsen and Friedman, whose personalities altered, not for the better, after one or two snifters or even sniffs of bourbon. Mostly, though, the parties were what parties should be, diversions from work and sources of collective amiability.

The department also held an annual spring barbecue in the woods an hour from Hyde Park. There senior members in aprons turned the spits and served cuts of beef and pork sliced from roasting torsos. The rest of us played softball or volleyball. Kids abounded.

Back then, almost everyone, senior and junior, lived in rented apartments. This domestic equality was another element of departmental cohesion. It was in the academic prosperity growing from the mid-sixties to the present that many of us managed to get mortgages for houses or to buy, like the Taves and Bevingtons, farms where they spent the summer.

Prosperity didn't end departmental cohesion. Nonetheless, there have been more divisions in the department in recent years than there were in my early years. Personnel and scholarly battles seemed to cause more bleeding and leave uglier scars. I myself think I have no scars, perhaps a couple of scratches. (This may be the sign of insensitivity or of being a professional outsider.) I have friends in every departmental generation (particularly those of Tom Mitchell, Beth Helsinger, Michael Murrin, Miriam Hansen, then of Richard Strier, Jay Schleusener, Bob

---

20. He used to visit Grace Hemingway, the writer's mother, in Oak Park, surely more devotedly than her mother-hating son did. Norman was in W-2 for alcoholic-induced depression the day his wonderful wife, Jessie, died. I went over and sat with him. It was a year or two later that he began the restoration and measured sobriety in which he would write his two famous books.

von Halberg. Lisa Ruddick, Ken Warren, Jim Chandler, Bill Veeder, Christina von Nolcken and, a bit later, Bill Brown, Josh Scodel, Janice Knight and Larry Rothfield), and although some of the work done by still younger colleagues has been out of my ken, I'd say that I've read and profited from three-quarters of my colleagues' work over the years. I have also greatly admired the extraordinary care with which the department has always treated promotions and appointments. My colleagues often write long, brilliant analyses of candidates' work, analyses which, in the way of the academy, often come to naught as the candidate finally turns down an offer or is turned down at a higher level of the university.

5

Perhaps my memories, gilded with nostalgia, are hiding much of the past from me. Proust writes about the different stages of acquaintance. At first, things are names which, reinforced by reading, become places, persons or ideas of greater or less enchantment. Then the places are visited, the persons encountered in the flesh, and reality complicates, adulterates and darkens them. Finally, there is remembering, and each person transforms what he remembers along the lines of his disposition, some of which is so powerful that it goes even deeper than the actuality of the middle stage. In memory, I treasure the department even more than I did in the forty-six years of my active membership in it.

Seventy-odd years ago, my father cautioned me about saying I loved Brown Betty. "You can't love what can't love you. You *like* Brown Betty." But I *did* love that grand fusion of apple, crumb and hard sauce, and I say that I love and have loved the English Department for over half a century.

On a Writer's Endgame

THE NEXT PIECE IS self-explanatory. It embodies a feeling strong in me then, much less strong as I write this several years later (in December 2006). It was my valedictory to my life's profession, half disinterest, half desire to lay down arms, though not against "a sea of troubles."

> Haven't I given specimen clues, if no more? At any rate I have written
> enough to weary myself—and I will dispatch it to the printers, and cease.
> But how much—how many topics, of the greatest point and cogency, I am
> leaving untouch'd!
> —Walt Whitman, "Last Saved Items"

In January of 2002, I retired from fifty-three years of teaching, forty-six of them at the University of Chicago. For tenured professors of my time, the decision to retire is one's own. I won't go into the pros and cons that weighed on me for more than a year. One pro, though, was that there would no longer be the slightest academic obstacle to writing. Since I was in the midst of writing what I thought might be my strongest novel, this was a large pro.

For about six post-retirement months, I did work reasonably hard on it. Then the excellent assistant to whom I dictated—I won't go into my compositional habits—left for the summer. I was partly relieved, for I felt that I no longer needed the stimulus of her pen poised over the pad of yellow paper waiting for my words. I'd spent the academic year 1999–2000 without such assistance and managed to write a great deal in the manner of my first twenty-five or thirty writing years.

I did, though, take a pause, partly to relax, partly to reflect on this span of experience in the lives of other writers.

Retirement from teaching had pushed my old friend and longtime colleague Norman Maclean through a door he might otherwise never have gone through. He'd not been regarded as an important scholar, had published fewer than a handful of articles, but was thought of as a great teacher.

Then in his last seventeen years, he shifted into a very different gear and produced two fine books at an age that sees most people, let alone most writers, rocking on the porch of recollection. The first was a best-selling memoir-novel, *A River Runs Through It;* the second, the posthumously published *Young Men and Fire,* was brilliantly carved by Alan Thomas and, to a lesser extent, Wayne Booth out of a much larger manuscript. Maclean became not only a celebrated writer, but a model for retirees (he was featured this way in such periodicals as *People*).

His two books had been stirring in him for decades. The first flowed from the death of his gifted daredevil brother Paul, not in a Montana bar fight—as in the book and film—but in a bar in south Chicago. The feeling that he had not taken proper care of his brother, that he had, because of that, been partly responsible for his death, fused with lyric, Hemingwayesque recollections of growing up fishing and fighting in Montana to create the groundswell of *A River Runs Through It.* Another source was the public and off-the-cuff sermonizing of his benevolent and competitively critical father, whose reactions to Norman's early compositions may well have led to his decades of literary silence.

My post-retirement pause from writing stretched from the summer of 2002 into fall. Only very occasionally did I work on my novel.

I wasn't worried. I'd never experienced writer's block and wasn't experiencing it now. What I did experience was a sort of creative lassitude, similar to the sort Gustav von Aschenbach, the writer-protagonist of Thomas Mann's *Death in Venice,* experiences. Perhaps mine was more a disinterest, an *it-doesn't-matter I-don't-careism.* Indeed, when I got an idea for something to put in the book, I not only let it drift, I pushed it away. After a few months, I told myself, "Maybe it's time to round things off. I've filled enough pages. I'm not going to just keep going like an industrial plant turning out clones or variations of what I've already written." I thought of other writers, mostly my contemporaries, who I thought were doing that. I wasn't angry at or disgusted by their activity. "Let them do what they want, I'll do what I want."

I believe that I've never *needed* to write; I'm not a *driven* writer. I wrote because I wanted to. Even when the work was difficult, even agonizing, whatever was necessary to keep going was there for me. Now it wasn't. I wrote a few small pieces, kept writing my notebook, read even more than usual, saw my friends, enjoyed the leisure of an undemanding life, and that was that.

In March, my wife and I went down to a seaside house in Georgia to spend a mostly isolated ten days in the sort of ease we enjoy down there. I read five or six books, and, as is my habit, thought how well or poorly their authors had put them together, but except for writing my journal, wrote nothing.

The eleventh day we flew into a bleak, rainy New York City during the evening rush hour, were threaded by an ingenious cab driver through Queens to the 59th Street Bridge, then to our hotel on East 57th Street, an area I know well but where I'd never before stayed. The room we were first shown was smaller than most jail cells, but for a few extra dollars we moved into a penthouse suite where we were surrounded by sky and skyscrapers. My wife was too exhausted to go out, but I went for drinks and dinner with the husband of my late sister and his companion, a woman whom, sixty years earlier, I myself had taken out. Meanwhile, I had a good conversation with my complicated oldest son and arranged to meet him at noon the next day. I also spoke with my agent, who told me that he'd decided to retire and move to France.

Three hours later, I was back in the hotel, ready for sleep, but tingling. My mind surged with thoughts that could not stop falling into patterns that surprised, even thrilled me. I felt too tired to get up and write them down—my wife was sleeping and I'd have to do this in the bathroom—but I realized that if I didn't, I'd lose something I didn't want to lose. I finally got up, took my notebook and wrote down a rough version of one set of thoughts headed "Autumn 1962," then, skipping a page, another set headed "Coda: 2003." These dealt with the day's rainy return to the town where my parents and I were born and raised and where my oldest son had spent most of his adult life.

Thinking about, more, *feeling,* this return somehow unleashed thoughts about 1962, when I worked in Venice as a Fulbright professor while back home, in America, the Cuban missile crisis boiled as close to annihilating the world as had ever happened. The public and personal events, the twelve years of my first marriage preceding 1962 and the ten years following that ended in divorce, the changing life of me and my children, cascaded in my head. Forty years after that Venetian year, I was about to see the son who partly blamed me for what he—but not I—regarded as the failure of his life. The morning after that, my wife and I would attend the bat mitzvah of our niece as another public crisis—the coming war with Iraq—boiled around us. These happenings, feelings and thoughts were bubbling in my head in a way I recognized as the desire, maybe even the need, to write, one I hadn't felt in months.

The next forty-eight hours were rich with these and other events: first, a moving four and a half hours talking and walking the packed, beautiful East Side streets with my son, then dinner at a good French restaurant with a very talented, very rich friend whose wealth had helped despoil her talent, then, on Saturday, taking the train from Grand Central Station—after coffee surrounded by cop-rousted, fearful, fearsome bums—to Chappequa where, in a beautiful synagogue designed by the odd genius Louis Kahn (who had, decades earlier, died in the old Penn Station, his body unidentified for two days), we rose and sat, rose and sat, recited, chanted and listened to the unending bat mitzvah ceremony of our dear niece. Its texts were full of a peaceful, pastoral Israel where swords were beaten into ploughshares; my head was full of tanks, barbed wire, blood, boys and girls not much older than my niece and grandchildren belting themselves into human bombs. Into the pit of Chappequa teenagers, the forceful young rabbi plunged, commanding them in vain to cease giggling, gossiping, gum-chewing. What a ceremony. Its finest moment came when my brother-in-law spoke directly and movingly to his tearing daughter. After, we went for lunch to their house, two hundred yards from that of our ex-president and his senator-wife, then, toward dusk, drove down the Saw Mill River and Henry Hudson Parkways, a drive that I'd first taken seventy years ago, before the George Washington Bridge had been built. There were the Palisades, the Cloisters, the bridge, Grant's Tomb, the mystic New York skyline, all more beautiful to me than ever. We headed for the day's final event—a raucous, rock-charged, DJ-led party of ninety thirteen-year-olds at the Columbia Faculty House, the girls and boys gawking at home movies, raising eyebrows at adult speeches, screaming, dancing and writing politically incorrect slogans on washroom mirrors with lipstick and mascara.

My literary machinery was processing as much of this as it could even as my stomach churned. Hours into the screams, music, proclamations, dancing, food and champagne, I made it into the air to throw up, first in a Department of Sanitation trash can, then for four hours back in the hotel.

Sick, one pays attention to nothing but one's misery, but later I realized that the vomiting was caused—in my writer's view—not just by my reaction to the noisome racket of the teenage party and my complex feelings of pleasure, warmth, anger and disgust at the bat mitzvah, but by the wonderful Virginia Woolf essay "On Being Ill," which I'd read two nights earlier and about which I'd been talking in connection with the film *The Hours,* which my wife and I had seen the week before in Georgia.

I will not add further to the ingredients in my literary pot. During my trip to New York, everything in that pot had begun, like a good stew or, better, a pot-au-feu, to affect everything else, and now it was my job—one I wanted—to finish cooking, serving and eating it.

It is now some months since my literary desires returned. Except for what I've put down here, I have not used the material conjured up in New York, nor have I yet returned to the novel I'd stopped writing eleven months ago.

Here, all I want to add are some thoughts about the retirement component of this endgame of mine. When one retires from a job one has had for a long time and begins living on what one has socked away, there is, for someone like me, a psychic gearshift. One is no longer earning, adding, accumulating; one is now subtracting, living off a comparatively fixed pile. It may be large enough so that one doesn't worry excessively about it lasting; it may be managed not by one of the great corporations whose shenanigans, criminality or mismanagement have broken the contract with—and the backs of—its workers, but by the good-as-gold managers of TIAA-CREF—nonetheless there is the gearshift into dependence. Since I no longer have a university salary, I can no longer claim on tax forms expenses I used to be able to claim. This loss reminds me that, as Shakespeare's Moor cries, "Othello's occupation's gone."

The armor of professionalism is largely gone, a relief in some ways—one is freer, lighter—but in others, not: one sometimes feels bare in the chill wind of the everyday world. Worst of all, the great force-field of one's classes is gone. Into those fields one was able to drop the ideas and observations that continue to bubble up in and around one. One can no longer say, "Oh yes, I'll talk to the class about this when we discuss Kafka next week."

As a writer, of course, I still have a force-field, I am still a professional, but, as I've indicated, after a few post-teaching months, I had more or less stopped being a writer. The writing life had for fifty years been part of a double professional life. Now, like a Siamese twin whose twin has died, it edged toward the void. In New York, where the writing life had started years before the professorial one, it revived, perhaps to live again on its own.

Perhaps.

END

Books by Richard Stern

Golk

Europe, or Up and Down with Baggish and Schreiber

In Any Case (reissued as The Chaleur Network)

Teeth, Dying and Other Matters

Stitch

Honey and Wax

1968. A Short Novel, An Urban Idyl, Five Stories and Two
Trade Notes

The Books in Fred Hampton's Apartment

Other Men's Daughters

Natural Shocks

Packages

The Invention of the Real

The Position of the Body

A Father's Words

Noble Rot. Stories 1949–1988

Shares, A Novel in Ten Pieces and Other Fictions

One Person and Another. On Writers and Writing

Sistermony

Pacific Tremors

What Is What Was?

Almonds to Zhoof. Collected Stories of Richard Stern

Still on Call

Edited:

American Poetry of the Fifties

Libretto: Golk (Music: John Eaton)

Selected Letters of Donald Justice and Richard Stern. Edited by
E. Murphy